# Snorkel Bob's

# Reality (& get down)

# Guide

# to Hawaii

by Snorkel Bob, Himself

HARA
PUBLISHING GROUP

**Snorkel Bob's**©
**Reality (& get down) Guide to Hawaii**

Published by:   Hara Publishing
                P.O. Box 19732
                Seattle, WA 98109
                206-775-7868

**Publisher's Cataloging-in-Publication Data**

Wintner, Robert,
Snorkel Bob's Reality (& get down) Guide to Hawaii.
1, Travel. 2, Hawaii. I Title
1997 919.69 93-073282
ISBN 1-883697-95-6 Softcover

For Snorkel Mom,
who 1st showed me, Snorkel Bob, the little fishes.

# Acknowledgements

I, Snorkel Bob, would like to thank every man, woman and child on the face of the earth, even though you multiply far past fruitful and maybe ought to slow down for a hundred years or so. And muy mucho mahalos to the managers, snorkel consultants, gear washers and fringe freeloaders at all of my Snorkel Bob's throughout the Hawaiian Islands. Further gratitude is due Mark Twain for his comments on Kona coffee and Mick Jagger for his comments on drinking alone and the nature of temptation.

And most of all, thanks to my, Snorkel Bob's, parents, teachers, snorkel buddies, dogs, cats, pigs, and you, my friends, who've opened your hearts and minds and wallets for the paltry few sheckels required to purchase this massive overflow of Truth.

# Aloha and Welcome to Hawaii,

If you read this from afar, Hawaii for you is still a frame of mind, untrammeled in its perfection and beauty.

If you are here, you can see, smell and feel in the air the wonderful discounts, cut-rate specials, all-you-can-eats, engorge-o-ramas, 2 for 1s or the 3rd for frees, free rides, free baked potatoes and $250 DOLLAR VALUES ABSOLUTELY FREE. I, Snorkel Bob, will not belabor the issue but will dive directly to the nit and grit you've come to expect from me, Snorkel Bob.

Rather than saying this is new, that's nice and the other is ugly, I, Snorkel Bob, will ease this edition of the Reality Guide into the reality of the 00's. The world gains density at maximum velocity; we hurl ourselves, our stuff, our children and their children inward toward implosion. I, Snorkel Bob, will repress the nay say here, because Hawaii is only a place like every other place. No place remains immune to ambient pressure.

Oh, look what they've done, you might think on arrival. This isn't at all how it looked on TV. You may wish you'd chosen that other tropical paradise, with perfectly-shaped women and the men who love them matted and framed on the shallow sea. But Jamaica has the biggest waste dump in the world. Nassau has more women for hire than New York. And South Florida speaks for itself with crowding, pollution, swamp shrinkage and hardly safe haven for a motorist to fix a flat. It may sound like faint praise to call social effluent more benign in Hawaii, but fairness requires comparison.

I, Snorkel Bob took literary sabbatical recently in Seattle. Call it a refreshing change, what with the clouds and rain, the jazz and caffeine, the eerie prevalence of over-educated people speaking English as a 1st language—right on the street! You get used to it. Then you take it for granted. You learn the value of a cell phone that lets you make calls when the traffic jams, so what little time you have in this life isn't wasted.

Time away from Hawaii offers a fresh perspective. Inured to what has become of America, I, Snorkel Bob, can now land on Maui and understand the K-Mart/Costco/OK Used Cars landscape. I, Snorkel Bob, can appreciate the amazing convenience now thickening Kapaa. I can value my cell phone in the gridlock in Paradise available daily between Kaanapali and Lahaina. The timeshare vendors in Kona and Lahaina and Kapaa want to give you $250 absolutely free, if you'll buy a Rolodex card for 10 grand, or 14 for the really best view. I, Snorkel Bob, understand that they too, must exist. Kihei resembles Beirut. Waikiki is still Wakiwaki, the only place in the world where T-shirt vendors pay 20 grand a month in rent.

1

But no matter where in Hawaii I, Snorkel Bob, am, a single calling remains true to its nature.

Of course I, Snorkel Bob, am partial, but the reef is still supreme in tropical essence. On the bright side, the fish who fled the silt and runoff from Hurricane Iniki have returned to Kauai's south shore. Most days there bode excellent for seeing more fish than humans. Snorkeling in Oahu is unchanged, and though the Big Island attracts many more visitors now, not-so-easy access to many reef areas along the lava coast make for wilderness conditions you can only mourn the loss of elsewhere in the world. And the big news on Maui is the sewer line in Kaanapali, where 10 pounds of #2 jammed the 5-pound bag for too many years, causing brown algae infusion and reef death. The sewer line got replaced to handle the greater flow. Conditions should allow continuing recovery.

Hey, I, Snorkel Bob, free dove the Med and wondered what? What are those strange and fluttery fish down there, the white ones, and look: some are translucent. Tampons, toilet paper, plastic diapers and Drink Coca Cola is what. And yes, syringes. Who uses all those syringes? And why? I, Snorkel Bob, would rather face big, hungry sharks than microbes in the Med.

I, Snorkel Bob, researched the Caribbean as well. Perfection there too, is most available on post cards. No sewer line problems in the Windwards; no sewer lines. That's right. The hot buffet runs directly to the reef. You can still find healthy coral a half mile out, but you better hurry.

Back in Hawaii, the snorkel market is knee-deep in muddy water, with timeshare and activity hustlers offering cheap equipment to lure you in. I, Snorkel Bob, believe that each snorkeler glugs and snuks according to karmic resolution. I, Snorkel Bob, am still the 1 and only snorkel outfitter in Hawaii with no ulterior, still the only 1 with Premium Brand Equipment. Would not I, Snorkel Bob, prefer the 65% savings on the stuff that looks like the good stuff? Yes, but would not you, my friends, soon ask, Hey, what?

Because when you get right down to it, you must hold on to what you hold dear. For me, Snorkel Bob, that means providing only snorkel gear that I, Snorkel Bob, would use myself, which is nothing less than the best in the world.

I, Snorkel Bob, hope you can penetrate the maze. This Reality Guide may help you. Beyond the discounts and fake freebies and all-you-can-eats and 2-fers and over-development, Hawaii still hosts the spirits of clarity and color, eruption and profusion. In spite of what they've done, the heart of the tropics still beats here for those who can find it.

Snorkel Bob, Himself
Maui, 1997

# Table of Contents

# Snorkel Bob's Reality (& get down) Guide to Hawaii

# 1
# Water

# Theory

Snorkeling is the best thing to do in Hawaii, and I, Snorkel Bob, ain't whistling Dixie. Hawaii has the best snorkeling in the United States of America, including South Florida, with its overpopulation, pollution and road hazards.

Snorkeling is contact with the ultimate tourist site. It is cheaper, cleaner and more memorable that stuffing your gob in a restaurant or shopping for stuff. You cannot match the efficiency of a day or a week on the reef.

The *How-to* does not change—swimming is optional, not required. The only requirement is relaxation, no short order for some of you, my civilized friends. But if you can muster a smidgen to start, the snorkeling will ease you further in. Tension is dense and wants to sink; relaxation is buoyant—just lay on the surface. Breathe slow, deep and easy. The kick follows the same pattern, slow and easy. Don't bend your knees. You are here, where the phone won't ring, the mate won't nag, the kids won't want, nothing is for sale—where life itself is a fluid dream, movement is graceful and colors are more vivid than the Fillmore West in '69. Imagine that.

*Where to* snorkel is up to you, but you should always practice safe snorkeling.

## SNORKELING SAFETY AND HEALTH TIPS

1) Snorkeling is a buddy sport. You help your buddy. She helps you.

2) Never turn your back on the ocean. It'll whomp you when you least suspect it.

3) Always assess surf, current, wave sets, surge, reef and rocks, submerged and exposed, before entering. Advanced snorkelers call this Snorkel Meditation and use the exercise to enter environmental data to their snorkel programs.

4) Avoid wana ("vonna"), black sea urchins whose spines break off in your skin. Use aspirin for sunburn; peroxide and antiseptic ointment for reef rash; and cigarette tobacco, meat tenderizer (except for MSG allergenics) and Benadryl (capsules or ointment) for Portuguese man-of-war, which is like bee sting. Making shishi on sting also kills pain and other trauma, but I, Snorkel Bob, know that this can sorely test a friendship.

5)  Enter and exit from sandy beach areas.

6)  Never swim against a current. Cross it diagonally. Extreme currents off windward Kauai and Oahu. If you get caught in a current, wave for help. Don't panic, unless of course the rubbernecks on the beach wave back.

7)  Avoid snorkeling at dusk.

8)  Friends don't let friends snorkel drunk.

9)  Don't snorkel in a strong offshore wind.

10) Duck or dive under breaking waves before they reach you to avoid their force. Don't jump over or turn your back to them.

11) I, Snorkel Bob, grease up liberally with Snorkel Bob Cares SPF 15 sunscreen in the intense Hawaiian sun—it's the mostest of the bestest for the leastest and will deter the gnarly wrinkles of old age.

12) If big fish swim up fast and hide behind you, you probably got bigger fish heading in, right on up the food chain to you-know-who. Arruuggahh!! Only kidding, ha ha. (HA!)

13) Don't forget your underwater camera—35mm–27 shots, cheap! Right now, with me, Snorkel Bob.

14) Fishfood in plastic wrappers is hereby denounced by me, Snorkel Bob, in particular LeSueur Peas and stale bread. The plastic wrappers tend to clog my, Snorkel Bob's, ocean, and all that crap constipates my, Snorkel Bob's, little bitty fish buddies. I, Snorkel Bob, further deplore so-called organic fish foods with biodegradable wrappers. This stuff fouls the eco-system, deranges mild-mannered fish and is baaaad. Bad. THE ONLY fish food allowed by my, Snorkel Bob's, Guidelines to a Better World is you, my friends, in final mode, aloha and adieu, down to nitrogen, phosphorous, potassium. This form can also free up some parking spaces.

# WHERE TO SNORKEL

## KAUAI

Call Surf Report (245-3564) for snorkel and boogie conditions.

POIPU BEACH PARK is down Poipu Road past the hotels, then right on Hoowili Road to the park, across from Brennecke's Restaurant.

KOLOA LANDING is out Poipu Road from Koloa Town to the fork in the road. Take a right onto Lawai Road, then a quick left over the small bridge, and 1st right on the dirt road to the old boat landing. Water entry is at the boat ramp.

BEACH HOUSE is adjacent to the Beach House Restaurant. Follow Poipu Road again south from Koloa Town to the fork in the road and again take the right fork (Lawai Road). But this time stay on it until you reach the restaurant. Park roadside. Many minions of fish here, even in shallow water.

LYDGATE STATE PARK, north of Lihue on the east shore, is prime for juniors or 1st-timers. Gentle snorkeling here inside a stone breakwater, as well as showers, picnic tables, and BBQ grills make this 1 a solid G rating. Take Hwy 56 to Leho Drive, turn east and follow your nose to just south of the mouth of the Wailua River. You are here.

KAPAA BEACH is a few miles north of Lydgate at mile 10 of Hwy 56, flanked by Kapaa town on 3 sides. The rare and formidable east swell here can remove you from the earthly plane, especially in Summer. And it's all sandy bottom, so the only fish here are lost or lolo. So why bother? Because sunrise is east, so you, my friends, may stop here for communion with the deep blue sea. Then it's onward, for example, to:

ANINI BEACH, north of Kapaa between Kalihiwai and Princeville. Turn off Hwy 56 onto Kalihiwai Road and go 0.2 mile, then go left on Anini Road to the end. Anini is good for snorkeling all Winter and a microfactotum safer from Ocean Whomp than Hanalei or Haena, 2 spots farther up the north shore. Waves break 300 yards out, leaving the water in front of it calm and serene. You could walk on the reef out to the breakers if you didn't use the brains God gave you to figure out that walking on the reef feels no better to the reef than the reef walking on you feels to you. I.e., my friend, the reef, suffers just like you, my friends, except that my friend, the reef, doesn't reproduce with nearly the fervor. I, Snorkel Bob, suspect my friend, the reef, doesn't practice as much.

HIDEAWAYS looks so far down, so far away, so engulfed by condomania. Fear not. Go right off Hwy 56 at Princeville Center into the complex to where the road dissects the golf course and passes multitudinous multihousing. About 1/4 mile before the road ends is the overlook and the beach—300' below. That's why they call it Hideaways. 1 path down is at the south end from the condominials. The other is at the north edge. Both take 5 minutes. If you can't find 1 or the other, ask around.

In summertime Hideaways is a best snorkel spot on the north shore. Turtle herds roam the depths here. Dolphins, Hawaiian monk seals and fishy hoards play the coral in crystal clarity and the thought bubble of me, Snorkel Bob, often fills with the question: Is this sweet?

HANALEI BAY provides excellent opportunity for those of you with degrees to cross reference your map index, post coordinates, interpolate, fix the interstices, plan the route, set the compass, dead reckon, allow for cross winds, traffic, mpg and go. Those of you without degrees can put the pedal to the metal and follow your nose.

Vast and epic is what it is. Here too an intuitive snorkeler may escape unharmed in big surf if she stays centered in the bay. Less coral here and fewer fish, big deal. So it's only great instead of pathological acid flashback. (See Boogie on this 1.)

HAENA BEACH STATE PARK is around 9 miles past Hanalei on Hwy 56, across from the ballyhooed and over-used Wet'n Dry Caves (seductive grottoes receptive to deep penetration). Haena Beach is a softer touch; long green rolls gently onto a sandy beach stretching to the horizon. I, Snorkel Bob, enter from the sandy beach and snorkel the rocks along the left side. Best in Summer, this 1; maybe break your head in Winter. 1/4 mile east of the W 'n D Caves is TUNNELS; flat here, and the outer reef is waaay out there, fending off freak sets, maintaining calmness inside during big surf outside. But don't take the ocean for granted. 1/3 mile west of the caves is CANNONS, reached via trail through a residential area.

KEE BEACH (KEE LAGOON) is on the north shore at the end of Hwy 56, with plenty room for parking. Best in Summer, this 1—bad in Winter. The sandy beach is fronted by a reef with plenty fish in the shallows—3-8' deep. You got a foot of water over the reef, then the bottom falls on the outside for some Snorkel Excellanté, but forget it if the surf is breaking over the reef!!?>#$%!! (Must I, Snorkel Bob, really tell you this?)

SALT POND BEACH PARK is on the lee side southeast of Hanapepe off Hwy 50. Watch for the park sign, turn left and follow the road past the airport, past Hawaiian Salt Factory. You are here. Great reef, few people, often good in Winter.

KEKAHA BEACH PARK is just past Waimea at mile 27 of Hwy 50. Roadside is a wide beach and usually a bunch of cars. It's a hot surf and boogie spot too (See Boogie)

PACIFIC MISSILE RANGE FACILITY (BARKING SANDS) is where you will most likely encounter Russian Spy Snorkelers. Don't worry. They're broke and fading now like we always hoped they would. You can penetrate the main gate to the military base with humility, respect, your driver's license and car rental agreement. Get a pass. Just for fun, you might want to dummy up some fake papers and hand them over with a nervous look, avoid eye contact and say strange stuff like Tenk you wery moch. Or better now would be Yusef Salaam, Salaam Yusef. So you see for yoorself we are not monasters, or even, Finish your soup!

I, Snorkel Bob, don't know exactly what will waken the missile range security guard, but a little test like this helps measure our front line security. It may also lead to the stockade, do not pass go, but who'll test the system if we don't? You think the problem got solved when the Russkies went broke? You don't think the 3rd Worlders want to horn in on our washers and dryers and 2.7 cars and stuff? You bet they do, with bad English too, and then what would we have to show for all the jack we blow on weapons and uniforms and K-rations and boots and guns and rockets and tanks and stuff if some dirt-poor peasant can come snooping around without so much as a Hey there fella why you talk funny like that?

Get directions with your pass and proceed to Checkpoint Charlie (the beach). Big and beauteous, this 1, the kind Saddam Hussein would call unreal if postcard shots of it were dumped out of helicopters along the Persian Gulf Coast—the 1 with murky water, big surf, dirty sand, oil slicks and intramural violence.

POLIHALE STATE PARK is farther west than west, through the cane to the end of the road. This is the biggest drowning spot on Kauai! So why do I, Snorkel Bob, include it here? Because A) akin to knowing where to snorkel is knowing where not to snorkel, and B) it's worth the trip just to see it. Death potential here is a function of killer current half the year and smash-yo-fockin-head south swell the other half. All this over shallow coral and sneaky drops with erratic sets, freak waves, surge and silt. And you're a long, long way from help. Otherwise it's a Teddy Bear's picnic.

# BIG ISLAND

NOTE: A.M. snorkeling is best; flat water, blue sky. After noon, Vog (volcano smog) often rolls down the mountain.

WHITE SANDS BEACH PARK on Alii Drive is 3 miles south of me, Snorkel Bob, in Kailua. Relief (shishi) units and picnic tables make this a social beach. A good break makes this a good boogie beach. When the surf goes flat, this is what I, Snorkel Bob, call a premium snorkel spot. Swim the point off to the right. AKA Disappearing Sands Beach—don't snorkel here if the sand is gone.

KAHALUU BEACH PARK is a mile or so south of White Sands, still on Alii Drive. A breakwater keeps the bay flat. The 4-6 foot depth makes it like a fishbowl, and fish census here ran 3.2 zillion in '97. A few turtles cruise by, and here too you can drink a beer with your elbows on a table or shishi in a little room.

KEALAKEKUA BAY is a deep marine preserve to remember forever. A sheer face on 1 side goes way above and 500' below the surface. Just past the point is a monument to Captain Cook (whataguy). I, Snorkel Bob, usually jump right off the old concrete pier, after whistling a tune and humming a mantra to remind myself that the bloodshot blalas in gauntlet formation on the approach are God's creatures too, and my friends, really they are, and would love me, Snorkel Bob, if only they knew what an engaging fellow I, Snorkel Bob, can be, once you get to know me, Snorkel Bob, and hey, they probably don't really want to have quick and unlubricated sexual relations with my, Snorkel Bob's, snorkel date, not at all, that's just a character defect in me, Snorkel Bob, (if you can believe that) suspecting that of friendly fellows like these. Then I, Snorkel Bob, hold my nose, grab my nuts, wish my date all the best and jump on in.
Ingress from a boat is another option.

HONAUNAU BAY (Place of Refuge National Historical Park, or, Puuhonua O Honaunau) is Historically Significant, so the park rules say: No Picnics! No Beach Bumming! And No Fooling Around! However, the abundant reef, prodigious fishes, flat water, barely surf nor surge with hardly cross current nor undertow, results in a ☆☆☆☆ USDA Prime rating—i.e., it gets no better! And since snorkeling is recognized by the Congress of the United States of America as a historical pastime, yes, you can snorkel Honaunau Bay.

Ingress is to the right of the visitor center, through the palm grove. A dollar more will gain access to the Historic Park too. An alleged criminal could reach the Place of Refuge only by swimming; once inside he was immune from further pursuit, unlike today, when even millionš and a dream team can't quell those pesky civil damages.

3.5 miles over the coastline road (rough) south from Kealakekua Bay is the park gate. From Kona take Hwy 11 south about 20 miles to Hwy 160 and go right to the park gate.

MILOLII BAY is 35 miles south of Kailua on Hwy 11 to the Milolii turnoff. Follow your nose 5 miles and park past the pavilions. Leave the doors unlocked so the playful boys won't have to break your windows to get your stuff. Follow the wall to the left out along the lava to the point. Ingress here and swim right. This is 1 sweet spot—but look out for boat traffic.

HONOKOHAU HARBOR is a couple miles north of Kailua on Hwy 19. Go left at the harbor road and stay left until you come even with the harbor entrance. Park on the lava and meander left to a sandy cove. Snorkel from the cove to the left. Drink beer, eat burgers, make shishi at the harbor restaurant. Look out for boats.

KONA COAST STATE PARK is 2 miles north of the airport, and about 12 miles north of Kailua, on Hwy 19—coral, sand, lava, G-rated boogie too.

ANAEHOOMALU BAY is the white sand beach in your dreams when you planned this trip, no asses, no elbows. From Kailua go north on Hwy 19 about 27 miles and turn left at Waikoloa. Take the 1st left and park. Best snorkeling is off to the left. Les shishoirs et les tables du picnic.

HAPUNA BEACH is 7 miles north of Waikoloa on Hwy 19. Turn left at the Hapuna sign, go 0.4 mile and park. The south point is best snorkeling and the north point is good too, where the rocks are. Follow the shoreline. Good body and boogie waves off the white sand beach. Uncrowded during the week. Big surf in Winter! Optimal BBQ break all year.

KAUNAOA BEACH is 8 miles north of Waikoloa and bordered by the Mauna Kea Beach Hotel. Go left at the hotel (ask the guard for a beach pass) 0.1 miles past the hotel and golf shop. Park and walk 5 minutes to the beach. Best snorkeling off the south point, where finger reefs reach over sandy bottom.

LAPAKAHI STATE HISTORICAL PARK is coral and rocks, no crowds and A-OK. Go 10 miles past Kawaihae Harbor (a couple miles north of the Mauna Kea) to the park entrance.

KAPOHO TIDEPOOLS at the opposite end of the Big Island in the seldom-visited Puna District, is a phenomenon and sometimes snorkel spot. Lava flowing along the coast developed shallow pools where fresh water seeps in and mixes with seawater, sometimes salty enough for reef fish. Beautiful, clean and safe (the pools are separated from the surf by natural lava breakwaters), these hidden places are a tropical paradise, waaay the hell out. Geography is generic here—i.e. a 5-mile radius with multiple centers might find you right on target, i.e., don't be shy. Local knowledge is currency on this 1—ask around (see sights to see). Take Hwy 11 all the way around the island, through Volcanoes National Park, to State Rte 130. Go south to Pahoa, stop and ask. From Pahoa you can take Rte 132 or 137 (they join in a big loop on the southeastern tip of the island). I, Snorkel Bob, take 132 to 137 and turn right, then take the 1st left off 137 and follow my, Snorkel Bob's, nose down to Mama Ocean.

# MAUI

Maui has more easy access snorkel spots than all the other islands combined. I, Snorkel Bob, will start south and go north, veering west, kind of.

AHIHI BAY is a United States of America Wilderness Preserve. That's heavy and it makes a difference. Boats can't even enter these waters much less drop anchor, so the prolific reef bottoms are pristine, no damage ever since when. Go about 15 minutes south of Wailea past Big Beach at Makena, past some beach houses to a small bay with a small beach. You are here. Caution! Ahihi is safe ingress and egress only from the right place, not from the jagged ledges.

Ahihi Bay teems with fish, eels, turtles, mollusks and coral habitat. Visibility goes to 150'. Potential hazards at Ahihi are:

1) South swell; most common in Summer. Ahihi is near the southern tip of Maui, so the open ocean rollers hit full strength when they're up.

2) Vandals; wilderness preserve areas are the petty thief's choice on Maui. The best deterrent is unlocked doors, open windows and no valuables in the car or trunk.

3) Navigation; Ahihi Bay is what I, Snorkel Bob, call a seductive body of water. It will lure you out, which is bad when you look up at 3 miles of shoreline that all looks the same.

Mark your entry point with the range marker method of navigation. That is, pick a landmark on the beach that will be visible from out in the bay. Then pick your angle of penetration into the bay. Now look up to the mountainside and pick another landmark directly above your beach landmark.

When you get waaay out there, find your beach landmark and swim left or right until your mountain landmark is directly above it. Now you're on course back to your entry/exit point.

MAKENA BEACH is dangerous for snorkeling (see Beach Awareness).

POLO BEACH is right in front of The Polo Beach Club. It's clear and deep with good habitat. Shower and lu here.

ULUA BEACH I, Snorkel Bob, rate Ulua Beach 5 Stars, and I ain't so easy to please. ☆☆☆☆☆, countum:

1) Easy ingress/egress.
2) 80-120 foot visibility.
3) 2-3 zillion fish.
4) Soft sandy beach.
5) A grassy knoll with all-day shade.
6) Good boogie waves most of the time.
7) Fresh water showers et les pissoirs.

That's pegging the meter. A lava rock promontory separates Ulua from Mokapu Beach to the north, but the Mokapu side is too shallow, turbid and surging and not good snorkeling.

The Ulua side is deeper. At the end of the rocks, maybe 80-90 yards out, you're in 20-25' of water. Most days you can see the ripples on the bottom. Some days go to 100' visibility.

Ulua is between the Renaissance Wailea and the Aston, down a public road marked by a sign that says Mokapu/Ulua Beaches. Turn onto that road, go down the hill, park it.

Or walk it from the Renaissance or the Aston.

KAMAOLE BEACH PARK 1 (KAM 1) is probably the last decent snorkeling you'll come to heading north on Kihei Road from Wailea, or 1st from the other direction. Kam 1 has a beach volleyball court, lifeguard station and restrooms visible from the road. If you walk to the water, turn right and go to the end, you'll be at Charlie Young Beach, characterized by big rocks jutting into the ocean maybe 40 yards out. Charley Young is good snorkeling with clear water, 20-30 foot depth and frequently sighted eels, turtles and bigger fish.

KAM 2 is the next beach park south, and KAM 3 is next after that. All the Kamaole beaches are good for ingress and egress with sandy bottom and usually passable shore break. Although sandy bottom makes entry and exit safe and easy, you won't see many fish unless you cruise to the rocks separating the sandy bottom beaches.

Find habitat, a place where reef fish can hide and live, and you'll find fish. All the Kam beaches are best in the morning, because they're often windy in the afternoon.

Fresh water showers at KAMS 1, 2 & 3.

OLOWALU is halfway between Kihei and Lahaina and is the only major snorkel reef on Maui with tradewind protection. Sheltered by the West Maui Mountains, Olowalu will stay calm and clear when most spots south and west are blown out.

South swell in summertime and Kona wind in wintertime can stir up the water. Otherwise Olowalu is often the only place to go on windy afternoons or unusual mornings with heavy trades.

The reef here is a few miles long and conditions are excellent. Visibility is up to 120'. The "beach" is narrow and plagued by kiawe thorns and road noise, and ingress can be tricky because the water is so shallow.

MILE MARKER 14, just south of the Olowalu General Store, is near the center of the reef. A post maybe 50 yards out in the water is just about in line with Mile Marker 14. Put your body between the mile marker and the post and go. You're in a shallow sand slough maybe 6' wide at the widest, with no coral to cut or otherwise impede your entry.

Depth stays about 15-18' out 200-300 yards, then it drops off to 25-35', where you may see some bigger fish. If you're lucky and in the snorkel groove, you'll find Turtle Heaven, a colony of 20-30 turtles who live out past the drop at Olowalu. I, Snorkel Bob himself, will not allow exact directions to Turtle Heaven. Those of you meant to find it will.

Olowalu is another seductive reef. You can get waay out there and wish you had a boat. So go ahead and forget who you are but pay attention to where you are. Maybe use a boogie board or other flotation if you plan to cover big sections of the reef.

Look out for swells at Olowalu. They can pick you up light as a feather and slam you on the coral heads just under the surface. These swells are easily visible from the shoreline when they're coming in.

No fresh water showers at Olowalu.

LAHAINA is best for snorkeling if you're staying there, because underwater you're away from the relentless heat, grit, honkytonk and stale history this quaint little village is famous for. The place is historical—where n'er-do-well misfits and drunks could find gainful employment in the casual massacre of large marine mammals in the calm waters just offshore. Most of the marine mammals are gone now.

About the best water in Lahaina, unless a heavy rain has caused a toxic runoff from the pineapple fields, is in front of the Lahaina Shores Hotel and 505 Front Street. Shallow reef with easy access, and the fish get thick beyond the drop off, maybe 50 yards out, 20' deep. Great visibility and it's in the lee of the mountains so no afternoon wind. Caution boat traffic!

KAANAPALI has okay snorkeling from the Hyatt south if you like a little bit deeper water, say 30', and wide open space. Visibility is usually 80-100'. Ingress and egress are critical here. Best entry at the Hyatt is by the Beach Services Center; look out for the northbound current. Don't snorkel in front of the Marriott or Kaanapali Alii—too much cross current sweeps the point.

From the Westin to Black Rock at the Sheraton is good; Black Rock is excellent, last to murk, 1st to clear after rain. The rock is sheer and a few stories above and below the water. Local hazards include the nearby golf course (Fore!) Also look out for stockbrokers jumping off the Rock.

Look out for a sudden bottom drop in some stretches of beach, especially the Hyatt. Close-out waves usually accompany that kind of drop-off. And beware the boat traffic. It's a scene down there, on the water and otherwise. If you're married, wear dark sunglasses so you won't be so obvious checking out the hard bodies. If you're alone, checking out is acceptable, possibly de rigeur. Wear gold if you have some, and a rolled up wash cloth in your Speedos can't hurt, unless you, like me, Snorkel Bob, have no room to spare.

AIRPORT BEACH is an old favorite, where the old Kaanapali Airport used to was, north of the Royal Lahaina Hotel. Take the last Kaanapali exit off the main highway and park in the old airport parking lot. Don't let the hospitable beach and easy access lure you more than 50 yards out, where another current, the Molokai Express, waits to show you the real meaning of treading water.

NAPILI BAY is like a saltwater swimming pool a quarter mile wide and 20' deep 200 yards out. 2 reefs run across the bay and both are prolific. This bay draws surfers and boogie boarders too when it's pumping. Then you'll see parts of the reefs exposed when the surface falls, just before the wave rolls over. You don't want to snorkel Napili Bay then, but those conditions prevail only for a short span in Winter.

Napili Bay access is easy, but parking gets tricky. 1 route is through the Napili Village Hotel, where I, Snorkel Bob, do bidness. Park along the beach road and cut through.

KAPALUA BAY is another postcard-pretty setting. Parking is easier here with a public lot. Turn left after the Napili Kai Beach Club onto the access road, then park in the lot and follow the path through the tunnel. The reef here is prolific. Be aware of some current farther out and surfer and boating traffic.

HONOLUA BAY is just around the corner from Kapalua Bay. If you stay on the main road, it's a 1/2 mile past Mile Marker 32. Paradoxically, the sign for Honolua Bay is actually at Slaughterhouse (MOKULEIA BAY), just to the south. Walk down a steep path from the parking area, then you're at Slaughterhouse. Honolua is a few hundred yards past the Conservation District sign. Park on the left. The path from here is a canopy of trees, which will tell you you're at Honolua. Sometimes it's crowded here, sometimes not.

This is the northwest corner of Maui, so it's exposed to tradewind weather. Depth is about 35' and the water may be a degree or 2 colder. The fish are bigger and the reefs spectacular. Because it's windward, heavy trades can generate big waves at Honolua and Slaughterhouse. Both are excellent.

Like Ahihi Bay far to the south, Honolua Bay is a Wilderness Preserve. So it's unimproved, undamaged, ever since when. You can test your free-dive skills swimming under the arches near the left side of Honolua, down about 20'. This reef separates the 2 bays and is good snorkeling all the way around.

HANA BAY fronts Hana Beach Park, and the point just past the old wharf is a good place for entry. Depth is about 15-18' between the point and the lighthouse island (Puuiki). The area is unique for snorkeling. Hana Beach Park has showers and restrooms and you can get a fair burger de Luxe at the snack bar.

# OAHU

Call Surf Report, 973-4383, for snorkel and boogie conditions.

WAIKIKI is not good for snorkeling; no coral, rocks, or seaweed. Waikiki is mostly flat sandy bottom; no habitat, no fish. You may well suppose that I, Snorkel Bob, get pretty hot under the goggles snorkeling south from Waikiki to Diamond Head and on around to find Nothing, Nada, Rien, Empty, No Life, Zip, Zero, Kaput, Finis, A Dusty Noxious Wasteland! And for what? For carelessness, poor sewage control and poison runoff (pesticide and fertilizer) in the name of sugarcane and jobs.

Is this what the mission hath wrought? Is this the saving grace? Never have so many given so much for so few.

Dead reef reflects sickness in the soul of a people. Keep this in mind, express your concern, get vocal, like me, Snorkel Bob, who am tired of pussyfooting around! However,

SANS SOUCI BEACH is just beyond Waikiki, out Kalakaua toward Diamond Head (east), across from Kapiolani Park. Just past the Waikiki Aquarium is the Natatorium, and Sans Souci stretches south from there to the New Otani Hotel. The beach here is also called Kaimana or Dig Me Beach, because of the gems and gold festooning the bodies rolled in Mazola. This beach is the start for the Labor Day Weekend Roughwater Swim, 2.6 miles to the Hilton Hawaiian Village. But it's not rough near the beach, and moderate fish populations cruise here.

KAHALA is nice, calm, clear, wide and sandy, behind the Kahala Hilton east of Diamondhead (out of the hubbub). The little island off the beach was built, yes, built in the 60's along with the hotel, but I, Snorkel Bob, can't imagine why. Anyway, the beach is set up to look like hotel property, but you, my friends, know better from me, Snorkel Bob: all beaches in Hawaii are public property.

I.e.; the old timers did 1 thing right, even though they lost all the land and let everything else get toxified with smoke, pvc, fertilizer and bug poison in the name of Sugar, God and Jobs. Park at Waialae Beach Park, 4925 Kahala, and walk down the beach to the hotel. Pleasantly deserted during the week, this 1.

SHARK'S COVE, on the north shore near Waimea, is on the northeast end of Pupukea Beach Park. This could be the 2nd most popular snorkel spot on Oahu (see Hanauma Bay). It's also part of Pupakea Marine Life Conservation District. Only Hanauma Bay on Oahu is similarly classified. Beware October through April—killer surf and bad current are common to the north shore. But don't worry about this place being called Shark's Cove—AARRGGHH! I, Snorkel Bob, had Oscar check it out. He's my shark pal in the picture with his teeth all set to chomp down on me, Snorkel Bob, and if you can't trust somebody in that situation, then who can you trust? Anyway, Oscar came over and cruised Shark's Cove and said, "Wha..? Sharks? I saw more sharks on foot in Waikiki."

Anyway, the cove and tidal pools form a beauteous stretch of the north shore. It's a scuba hot spot in Summer, with flat water and easy access, unlike Winter, when you can break your toe just sticking it in, it's that rough, and I, Snorkel Bob, mean really.

Also at the Waimea end of the beach park is 3 TABLES, a reef in 3 sections. In the middle, between 3 Tables and Shark's Cove, is a big tidal pool (Kapoo). Too shallow for snorkeling, unless you be Tom Thumb. Tennies or tabbies will save your feet, but nothing will save your ass if you hang out here in wintertime. Summer Only!

WAIMEA BAY BEACH PARK across from Waimea Falls park is also hurly burly kablammah in wintertime, so don't go except May through September when it's flat. A world famous surf spot, this 1, with the biggest rideable waves in Hawaii—20-30' sometimes, which is bigger than The Empire State Building and much steeper. However, on the Haleiwa side of this vast and epic bay is a high islet, the Rock. Swimmers jump off the Rock. Beneath the Rock is a big subaqueous tunnel, good for snorkel exploration if you be A-1 in the water. (I.e., novice swimmers keep out.)

On the bright side, Waimea Bay could be the mostest of the bestest at Waimea. Pupukea Marine Life Conservation District is the only such classified water off Oahu besides Hanauma Bay. The old quarry in the center is deep, coming up shallow on the side where you, my friends, can nose-to-nose with some cold and scalies if you want to. ☆☆☆☆☆ Excellanté here, but only in Summer with flat water!

WINDWARD OAHU NOTE: Long stretches here are bleaked out with souvenir shops—big conch shells from Florida, seashell plant hangers from the Philippines and fresh pineapple from Safeway. Don't be discouraged; windward Oahu won't be thoroughly trashed for another few years.

KUALOA REGIONAL PARK is northwest of Kaneohe, 9.8 miles off Rte 83 going north. It's a popular regional park avec les shishoirs et les tables du picnics. The earthy contingent can camp at Kualoa too. This long, sandy beach is good for swimming, but the water is sometimes murked. The little island off the beach is Chinaman's Hat, with a big Chinaman living the sedentary life thereunder. It's on the National Register of Historical Places because it's so important to Hawaiian culture.

Beside the park is Kualoa Sugar Mill Beach. You'll scrape your hull in the rocky shallows unless it's high tide. Once beyond the shallows you'll see many of my, Snorkel Bob's, eency-teenciest of little bitty fish buddies and some of my most-legged mucaceous friends too, i.e. tako, or octopuses. (Octopi sounds so angular and crusty, like with hard edges and blueberries.)

And remember: Don't molest the tako. They're shy, sensitive, easily stressed, just like me, Snorkel Bob, and smart as doggie woggie waiting back home. Handle them gently, with a little bit shoyu and wasabi maybe. (Then again, would you do that to Fido?)

KAILUA BEACH PARK is 30 acres of good-as-it-gets. Windsurfers here, so look out for melon cleavers when swimming or snorkeling. The little island in the offing is Flat Island State Bird Refuge. Next to the beach park is mile-long Lanikai Beach, all good for swimming and/or fish-watching. And check out Bob's Twogood Kayaks [Hahani St., Kailua, Oahu (808) 262-5656.] Bob's (no relation) rents for $28/day for a single, $39/day for a tandem, with free delivery to the beach.

HAUULA BEACH PARK and PUNALUU BEACH PARK am connected by a fur piece o' beach and, out a ways, a reef. Nice, the water, inside the reef. Tumultuous, deep and tricky outside. Big surf breaks over the reef sometimes in Winter, so those of you, my friends, with degrees can apply them here. Those of you, my friends, without degrees must trust your instincts. Also bad sometimes at this place are the Portuguese man-of-wars. Don't mess with. They look easy enough to avoid—little blue plastic bubble is all you see, maybe an inch around and fun to pop on the beach, if you wear shoes. The bad thing is they trail gobs of hot blue snot, 10 - 15' strings of it. Worse yet, the blue snot comes free when the animal crashes on rocks or reef, then it drifts, still hot for a day or 2. It's not a chronic problem here but happens occasionally on blustery days.

IF YOU GET STUNG: The toxin is similar to bee sting. Allergy to bees indicates serious consequence to man-of-war, e.g., short breath, rapid heart beat, maybe a touch of shock and/or death. Common reaction is intense burning, rush pulsation from sting to nearest lymph network (armpits or groin), mild shock. You, my friends, should stay calm in any event. 1st aid requires Benadryl ointment or tablets, or meat tenderizer—either will neutralize the poison. Or, tobacco poultice on sting will neutralize in mere moments.

Short of that, since most of you, my friends, gave up smoking (and now your good behavior could cost you your life), shishi right on sting will also neutralize the toxin.

I, Snorkel Bob, remind you, my friends, that this last remedy can sorely test a friendship, usually in direct relation to location of sting—chin, nose, forehead worst of all. Relief can also vary directly with stream duration. So I, Snorkel Bob, always carry an extra 6-pack for emergency. What the hey—better a pissed-on, pissed-off friend, than 1 who can't talk back.

KAHANA BAY BEACH PARK is on Rte 83, 15.4 miles past Rte 63 going north and is only good with no breeze, no murk, flat water.

SWANZY BEACH PARK, however, is a narrow, rocky beach usually underwater at high tide and home to my, Snorkel Bob's, most noble colleagues. Beware the tako takers—they got spears and hearts with barbed points. Scientific Fact: The octopus is most intelligent of all invertebrates. And I, Snorkel Bob, can promise: They're smarter than a few spinals around here too.

Beware the outrushing sandslough at Swanzy—stay inside the reef and out of this little channel. If you, my friends, perchance get swept out to sea like flotsam on a freight train, relax. Let it take you. It will tire of you as your mother once did. Then swim parallel to the beach, then come back in, older and wiser.

KAAAWA BEACH PARK must roll off slowly, giving each "a" the independence every 3rd world outpost longs for—Ka-a-a-wa. Go faster if you feel safe. Better than Swanzy, this 1, with picnic tables and lifeguard. But look out for surf.

LEEWARD OAHU NOTE: Tradewinds blow from the northeast, often 35 knots, often nixing windward snorkel spots. The west (leeward) coast is sheltered from trades by the Waianae Mountains, but you must watch for the wicked northwest swell on leeward shores which can maim and/or crush. Check on conditions before the trip (about 1.5 hours west from Wakiwaki).

PAPAONEONE BEACH near Lahilahi Point is west on U.S. Interstate H1 past the Barber's Point Naval Air Station where the federal road changes to State Rte 93. Go north through Waianae toward Makaha. Look for 2 beachfront condos just past Makaha Valley Road. Access betweenum & snorkel the left shoreline out to the point.

MAKAHA BEACH is famous for surfing. If der surf is down, it's good fer schnorkling too. Ask Herr Lifeguard, Vhere? Vhen?

YOKOHAMA BAY at Kaena State Park is past Makaha at the end of the paved road. No burgers here—and no life guards. This reef parallels the coast for miles. Beware big surf—calm water snorkeling only. And then it's very good.

ELECTRIC BEACH, or KAHE POINT, is across from the power plant (take H1 thru Ebba Beach and Makaha) and is excellent, with a 30' reef wall along the side of the point.

# BEWARE PETTY THIEVERY AT ALL OAHU BEACHES

HANAUMA BAY is now $3 per person, 13 & up, and $1 to park. It's a wonder of nature, once a volcanic crater, now a vast deep water bay with a bottom coming up to shallow reef 100 yards out. Inside the reef is habitat for nearly all my little fish buddies—sheltered from current and big surf. It was spawning grounds and nursery too—was, because Oahu ain't your typical tropical wilderness. You got your cars, your condomania, your highrises, freeways, mass transit, gridlock, drugs, crime, hookers, suburbs, neurosis, neuritis, neuralgia and a city in Collective Profit Mode (collective consciousness for money).

I.e., some guy discovered the scene at Hanauma Bay. The next discovery was that Beta Normals from America and Japanese tour gangs would pay big dough to have their hands held out to the Snorkel Adventure Grounds. But 10,000 people a day left enough oogies, toe jams, pubies, and ammonia nitrite (the yellow tinge) to kill the inside reef. It's alive outside, but that's safe for intermediate to advanced swimmers only.

The fish at Hanauma survive on fish food. It's been a marine preserve since '67—you can't hook, spear, capture, kill, alter or take any sea shells, animal life, sand or geological features. But it's no longer an ecosystem; it's hand-fed fish. Now the suits downtown want to limit the body count to 2,000 daily. I, Snorkel Bob, say Yes! They want to ban fish food, but I, Snorkel Bob, say No! On a dead reef, the fish won't eat if they don't get fed. More fish food on other dead reefs would bring fish to otherwise barren coastline. I.e., once you kill it's natural spirit, you must maintain it.

No ecosystem means no live coral. Coral is the base of the food chain, from eency-teency to quarter-pounders to my pal, Oscar. Hanauma Bay is all fish from the midrange of the system, the only size fish who can live on fishfood. (Far removed from the natural order, the more aggressive among them now insist on fishy values and the same fish pellets for all.)

You got a ton ofum–80 species–but Hanauma Bay is still to snorkeling what the Boat Show is to trout fishing, and the beauty is tainted by so many asses and elbows. Even so, 10 Oahu pedestrians asked where to snorkel will say "Hanauma." Giant tourbuses offload all day except early morning, when you should go, if go you must. You'll have easy parking and calm then. And "Hey! Where in hell is breakfast already?" all the arrogant fish will ask at 1st light.

For historical iota: When Burt and Deb lay on the beach in From Here to Eternity, little wavelets lapping up on their young, writhing bodies, guess where that was? Exackalackaly—Hanauma kind, but at night, no tourists. Sheesh, can you imagine that scene in the daytime with 10,000 pasty-face lard-asses sloshing up the shallows? They'd have called it From Lunch to Yehupet or something.

You go east on Interstate H1 until it becomes Rte 72, then follow your nose, eyes open. They got a snack bar & 2 shishoirs.

# SNORKEL 101— THE MOVIE A REALITY AT LAST

*--Tell me Snorkel Bob, Can I Ever Learn How to Snorkel?*

Everything you wanted to know about snorkeling and then some is now available in the privacy of your own home, thanks to the public-service video, *Snorkel 101*.

Snorkel Bob, the best-known snorkeler in either hemisphere, appears in his 1st starring role. Snorkel Bob said, "It's time for *Snorkel 101*. I've felt for awhile that many beginners are less confident than I was when I asked my 1st mermaid for a date. For years I've seen scads of people coming to Hawaii to snorkel—but I realized that many don't snorkel, because they think they can't."

Filmed at 4 of Maui's popular snorkel sites, *Snorkel 101* is hosted and narrated by Matt Roving. "I think Snorkel Bob worries too much," Roving said. "Who would ever think they couldn't snorkel? But I agree that it's time for *Snorkel 101*. You hang out at Snorkel Bob's for 10 minutes, you'll see what I mean. It's the Smiths from Seattle asking, 'Do I breathe through this thing?' Or the Browns from Keokuk: 'Do these things go on my hands?' It can drive a Snorkel Exec nuts."

Roving said the half-hour epic answers the 400 questions most asked by snorkelers. Equipment selection, basic skills, relaxation techniques, health and safety, where to go and some exciting snorkel-tech are the highlights.

"Hawaii without snorkeling is like Paris with no cheese, Aspen without the eye contact, New York with no bickering," Snorkel Bob said. "But we saw some bone-dry snorkel lessons and knew we needed some color. So we got some bathing beauties and blew the rent on fancy shirts for Matt. We got a Hollywood director for cheap because he's still undiscovered. I thought *Snorkel 101* would be good, a cut above Geraldo maybe. I never dreamed we'd be as good as Oprah, or Sonja. I mean really."

Snorkel Bob said many snorkel sites are accessible to anyone who finds them. "These 4 are based on safety and fish—and plenty other snorkelers should be there too.

"*Snorkel 101* in VHS Home Video format is yours to keep forever for only 20 bucks from me, Snorkel Bob. Or, you can keep it for a 1-night stand for free, and if that ain't love, then what?"

# WHERE TO BOOGIE

Now I, Snorkel Bob, and you, my friends, play CYA. I, Snorkel Bob, C my A by giving you these handy tips. You, my friends, C your A by reading them and playing safe.

I, Snorkel Bob, realize that not all of your degrees are paid for but if you, my friends, are ever going to use them, use them now. Ask around. (Is this good for boogie?) Look around (Hmm...Do I see anyone else dropping in?). Meditate. (What is the feeling? What is the not feeling?) Furthermore, an apparently calm beach can be hit with huge sets. Meditate 10 minutes to be sure. And no solo boogie!

1) Don't boogie close-outs (waves that collapse).

2) Don't boogie shore break (waves that break close-in over shallow bottom). Shore Break Can Knock You Down, Beat You Up, Break Your Head!

3) Don't boogie unfamiliar areas. (Ask around.)

4) Don't boogie secluded areas. (Don't ask.)

5) Don't boogie alone. (Use a boogie buddy.)

6) Don't watch small local children boogie killer surf and say Hey, if they can do it I can do it. Small local children boogie 1st, crawl and walk later.

7) Don't break your neck (or your back, usually from thrusting into shallow bottom like a pogo stick, head where rubber bouncer used to be).

8) Don't do this.

9) Don't do that.

Have a nice boogie. I mean really.

# KAUAI

Call Surf Report, 245-3564, for snorkel and boogie conditions. Check snorkel listings for additional directions to these spots.

HAENA BEACH STATE PARK has a seductive break but it's No Place For Beginners! Shallow reef makes for vertical (straight down) drop-ins. I, Snorkel Bob, call this over-the-falls; you, my 1st-time-boogie friends, will call it assault and battery.

HANALEI BAY may be the best surf on Kauai. The breaks to the left, however, and out in the middle are far from terra firma and therefore dangerous for beginners. To the right by the pier be more better—sandy bottom and excellent boogie swells. Farther right outside is a long right break: Expert surfers here.

HIDEAWAYS in Winter has waves nearly everyday. The paddle out is a few hundred yards and the surf can get tricky. Beginners go away. Intermediates with strong swim strokes can stay for some excellent boogie on a steep break in fairly deep water. (Deep good; no go boom on bottom.)

ANINI BEACH looks maaarvelous. So did Rock Hudson. Don't go. Long paddle out, aggressive reef, strong tide, cross current, undertow, quicksand, slime, gore, nails, broken glass, terroristic threatening, assault with attempt to kill, rape, pillage, plunder, 1st degree murder, Sodom 'n Gomorrah, bamboo spikes under the fingernails, 40,000 volts, raw sewage, hemmorhoids, bunyons, terminal dandruff, impetigo, pink eye, gall stones, halitosis, chain smokers, soy bean farts, guns, knives, ninja death stars, bad manners, hostile locals and much much more make this a less than perfect boogie spot. It's pretty good for snorkeling though. (See Snorkel, Where to)

KAPAA has medium waves over sandy bottom and could be the place for you, my friends. Add blue sky, sunshine, sunscreen, beach chairs, some o' my, Snorkel Bob's, T-shirts, and you're ready for action, even if you never tried it before. This is the place to learn how. Highlights are: 1) an easy paddle to the break and 2) nearly no current whatsoever, hitherto or forevermore.

BRENNECKE'S BEACH is left of Poipu Beach Park past Brennecke's Beach Broiler, if you face the ocean. This was the best body surfing on Kauai until Hurricane Iwa gobbled 50 yards of beach in '81. Now watch for bigger surf and beware the rocks.

SHIPWRECKS, in front of the new Hyatt is past Poipu Beach Park. Rocky ledge makes for iffy entry, but good depth allows beginner survival, intermediate and advanced thrill. Don't feed the monk seals who bask on the beach and love finger meat best of all. Cliff jumping is permitted from the left shoulder but I, Snorkel Bob, advise the safe choice.

KEKAHA is A-1, beginners or advanced. You can work your way up the wave chain—Intersections, 1st Ditch, Rifle Range—or stay in the baby wavelets (like Chicken of the Sea).

PACIFIC MISSILE RANGE FACILITY (BARKING SANDS) is vast and beauteous with swells to knock you down and beat you up (head 1st). But that's only where you arrive and park, Major's Bay. A walk down the beach (northward) maybe 10 minutes will bring you to a popular surf break—Family Housing. (So named by wave-people on welfare).

Barking Sands is what boogiers in the know call awesome. The weather here is excellent with a tropical ion rating to peg the meter. And the short hike north will put you at the door of the Green Room, iris to iris with the Almond Eye, i.e., tubed, if you want it. 5' deep 100 yards out, sandy bottom.

Negatorily, however, both Major's Bay and Family Housing generate Killer Surf in Winter, and in Summer, either 1 can pump a south swell that will close your account. Rip currents are a Winter fact at Major's. Furthermore, access here requires interface with the United States of America, i.e., a gate with a guard who will ask, "Veh iss cho peppahs?" You must show your driver's license, at least. On the whole, I, Snorkel Bob, rate this 1 worthwhile, if you take some eats and drinks and understand that on a calm day in Summer, it MIGHT be good for boogie. NOTE TO COLLEGE GRADUATES: If it's holy screaming Cheez-its, it ain't.

# BIG ISLAND

WHITE SANDS (DISAPPEARING SANDS) The small, quick left break here is usually over sandy bottom. If in doubt, reconnoiter. When surf go big, he break nice left off south point. If you like ride him big left, Cut hard, Foo! (Or rock touch face like French kiss from freight train).

LYMAN'S BAY Practice, practice, practice and a car ride south 1/4 mile past Banyan Tree Condominials and the Banyan Mart will lead you, my friends, to More Advanced Conditions (bigger the ante, greater the payout—or the loss). For ingress, walk left on top of the lava wall, down steps, past house, around grassy knoll to small, rocky cove. The surf breaks big off the south point for 150-yard ride. But bail out, Harry! Before the wave closes out and the sky falls on your head.

KAHALUU BEACH PARK Boogie near the little blue church but look out for surfer traffic in Winter months.

HAPUNA Big surf in winter be good if you win, bad if you lose. Sandy shore softens landing here. Read the caution signs.

HONOLII BAY Take Hilo Beachfront Highway about 1 mile from Hilo towards Honokaa. Just past the cemetery turn right on Alae. Go left at the dead end, park and go downstairs for a nice, rivermouth break.

# MAUI

KAMAOLE BEACH PARKS 1, 2, 3 are all are good for boogie, and so is Charley Young at the north end of Kam 1. Like all beaches, the Kams are subject to big surf; watch for red flags near the lifeguard stand. And a few days a year Kam 1 gets killer surf, when usually normal people get out in it and cheat death, diving under at the last instant.

These beaches can get 8-10'. I, Snorkel Bob, took on a 5-footer once and got pummeled worse than a man seeking freedom in a nolo contendere divorce proceeding.

SIDEWALKS South of the Kamaole Beach Parks is the Mana Kai Hotel. The Mana Kai has a grassy lawn and a good beach. The surf there is called Sidewalks, a clean 2-3' break for good boogie rides most of the time.

Be aware of shallow rocks at Sidewalks. 5-10 minutes of boogie meditation is required here. If you know where they are, you won't hit them, maybe.

ULUA BEACH is usually good for 1-3' waves, although they sometimes close out.

WAILEA BEACH is the next beach south and POLO BEACH is after that. Both are good for small (3' and under) waves. Wailea Beach is 1/2 mile long.

MAKENA BEACH—DON'T BOOGIE MAKENA—However, if boogie you must, walk north (hang a right at the waterline) until you get to the cliff at the north end of Makena (Puu Olai). You'll find a path leading up and over. It's steep and requires both hands, so either prepare to sling your gear over your shoulder or hand it up to your boogie buddy.

The far side is Little Beach. Some people call this a nude beach, others call it clothing optional. Anyway, the surf here gets big but it doesn't close out nearly as bad as on Big Beach. It'll still knock you down and beat you up, but it won't kill you, or at least it won't kill you as quick.

If you paddle out toward the tip of Puu Olai (the cliff you just scaled) you can pick up a perfect left coming back in. The water at Makena is the clearest on Maui—you boogie over some rocky areas, but you got plenty depth. The perfect left boogie is optimal early morning.

NAPILI BAY is as good as it gets for boogie on those days when the waves are big enough to break through the ho-hums but not so big they smash you to smithereens with indifference. Reading conditions for most boogie and snorkel conditions becomes obvious with experience. Reading Napili is like that.

The 1st reef, out 50 yards or so, runs across the bay except for about a 30-yard stretch in the middle. Some days the waves are big enough to suck all the water off the right hand (northwest) half of the reef, exposing it, before rolling over. Then the area just inside the reef sloshes like a washing machine. The wild young boys like to hang out there for the shake-up. If you see them there, it's probably safe.

On big wave days you catch waves farther out, closer to the 2nd reef and ride in. Advanced boogiers often ride right over the reef, since the wave gives them altitude for clearance. Beginning and intermediate boogiers should aim for the open slot in the middle. That way if you eat it, with luck, you eat it little.

SLAUGHTERHOUSE is just past the Mile 32 marker on Rte 30. You'll see a Conservation District sign for Mokuleia. Take the trail about 50 yards downhill to a beautiful white sand beach. ☆☆☆☆ beaching and boogie are here. But beware Winter surf and close-out sets!

# OAHU

Call Surf Report, 973-4383, for snorkel and boogie conditions. And remember: You, my friends, can get slammed at:

WAIKIKI BEACH is excellent for watching people who are right up next to naked but I, Snorkel Bob, must caution: Some of them are unlovely!

But the surf is good for boogie every now and then, and 1 place worth checking is the Wall. It juts seaward off Kalakaua right at Kapahulu, which happens to be the soulful street of my, Snorkel Bob's, place, where you, my friends, may equip yourselves for perfect lefts on a Kauai Challenger, or a Mach 7.7, or an Edge, or a Body Glove.

Shallow water and rocky bottom here may bump your noggin, so don't say I, Snorkel Bob, didn't tell you.

SANDY BEACH is 1.7 miles past Hanauma Bay and is most popular for boogie, because the break here is good as it gets. However! The red flag flies here—conditions vary, always dangerous. Strong current, hefty undertow and kaablaammaa shore break account for Sandy's rank as #2 in all Hawaii for lifeguard rescues. (#1, Makapuu, coming up).

Sandy is for those among you, my friends, who understand the Green Room, especially when the ceiling falls, the walls collapse, the floor buckles. The red flag on the beach means DANGER: Don't go in. The yellow flag means mixed conditions (You might die, might not). A green flag means go ahead on.

A few years ago this guy comes down to Sandy when it's breaking size Killer, Triple E. He testified later at the trial that yes, he saw the sign posting extreme danger and yes, he saw the red flag too. But then he also saw the little kids out in the break having fun. What he didn't know was my, Snorkel Bob's, Boogie Safety Tip #6 (Don't watch local kids boogie and think if they can, you can. Local kids boogie 1st, crawl and walk later).

So the guy heads out head 1st, drops in and eats it—broken neck, quadriplegic for life. He sued the city for 2.3 or 8.6 or whatever on the grounds that the sign and flag weren't enough. The kids in the surf were misleading. He lost again.

The lifeguard at Sandy knows the conditions. Ask. And don't forget your boogie etiquette.

MAKAPUU BEACH PARK is 4.3 miles past Hanauma, just before Sealife Park. This may be the most famous bodysurf beach in Hawaii and is not a beach for boogie novices. In Winter, September through April, you got bully current and psychotic shore break. It's calmer in Summer but still good for the experienced only; warning flags here too. When it's good, it's the eternal moment, and isn't that why we reach for the edge?

WAIMANALO BAY STATE RECREATION AREA has the biggest break in Waimanalo Bay, so it's the busiest stretch of the bay. It's next to Bellows Field—military name but state-owned since '66, unlike Bellows Beach. (see below) The beaches are similar, but the break here is bigger and steeper; bigger stakes mean greater loss, higher pay out.

BELLOWS FIELD BEACH PARK still belongs to the military and is only open to civilians on weekends and holidays. Smaller waves make this place A-1 for beginners, families and other unaggressive types. Sandy bottom with gentle slope here means if you eat it, you got time to chew—none of that slam-the-beach-down-your-gob foolishness. This clean and easy break may remind you, my friends, of your 1st encounter with me, Snorkel Bob. This is a windward beach, so strong trades can blow the Portugee man-of-wars in. (See Where to Snorkel, for Oahu—Hauula and Punaluu Beach Parks)

MAKAHA BEACH on the westside gets the biggest waves in Hawaii in Winter, when you should look, don't touch, unless of course you happen to be congenitally deficient in fear, like the guy who got dropped from a helicopter outside a 30' break because no way could he paddle out through 30-footers. Then he drops in—don't look back. It's straight down from there, just you and Mr. Gravity, Mr. Speed and their pesky friend, Mr. Death, who hovers uncertainly in the 10 megaton waterwall overhead.

Some guys carry spare air—a mini-cylinder of compressed air with a tiny regulator for the 3-7 minutes they need until mean old Mr. Undertow spits them out. He's there too.

Meanwhile, it's 1 of the 7 Wonders of Oahu and is also the scene of the biggest surfing competitions on Planet E, because some guys just can't get enough.

And a beautiful sandy beach off to the side is where, in Summer months only, the surf isn't too big. It might rough you up if you're careless but usually only assaults with a light mugging instead of sincerely trying to kill you.

# SCUBA DO

If you stop in at Snorkel Bob's on Kauai, Kona, Maui or Oahu, we'll recommend a dive shop. Recommendations change according to whose boats are broke down, who owes me, Snorkel Bob, money, whose customers appear satisfied and other sundry considerations of the local nitrogen industry. I, Snorkel Bob, have mixed feelings on scuba. It's better here than most places, because Hawaii has warm water all year long, no thermoclines, plenty good dive spots and plenty critters. On the other hand, who needs all that equipment to have fun?

If you never dove before and want to try it, most dive shops here sell an intro dive. You'll get a lecture on the equipment and a brief lesson on the purge valve and its function, and how to clear your mask at depth.

Then you'll dive, 35' maximum, where you'll experience the Oh my God phenomenon—breathing under water. You'll practice with your purge valve, take off your mask, put it back on and clear it. In fact, these 2 skills comprise the 1st dive of the certification class.

If once is enough, it's aloha. Or you may continue for 3 or 4 more dives plus 3 classroom sessions. Intros run $60-$70 here depending on economic strife and competition. You, my friends, will instantaneously note the difference between this fluctuant pricing and that bedrock, cornerstone, Mother of All Prices, $9/week for Mask, Fins, Snorkel, Snorkel Map & Tips, the bag, the card, the goop and the Legend of Me, Snorkel Bob, the price to beat ever since when, including but not limited to The Beginning of Time.

Scuba certification runs $300-$350. Some shops here go as high as $120 for the intro experience but I, Snorkel Bob, suspect a shoe shine and back rub in the deal. If the shop is good, the intro-dive cost will accrue toward certification cost. Why should they quibble over a few bucks anyway, when they'll probably peg you another 2 grand for gear you have to have to have to have? (How about those color-coordinated, calf-wrap dive daggers for the Now Woman who knows who she is, where she's going?)

You'll learn and practice more skills on each dive, like ditch and don, buddy breathing, ear clearing, emergency free ascent and much much more. In the classroom sessions, you'll learn about volume exchange, air embolism, nitrogen narcosis, the bends and tons of other fun and valuable info.

Once certified, you'll get a card with your picture on it that enables you to get compressed air anywhere in the world. That doesn't mean you're ready to deep dive Colombo tomorrow. It means you can go to the local dive shop anywhere, show your card and then tag along with the divers from the local shop, who got the local knowledge.

Most dive shops run 2-tank boat trips, and most of the good dive spots are easy access, a mile or so off the south shore. 2 tanks run $85-$135 depending on how much gear you don't have and the mortgage balance on the boat.

# KAUAI

SHERATON CAVERNS is a series of dark holes but not that dark. A cave is dark and dangerous. A cavern is a dead end or has light-emitting fissures overhead. Flutter-kick silting is a chronic nuisance and heavy hazard in caves or caverns. Sheraton Caverns has passed the silt test.

BRENNECKE'S LEDGE is just that, a ledge off Brennecke's Beach. The attraction here is black coral. Alas and alack, however, the black coral remaining is a mere smidgen of what it was when men were real (fearless), and a decompression stop at 15' was called hanging out shallow till the buzz goes away. Then the subaqueous slopes were festooned with black coral for the plucking. And all the divers with fat pockets would belly up for rum and fights and talk of bowlegged women.

No more. Now you look, don't touch. Go home for a light beer, the evening news, a hark, a wish, a sigh.

OASIS REEF is neither an oasis nor a reef but is a refreshing surprise in the deep blue sea. A single pinnacle rises to 35' below the surface, so it's usually a 2nd dive. Many critters gather here, including eels, lobsters and dense populations of my, Snorkel Bob's, little bitty fish buddies.

TURTLE HILL has many turtles.

CATHEDRAL HILL has many churches. Not really. Its open chambers hint sublime habitation. Divine ether is abundant in Hawaii and since the advent of missionaries in the recent century, many such atmospheres bear churchly names.

GENERAL STORE has caverns, a shipwreck, eels, turtles, sharks, rays, big fish, little fish and most likely coming soon, post cards and T-shirts and incredible discounts on activities.

LOST CONGER CAVE is a cave named for an eel that isn't moray; i.e. conger. They go about 8' and despite my, Snorkel Bob's, heartfelt love of nature and its bounty, et al, ad infinitim, these guys are ugly—UGH. LY. Long pointy snoots with long uppers, interweaving lowers and thin lips are remarkably similar to those of my, Snorkel Bob's, certain ex-in-law—don't get me wrong, her daughter was a wonderful girl who gave me, Snorkel Bob, the best years of her life. And Oh, could she cook! Especially after I, Snorkel Bob, got her a book on it. And if she didn't look like the Queen o' the Prom in the a.m., I, Snorkel Bob, sometimes look a little soaked down and dried out then too; it's only human.

Who knows? Maybe you'll experience a nostalgia or 2 too, deep in Lost Conger Cave.

You have maybe 15 more spots to choose from. These shops are good, members of the Professional Association of Diving Instructors (PADI), the scuba documentation cartel:

**FATHOM 5 ADVENTURES**
Poipu Rd.
Koloa, Kauai
(808) 742-6991

This is a ☆☆☆☆☆ shop, which isn't easy and means they pump their own air. $135 for the intro here includes 2 tanks, 2 dives. But it's a good place to continue the cert program at $369.

**DIVE KAUAI**
Kapaa, Kauai
(808) 822-0452

Michael runs 2-tank dives from 9-1 to sites like Tunnels, Cannons, Turtle Bluff, and the island of Niihau during summertime on his 28' Delta. Max 11 divers per trip. The boat has a shower, stereo, and shade. Trips include beverages and snacks. The $85 intro includes 1 tank. Certification is $395. Now offering I.D.C. (Instructor Development Course).

# BIG ISLAND

Most dive shops sell the intro for about $95, same format as Kauai. Certification here runs about $425—higher than other islands, but Kona is best for scuba because of:

THE GOLDEN ARCHES sells no burgers, but has 2 lava arches covered with coral—all that glitters is not fluorescent.

SUCK'EM UP No brewski here, but caverns with skylights. Big entrance, little exit allows surge to spit scuba doers like Zeke Dribble squirting juice gobs.

LONG LAVA TUBE is a 65' lava tube with a skylight, plus another 25' tube nearby. My, Snorkel Bob's, lionfish and manta ray buddies like this spot too. Not to worry, except to know that lionfish have big spikes in their fins, and they hangout upside down, belly to ceiling—and red hot sauce comes out the points. So be aware under those ledges—stand up quick and you could take a shot to the head you'll never forget.

AMPHITHEATER Natural sea caves interconnected by underwater passageways. Imagine that.

MAUNA LANI CAVES are at 60', optimal sport diving depth for maximum contact with gill breathers, and your air lasts longer. Some of my turtle friends tell me, Snorkel Bob, they may never leave the lava tubes here, unless of course some Big Money moves in with a hot new condominial project.

THE PENTAGON has no $600 nail installation devices, but it do have 5 lava tubes converging at 35 foot depth.

THE 6TH HOLE is basics for an excellent dive; coral and fish, fish and coral, and on and on at 60'.

PUAKO I and II is another basic great 1 in Puako Bay at 45' with BIG coral.

# MAUI

Maui intros run around $59-$89, certification about $99-$275, depending on what gear you need. If you're certified and experienced, say 30 to 50 dives, and want unique diving here, choices are good.

ULUA BEACH (Wailea) and BLACK ROCK (Sheraton Kaanapali) are good refresher dive spots, no surprises. Other good spots are the WWII tank and landing craft a mile off POLO BEACH in front of the 15th hole. The boys were knee-walking drunk around Puu Olai in '45, when they barged the tank and landing craft from the bunker at Makena to somewhere else. The tank went over, and nobody said much, so the landing craft went over too. A zillion fish live in the crusty remains now about 80' down. Some big lobsters hang out in the turrets and a hunky eel took up the tank driver's seat a few years ago. He now shares the cockpit, however, with a smaller, more feminine hunky eel who likes to ride shotgun and navigate.

But don't get me, Snorkel Bob, sidetracked. The best dive in Hawaii is the backside of Molokini:

MOLOKINI is the same place you'll see in pictures ad nauseam everywhere. The front side is a relatively shallow crater, maybe 200' deep along the outer edge, and the pictures would look real if they overlaid another shot of the Foodland parking lot—so many charter boats now it's hard to find a spot to dive in.

But the back side facing the ocean is sheer, 4000' down to a ledge, then down another 4000' to the bottom, and not nearly as crowded. Of course these depths are incidental to the sport diver—backside Molokini is a bottomless dive. Current hits the back wall near the center, then flows to either side—on a good day you'll drift at 3 knots. Diving the backside shallow, less than 60', can be difficult with the upsweeps. So most divers drift the backside at 80 or 90'.

Backside Molokini is an advanced dive. You may see some big white-tip reef sharks or grays or some rays running to 25' wingspans. Whale sharks hang out there once or twice a year. A big temptation am the big dog lobsters, 7-8 pounders, walking arrogantly down the ledge just below your dive plan at 130' or 140', only a stone's throw really if you could just drop down there and pickumup. You can't because a) Molokini is a Marine Preserve; no take notting, and b) you get bent at those depths, chasing the big bugs.

Backside Molokini is a 25-30 minute dive. The dive boat picks you up at 1 end or the other, then you hang out inside the crater for your 2nd dive around 40'.

CATHEDRALS is another unique, spectacular dive just off Lanai. It's a natural formation on a 60' bottom with an entry, some windows near the top, an altar in the center and some rough seating around the periphery. Cathedrals appears to be more than a coincidence of natural formations. Most days sunlight hits the altar with a rippling effect. Most dive groups exploring Cathedrals scurry like mice in the pantry, seeking crumbs. Cathedrals is 1 of those rare dive spots, however, where some meditation at 60' makes the trip worthwhile.

For awhile now I, Snorkel Bob, have been particularly satisfied with:

**DIVE MAUI**
900 Front St.
Lahaina, Maui
(808) 667-2080

They run 2 boats with several formats starting with an intro beach dive at $59, up to the 3-day cert for $139. I, SB, especially like their Cathedrals trip. Scuba gear rentals too.

**MAKENA COAST CHARTERS**
Kihei, Maui
(808) 874-1273

MCC runs out of Kihei with an intro at $85 and certified dives for $99. Their 25' Force Marine has shade and can take up to 6 divers. No cert course here but a good Molokini trip.

# OAHU

Certification on Oahu should run $300-$400. Most Oahu shops run 2-tank boat trips, and most good dive spots are easy access, a mile or so off the Waianae Coast.

THE MAHI is a 165' mine sweeper from WWII. Mahi became a research vessel after the Great Conflagration but the data musta been bad, because it got sunk in '84 by Scuba King Ken Taylor, who swore up and down he had plenty depth to sink the whole damn thing but the mast was still sticking out of the water so he went down and strapped on some plastique and blew the mast to smithereens. So now it's about 50' down to the mast stub and 65' down to the deck. You can cruise the ship in and out and visit the hand-fed eels who live there. I, Snorkel Bob, prefer this 1 after brunch, when the eels are already full of hands.

TWIN HOLES is how I, Snorkel Bob, think of my ex-brothers-in-law. The holes begin on the 65' bottom, wide and well-lit. They lead down to 95' and go horizontal to a canyon wall at the far end. Dogies.

THE AIRPLANE is a twin-engine 12-pack on a 100' bottom, stripped down so you can go in the cockpit and push the beefcake eels out of the way and take control and pilot a drowned bird that used to do 200 knots but now can't even blow bubbles, except maybe when an eel scores a can of beans or something. Maybe you'll get narced down there and try to bring her in on instruments. Who the hell knows?

MAKAHA CAVES is an excellent 2nd dive at 30-50' with lava tubes, turtles and other marine life in prolific preponderance. The lava tubes here are through streets, no silt, plenty light, leading to extravagant terrain with arches, tunnels and canyons.

3 shops on Oahu with strong service are:

**ALOHA DIVE SHOP**
Koko Marina Shopping Center
Honolulu, Oahu
(808) 395-5922

Jackie has owned this outfit for 27 years and runs intros at Manalua Bay, a good spot for beach dives. The $85 intro includes all equipment. A 3-day PADI cert is $398.

**DAN'S DIVE SHOP**
660 Ala Moana Blvd.
Honolulu, Oahu
(808) 536-6181

Good for intros and certs. Dan wants $70 for a boat intro on his 32' catamaran, and $300 for certification. But with 2 or more people the price drops to $250 each. Dan offers Japanese instruction for $450. Shouldn't they pay more?

**SOUTH SEAS AQUATICS**
2155 Kalakaua Ave.
Honolulu, Oahu
(808) 735-0437

South Seas runs 18 people on a 38' Delta, a great dive boat, with 6 certified divers per guide. 3-day cert course offered.

# BEACH AWARENESS

All beaches in Hawaii are public. All humans have access everywhere, even the beach at the Ritz. A beach is terrafirmally defined between its high water mark (no weeds) and actual H2O.

Many beaches have particular characteristics. Beach awareness factors these details for enjoyment and longevity.

For example, Yokohama Beach on Oahu is known for unimpeded mileage, allowing meditation at a steady clip until arrival at the crux of the situation.

North shore beaches account for disproportionate drownings on all islands, because currents are swiftest on the north shores, with swirls, eddies and murks. Many north shore currents are faster than Mark Spitz and can prevent landfall, but they will eventually tire of toying with you. However, north shore Kauai currents are much stronger and must be respected.

Kona has few beaches, and many great Kona snorkel spots are 4-wheel only, over the lava. No beach means thinner crowds. No sand or course sand means clearer water.

A beach most revered by me, Snorkel Bob, near Hana on Maui is like most beaches in its need for respect. It was only with a wince and a grimace that I, Snorkel Bob, heard of the 2 guys not long ago who went maki because they went into the ocean, because they had to, because they'd just arrived and it looked so different from Cleveburg. But no sooner did they clear the break than a tremendous set came rolling in. The waves seemed endless and growing. So when they'd waited for maybe 20 minutes for a lull in the action, they decided a lull would never come. So they made for the beach because they were tired of waiting, and now they wait no more, or as they say in Hana, no mo stay. If they had to wait 2 hours and then 2 hours more they could have eventually cruised on in, casual, dog paddle even.

Black Sand Beach in Hana, on the other hand, is a sheltered cove lined with polished coarse sand, gloss black. Makena Beach on Maui can pluck a heartstring gently as a muse but accounts for a dozen broken necks and shoulders every year—southern exposure, bad bottom. Waves roll in from 7,000 miles of open ocean. A south swell, usually in Summer, can pump 12' surf. Most beaches descend gradually, for an even break. Makena bottom drops off, so the waves collapse.

Remember Boogie Rule #6 (Don't watch local children boogie killer surf and say hey if they can do it, I can do it). You like die? I, Snorkel Bob, have seen grown, rational people stroll into the Valley of the Shadow of Death, into the monster maw to learn instantly the rule of slam, the reality of tonnage. And alas, in that bleak epiphany they slide to the realm of Kablammaa! to the next moment, the next lesson: Chaos.

But enough bad talk. You can hit the warm and wet anywhere in Hawaii and think, *Now what in the hell is that guy, Snorkel Bob, so worried about?* Calm and serene is what you'll see. I, Snorkel Bob, only advise sitting still to see if it sticks, the calmness, the serenity. If it does, so much the better—so much easier to see what lies out front, what is real, as in real life.

Makena is excellent for swimming; visibility to 120' with no surfers, windsurfers or boat traffic. The catch is: Don't hang out in the surf line. Get in or get out. You can watch the set pattern—even on a monster day, you'll get 30 or 40 seconds between sets when you can get in. Same goes for getting out.

If you swim Makena and think you'll never get a break between sets, wait anyway, you will. If you make your move and another set overtakes you, turn around and dive under it. If you succeed, it's a rush.

And a half mile out can be too far (strong current), so be aware between the devil and the deep blue sea.

Little Beach is just north and over the promontory (Puu Olai) on a steep path that takes 2 hands.

Little Makena Beach has a perfect left boogie break (see Boogie, Where to). It's also known as the nude beach or the clothing optional beach. It too, is a most beauteous matrix of sand and sea, and some days it's like it was, with a few people hanging out naked. Other days it's crowded, asses and elbows. Some days it's strange, thick with alternative sexual preference. And some days it's like it really was; solitary.

The ex-Mayor (Hannibal) long ago sent in SWAT teams to bust the nakeds. What a scene, all these guys in their camou-fatigues, berets, machetes, guns and walkie talkies, rounding up the naked threat. But you can't suppress the sinners.

Cane fields plumed polyvinyl chloride into the atmosphere then. They still do, and sugar sucks up 900 gallons of fresh water per pound for personal profit in the name of Jobs with heavy federal price support. The green berets haven't stormed Little Beach in awhile and I, Snorkel Bob, promise to say nothing more of a political nature. I, Snorkel Bob, am not a candidate. If nominated I will not run. If elected I will not serve. I mean not for County Council in '98, or Mayor in '99, or President Of The United States of America In '00.

And it's waay too soon to talk about my reelection campaign for '04, agenda for the 21st, etc, et al, ie.

DON'T FORGET YOUR SUNSCREEN!

(Or you might get burned).

# DAS BOATS

*"Can you tell me, Snorkel Bob, is this boat thing really worth it? I mean, can't I snorkel just as well at the beach, or eat generic baked chicken in a cheap restaurant, or see whales at the scenic lookout, or get cold, beat-up and constipated during rush hour in Cleveburg?"*

Yes, she said yes, again yes. Howsoever, the boat thing can be worth it, if you choose a good boat.

## KAUAI

Na Pali coast (northshore) rubber boat trips are big on Kauai, because the guy who started the brass-balls business of taking tourists (of all people) up that jagged, bumpy coast made a ton o'dough. The dough drew a crowd of other guys into the biz too. I, Snorkel Bob, think the 1st guy was smart, because he knew who should drive his rubber boats. Inflatables are safe as any boats in these conditions, and if they go kapa kai (upside down) on your head, they may only dent your skull rather than pounding it to a tasteless pulp. On the comfort side, however, they are neither a) dry nor b) smooth riding. They say no bad backs or pregnant women, which I, Snorkel Bob, find sexist and/or redundant, since who else can get pregnant? Oh sure, they could allow pregnant dogs, but I, Snorkel Bob, bet they wouldn't. So why don't they just say No bad backs or pregnant humans?

Back on the plus side, however, they don't draw much water, allowing you, my friends, to glide serenely over rocks near the surface without scraping your ass. These big, lovable toy boats can even run right up on the beach, but beware the hernia waiting in the shove off.

Anyway, where was I, Snorkel Bob? Oh yes, the right guys. No Barnacle Bills here, these guys stay calm when the sea gets steep and dark. These guys can fake a smile in fonky conditions and tell you it's A-OK. And it is, sometimes. The Na Pali coast rubber boat trip is extremely popular and I, Snorkel Bob, think at least half that popularity is warranted.

Like most adventures for sale in Hawaii, this 1 too, requires discretion (caveat emptor). Also keep in mind that some of these captains, especially the newer ones, are subject to the lure of showbiz and general bad judgment, the "Hey, look at me now!" syndrome, such as approaching a cave for the drama when the approach is a no man's land of steep breakers, size XL, going kapa kai, embarrassing himself and his employer, getting everybody wet and nearly drowned and calling their lawyers and ruining the whole day with talk of pain and trauma, punitive damages, we'll settle out for 2.3.

Relax, it only happened once. And I, Snorkel Bob, ain't whistling Dixie by calling it a great trip. So you get a little bit cold, wet, plugged up, beat up, yelled at—hey, that's life at sea. I, SB, recommend it. These outings include a snorkel stop, unless of course it's seas 6-8', trades 15-30, for which surplus adventure you will pay no more, except of course for nerve tax, wear and tear and the horror, the horror, the horror... Stop!

It's a great trip, and I, Snorkel Bob'm, not kidding either! And if that ain't enough, at least 2 outfits (Captain Zodiac and Hanalei Sea Tours) are licensed to drop you at Kalalau Trail—makes Shangri La look like Kansas—from whence you can hike back to civilization or hike farther and get picked up tomorrow. Extreme gravity hazard on cliff trails here. Boat drops available in Summer only, when the surf is smaller. State permit required. (See Hiking.)

Among those pounding the waves off Na Pali coast:

## CAPTAIN ZODIAC
Hanalei, Kauai
(808) 826-9371

Captain Z runs 5 trips per day, 3 to the Na Pali Coast, and 2 to Kipukai. The full day trip (approx. 6 hrs.) to the secluded beach Nualolokai for a picnic lunch is $108 for adults, $98 for kids; a 3-4 hr.

sightseeing/snorkeling trip is $78 and $63; 2-3 hrs. (no snorkeling), $68 and $58. This is the oldest rubber boat outfit and has an excellent reputation on all islands.

### NA PALI ADVENTURES
Hanalei, Kauai
(808) 826-6804

This outfit has all the above, more here, less there, with a difference: No mo da rubber boat. Catamaran motorboat this 1. Try it out maybe, and if you do, let me, Snorkel Bob, know if it's a good 1. 4-hr. morning trip is $90 for adults, $50 for kids. 2-hr. afternoon trip is $65 for adults, $30 for kids, less for cash or traveler's checks.

### HANALEI SEA TOURS
Hanalei, Kauai
(808) 826-7254

Rubber boats and power cats and many trips ranging $55-$110. 4-hr. morning snorkel trip is $75; 2-hr. sightseeing trip is $55. This outfit is "1 of the oldest" Na Pali coast boat trippers, which must be worth something, since most claim oldness or 1stness. This 1 is good, with state permits for those behaviors states like people to have permits for.

The latest development in the northshore fleet is the 33' power cat, less bumpy, some say less fun. But boats are like life: you get your comfort, or you get your speed.

REMINDER: As a reactionary with your comfort in mind, I, Snorkel Bob, will herein spend 2¢ more: Most Na Pali outfitters provide snorkel gear but with no reverence for snorkeling, as if you too should be oblivious to utmost communion with Mama Deep.

Most snorkel gear on these boats is junk. No names mentioned, but 1 outfit got to the snorkel grounds 1 day and said all the 4-eyes on board were in luck, because Rx masks are right here, have at um. Then they pulled out a milk crate full of dingy, scratched, unclean and unlabelled Rx masks. Sheesh, what a scene—all these squinters groping for the right Rx then fighting like fat ladies at a rummage sale over the 1 pair that worked. Take the stuff you got from me, Snorkel Bob.

The southside fleet on Kauai is more divergent, several boats promoting custom charters. Again, enjoy the process, eyeball the boat, the crew, the chart. Look past the brochure; photographs can be airbrushed, boats can't.

You also got some motorboats to choose from, and some little daysailers running off the south end up and down the coast.

## CAPTAIN SUNDOWN'S CATAMARAN CRUISE
Hanalei, Kauai
(808)826-5585

This is a good, traditional snorkel sail, or just a sail on a 40' 15-passenger catamaran out of Hanalei Bay. Standard fare is a 6-hour snorkel trip for $95 to a secluded beach, Kipukai.

Captain Sundown also has the Private Charter, $950 for 3 hours, $1000 for 4 hours; "Hey, I'll stay out there till they get sick of it."—Captain Sundown, himself.

I, Snorkel Bob'll, give this to Captain Sundown: He be Captain Sundowning 26 years now, going on 27, no crash, no burn. He's a small operator with a personal approach. So there you are.

THE WAILUA RIVER is the only navigable river in Hawaii (not like the cute little creek the kayakers use on the way to Hanalei). The Wailua River is like what you saw in the old Tarzan movies, sans crocs of course, but with the same jungle foliage on the passing shoreline. The stories you hear on the way are good and historically correct. Up the river used to be sacred, heavy mana, and the route passes what modern students of the old way call Power Spots.

## SMITH'S FERN GROTTO BOAT TOURS
Wailua, Kauai
821-6892
8-3 Daily

Smith's is north of Lihue on Hwy 56. Turn left into Wailua Marina. The Smiths pack a passel o' people on an object that displaces water heavier than its own weight. It's like an open-air cane house, the boat, unlike river trips I, Snorkel Bob, have seen elsewhere, like, say, up the Navua River in Fiji in 30' skinny canoes with 45hp outboards that go 12 miles up at 25 knots with nary a bump nor splash but only a hiss and a slice...

Into the heart of darkness, to where rapids cancel 20 of the 25 knots, yet a white man like me, Snorkel Bob, derives small solace knowing that going over will carry me home. Cold, swift thoughts rush in a current on hearing Prince Mjmoubji say how glad he is to see me, Snorkel Bob, and how his grandfather would have been even gladder, so tender I appear to be on the upper gams. Yes! Eating me, Snorkel Bob, in the real and literal

sense is what Grandfather Jmjuojbi would have proposed.
Even my Nike Airs? Ah, his most very favorite part of all! Olobongo!
Jambo Bula Matari! Gobbogobbogobbo...

Meanwhile, back on Kauai, you got 1 large floating device, slow and
comfy and cool (1/2 acre shade, under roof) lumbering up the river to the
Fern Grotto, a formidable cave worth seeing. In my, Snorkel Bob's,
opinion, it's a nice trip.

It will not satisfy your appetite for adventure, and they don't "sail" up
the river, like the brochure says. But it's only $15 for a 1.5-hour ride
($7.50 for kids) so what the hey. It's a great deal. They run every half
hour, 9-3:30.

# BIG ISLAND

On the Big Island, the Kona Snorkel Fleet goes to Captain Cook's
Monument in Kealakekua Bay or Kaiwi Point near the old airport north of
Kailua. Either place is accessible by car, with some minor hiking and
swimming requirements too. Captain Cook's is a marine preserve (see
Where to Snorkel) with extreme clarity, 120-150', and more fish than
gnats on Snorkel Dog's ass in July. That's some fish. Steep coral walls
drop 500' so it's a vertical plane with reverse hierarchy—the lower you
go, the bigger they get, kind of like Wall Street.

Kaiwi Point is just off a lava coastline. It's a vertical wall here too, but
in lava and coral that levels at 20', an easy dive with a little practice if
you lay off the liquor and smokables. Once down you can cruise the coral
garden. These fish have been on welfare so long they get hostile if you
don't bring a handout. I, Snorkel Bob, remind them that fishfood is
baaaad. Bad. Still, they insist.

Most head boats pump up the jam with luau hoopla, with a PA
system, an MC and some "entertainment," like you're the Brady Bunch
and actually appreciate that crap. I, Snorkel Bob, in gentler moments
suspect some people do enjoy that sort of thing.

**SEA QUEST RAFTING ADVENTURES**
Keauhou Bay, Big Island
(808) 322-3669

Sea Quest runs rubber boats, 2-6 people, on 4-hour tours in the
morning to Captain Cook's monument and the City of Refuge at $59 per
person, or 3-hour tours in the afternoon to Kealakekua for $44 per

person. I, Snorkel Bob, am told these guys run a good trip with good boats.

## CAPTAIN ZODIAC
Kailua, Big Island
(808) 329-3199

This outfit takes 2 excursions daily, max 16 passengers per, to Kealakekua Bay for snorkeling and tropical lunch, whatever that is. $62 for adults, $52 for kids.

## BODY GLOVE
Kailua, Big Island
(808) 326-7122

More of the same on a 55' trimaran, plus scuba, breakfast and lunch; $36 for adults, $19 for kids. During whale season, the Body Glovers run a Greenpeace whale watch from 2-5, but I, Snorkel Bob, tend to believe Captain Paul Watson (the Ocean Warrior) when he calls Greenpeace a top-heavy, namby pamby bureaucracy. Paul Watson went offshore and rammed a Japanese driftnetter or 2 and sunk half the Norwegian whaling fleet. Greenpeace calls him radical. I, Snorkel Bob, call him effective. So what am I, Snorkel Bob, supposed to do? Get excited about a Greenpeace whale watch? NOT. I, SB, am tired of pussyfooting around. Send your money to the Sea Shepherd Conservation Society. Greenpeace is puff.

Meanwhile, Body Glove runs a terrific trip, once you overlook the naive approach to conservation.

# MAUI

The main Maui excursion is the Molokini Snorkel Adventure, so promoted that the Molokini Marine Preserve is no longer an ecosystem but is home only to those species adaptable to crowds. By 10 a.m. every day, except those days blown out by gale-force winds, the place looks like a continuous deck. And that's only on the surface. Below it's yellow clouds—decomposing bread heaved overboard for fish arousal, and several hundred Alpha Normals after coffee or tea and the 90-minute cruise out.

But hey, sometimes you got to overlook the small stuff. Maui boats sell a westside beach snorkel too along the Kaanapali coast, and many cruise the reefs off Olowalu.

Again, beach snorkeling will show you as many different species, especially in the wilderness preserve areas. The Molokini thing is as much as a boat ride as a snorkel trip.

Molokini is 8 miles out in deep water, so sometimes a big sumbitch'll cruise through, like the 25' manta ray that hung out for a few weeks this year, or the whale sharks drifting by.

But since the trip is 4-6 hours, and snorkel time is an hour or 2, you can see the importance of the boat.

Standard fare on most of the boats is tropical fruit and/or juice on the way out; deli buffet lunch, soda, beer and bag wine after snorkel adventuring. Standard fare is also $50-60 a head with kids $10-20 off depending on how old they look. (Remember: Caveat emptor. You get what you pay for, sometimes).

I, Snorkel Bob, happen to like:

## SUNTAN SPECIAL
Maalaea Harbor in Maalaea, Maui
(808) 874-0332

Suntan Special is a real boat for 1 thing, and I, Snorkel Bob, can tell you, you can make a good-looking Molokini thang brochure a whole heap cheaper than you can buy a good Molokini thang boat.

Some of the Molokini fleet are 6-pack sail boats with a maximum speed of 6-8 knots. Others are head boats with 80-300 people aboard and a showbiz, luau glitz that presumes you cannot enjoy life without noise. Damn! I, Snorkel Bob, find that stuff irritating. And when I, Snorkel Bob, see 1 of the headboat bilge rats pluck an innocently bystanding octopus from its home so a bunch of Gamma Normals can go, "Uuuu!" while it slowly writhes and dies on deck, you may well anticipate my, Snorkel Bob's, shark frenzy impersonation. I mean really.

I, Snorkel Bob, like a boat like Suntan Special because it's maybe 18 people on a racing yacht. They let me, Snorkel Bob, drive it 1 time, and the speedo got pegged at 24 knots, which feels like 90 mph on a motorcycle, which feels like 450 mph in your father's Oldsmobile. The ride is $60 plus tax for bigs, $39 for smalls, free for miniatures (2 and under).

## MAUI DIAMOND II
Maalaea Harbor in Maalaea, Maui
(808) 879-9119

Out of Maalaea at 7 to Molokini, then to a 2nd spot off Makena. MD II has room for 18 divers and snorkelers–snorkelers usually rule. $50 gets the 5-hour snorkel trip with breakfast, snax, deli lunch, a cabin for shade and a baño in case you can't free'um up for whizzing over the rail.

No QE II, this, but BIG on skills and service. In the words of a mermaid I, SB, happen to know: "Mellow, intimate and fun."

## NAVATEK II
Maalaea Harbor in Maalaea, Maui
(808) 661-8787

I, Snorkel Bob, must defer to the 100 people daily who take this trip to Lanai and love, love, love the Belgian waffles with blueberries, the air-conditioned dining room, the burgers, drinks and beer. The crew is up to the task with impressive manners and info. An on-board masseuse goes 15 minutes for $15 and will not say, "Arrr Billy."

It's a smooth, fast ride to Lanai with lounge chairs and big bathrooms. Lanai is as pristine for snorkeling as Molokini was 20 years ago. The crew is helpful in the water and hurls into 3rd world crafts après snorkeling, making hats, boats and flowers from palm fronds as prizes for the Hawaiian Trivia Contest during the trip back to prevent depression. The music is Hawaiian with a real guitarist, but not oppressively loud.

It's a late departure, 8, with an hour between check-in and cast-off. It's $112 booked through me, Snorkel Bob, or $140 otherwise. The snorkel gear on board is generic but sanitary.

## PRIDE OF MAUI
Maalaea Harbor in Maalaea, Maui
(808) 875-0955

A friendly, attentive crew is well-informed and alert. This is a big, comfy bucket for those prone to the ho heave. The lower deck is shady and a swim step makes the old in-out a breeze. You will get good snorkel instruction, flotation if you want it, breakfast, snax, BBQ chicken, burgers or garden burgers for lunch and keg beer and/or (oy) Mai Tai's after the 2nd snorkel.

It's a load o' beef with 100 humans churning the azure serenity to spin cycle, but hey, you won't get lost. And what could you possibly have to discuss that's more important than Jimmy Buffett at 168 decibels? Check-in is 7:30, then you wait an hour and get to Molokini about 9 to join the jam-packing.

The snorkel gear appears dirty enough to warrant a condom, and gear fitting is down to: Here. Use this.

Again, I, SB, must defer to the hundreds who take this trip daily and love it at $69 a throw plus $35 for a 1-tank dive or $55 for 2 tanks. $15 will get you a family photo, and $30 buys an underwater video, or you can rent an underwater camera for $20.

# OAHU

The boat thing is different on Oahu, where the booze cruise began, and where some say boat rides were 1st called awful. But some people just don't understand the joy of cheap liquor and sunburn. 1 outfit here advertises a "Hearty Picnic Lunch & Snacks, Open Bar of Beer, Hawaiian Entertainment, Wading in Shallow Water." A volleyball net, knee-deep, rounds out the action, and the picture shows a big fat guy lunging for a shot that will obviously get him all wet. What a laugh that will be at the open bar of beer. Some cruises even barbecue, right there in knee-deep water. Did you ever dream it could be this good?

THE DINNER CRUISE is 1st cousin to all cruises on Oahu, and is available on the other islands too.

I, Snorkel Bob, am not the best person to ask about the Dinner Cruise, because I, Snorkel Bob, take a Blue Plate Special as it comes. Sticky white rice, succotash and cold beets are 3 of my favorite things. But I want 1 at a time. I might vary the order, why mix the peas and the beets? It doesn't make sense.

That's why I, Snorkel Bob, think you oughta have dinner (see Eateries) before or after your sunset cruise. Again, I, Snorkel Bob, emphasize the boat—not the menu.

Don't get me wrong. It's not like I, Snorkel Bob, got my head in the sand. I'm perfectly (painfully?) aware that some people want to go out on the bay and eat dinner, or at least they think they do. Why are so many gratifications in our culture hinged on immediate return? And why are so many gratifications orally based? All fulfillments are in easy access on the lovely island of Oahu, so why mush them up together?

What many people get on a dinner cruise is a growth opportunity. If they're de rigeur on cruise paraphernalia, another opportunity rises to their Snorkel Bob Barf Bags.

At best it's generic baked chicken, a rebaked spud and salad dressing from a bucket on rusty iceberg lettuce pressed to your chest by the dreamlike balmy breeze. Once aboard, your only choice is Italian, Thousand Island or Blue Cheese.

A typical Booze Cruise runs in the low $70s, for which you will be subject to mass-production Mai Tais, Acme brand vodka, teriyaki beef, salad, rice, corn on cob. **YOU WILL DANCE** to a live band playing electric Hawaiian, and the more sentimental among you may thrill to a coconut brassiere and grass skirt.

Please keep in mind that I, Snorkel Bob, am a real prima donna on this subject and am perfectly aware yet again that many people enjoy the traditional music, the fabulous grinds and the Mai Tai drunk so accessible on the Dinner Cruise.

Many people go and love love love it.

Yet not from me, Snorkel Bob, will you be encouraged to board a snorkel boat or dinner cruise on Oahu, or a dinner cruise on any other island, unless I, Snorkel Bob, book those cruises. But cheer up! Alternative prevails.

THE WAIKIKI BEACH CATAMARANS are traditional since the mid-50s, developed when beach boys turned a few bucks selling boat rides to tourists in this swamp. These beach cats are designed to haul people, sail fast and draw shallow, so they can board on the beach. 1-hour rides are about $12, which is a red-hot, 4-square value you won't see that much of in Hawaii.

It's a great deal because sailing is like roller skating, or like the all-you-can-eat buffet. Hey, who you think you're kidding? How much of that swill can you pack down, anyway? How long can your ankles take the pressure, your toes the blisters? You think sailing is any different? You think you can't get too much sun and salt and carefree breeze? I, Snorkel Bob'm, here to tell you: Cold, wet, tired, sore, constipated, beat and broke is where yachting will get you, unless of course it's on OPB (other people's boats.) And at $12 down with a 1-hour back door, the inevitables are easy to weather.

About a half-doz beach cats work it at 100-yard intervals. They're all great, and all give you a drink and snacks and a run around Diamond Head in fair trades. The only downside is the body count; some of them carry 30 or more, which is a push, but it's only an hour. Sometimes smaller boats mean smaller crowds.

Sunset is at a premium, it's so beauteous and romantical, in many cases leading to sexual intercourse between married people. It costs a few bucks more because you get another 30 minutes for that extra prime in your pump.

If pressed to the wall for my favorite beach cat of all, then I, Snorkel Bob, would have to fess up and say:

**LEAHI**
By the Sheraton
Honolulu, Oahu
(808) 922-5665

All-aluminum with a high-aspect ratio and low profile makes her lean and mean. Reverse sheer, plumb bows and skinny little beams (2.5') give her that razorblade relationship to Mama O. With a 57' stick, 22' rail to rail and 44' x 2 waterline length, Leahi is fastest on the beach. Goofy green all over the sails, but she still looks good in the dark, and I, SB, am a sucker for the speed. And what a deal, $16 for adults, $8 for kids and it's only $6 to go again. The sunset sail is $24 with an open bar.

WHALE WATCH CRUISES happen from about January 10 to the last of April. The hype and promo starts about Thanksgiving because the charter people must sell to eat.

I, Snorkel Bob, get a good laugh when you, my friends, ask for a combination cruise, 1 that includes a whale watch. What? You think the whales know which boats with what people who bought whose tickets to perform for? Not.

The big whales breath every 21 minutes, the babies every 8 or 9 no matter what, no matter who or where.

I, Snorkel Bob, get caught up in whale frenzy mania too, and sometimes can't get enough. Did you know that an adult whale's lungs are as big as a Volkswagon? I, Snorkel Bob, forgot to find out if that's 2 lungs for 1 Volkswagon, or if it's 2 Volkswagons per whale—Whoa! That would be something, wouldn't it? I, Snorkel Bob, assume they mean the kind of Volkswagon that everybody naturally thinks of when somebody says Volkswagon, i.e., a bug.

But like my old painting teacher, Dewey Sewell ("You just dip her in a can 1 time 'en slap 'at sumbitch on'ere 'n 'at's all 'ey is to it.") once told me, Snorkel Bob: "Boy," he said. "You take 'at word, assume, 'n you know what you got? You got ass, for starters. Then you got you. And then you got me. That's where assume'll getcha."

Sometimes old Dewey comes back when I, Snorkel Bob, think I got it all figured out. I mean, what if they meant Volkswagon like in the new Vanagon? And then it did turn out to be 2 Volkswagons per whale. Boy oh boy! That's big! That's about as big as The Empire State Building. Once I, Snorkel Bob, went so far as to imagine 3 Volkswagons.

That's why I, Snorkel Bob, am such a fanatical whale watcher. Because there's so much stuff to learn, and it's so fascinating. Some days I, Snorkel Bob, just watch and watch and watch. Boy oh boy oh boy oh boy.

Hey, you know what else? I, Snorkel Bob, heard that each baby whale is as big as a Volkswagon, and if you stick your head underwater while the whales are in town, sometimes, if you're very very lucky and possibly blessed by the Cosmic Whale, you can hear the itty bitty babies crying out in their teency-tinecy voices, "Maaa Ma. Maaa Ma." It's so cute. I, Snorkel Bob, am thinking of putting them up all over my room—putting up their pictures. I mean you couldn't get that many Volkswagons in my room, not to mention Mommy and Daddy whales as big as...as big as elephants! And all those Vanagons for lungs. Boy oh boy oh boy oh boy.

How about them whales? My, Snorkel Bob's, very most favorite part of the whole whale shebang is these tourii (present company excluded, of course) you see walking the promenade who suddenly jerk sideways, hunker down, hood the eyes, squint hard at a foamy speck on the horizon, inhale deep, stand up straight and scream bloody frigging murder:

# WHALES!

That's my, Snorkel Bob's, very very most favorite part of all. Say, did you know that a whale's tail is as wide as a Volkswagon? Boy oh boy oh boy oh boy oh boy.

But really I, Snorkel Bob, suppose my very very very most favorite part of whale madness is the hourly update they got now on the radio: The Whale Report. I, Snorkel Bob'm cruising down the road trying to keep up with Fonky Holliday on Broadway with the radio way up. And right in a part I knew all the words to, about 4 bars from the end, this guy comes on all crackly like he's on a VHF at sea and says he's Fuzzy Bollinger with the Whale Report:

Cchhh...chhh (static on the wire)...We got a sighting this morning at 0800 hours—a very big mommy whale and her little baby. Chhh chhh... They swam along, then they went down, then they came up again. She rolled over and raised 1 of her side fins up in the air. Boy oh boy. The baby headed toward us, much against her wishes, I might add. But she didn't do anything to stop him. He came alongside and then he rolled over too. Boy oh boy. Then he swam back toward her and they swam along for awhile, right there in the water mostly. It was something. It was really something. This is Fuzzy Bollinger coming to you live with...the Whale Report... Cchhhhhh

Boy oh boy oh boy.

Anyway, if you get seasick or just generally nauseated but you still want a glimpse of those big, lovable, huggable, adorable (used-to-be squeeze-down-to-oilable) galoots, then I, Snorkel Bob, recommend a casual stroll near the water in Waikoloa or north Lapakahi State Park, on the Kona coast. If you're whale crazy, then you should go, like most of the whales do, to Maui.

Hey! You know what? A grown-up whale is as big as 10 Volkswagons bumper to bumper and weighs as much as a Volkswagon per foot. You smarty-pants guys who always had your hand waving 1st in math class already figured out that whales are much more dense than Volkswagons, even though, just like Volkswagons, they're hollow inside. 1 whale can weigh as much as 40 Volkswagons, not counting luggage and ski racks, and the little itty bitty baby whales hit the water at 3 Volkswagons long, 2 Volkswagons on the scale.

My, Snorkel Bob's, ex-mother-in-law was around 2 Volkswagons. But she had to bust her chops to maintain that kind of weight. 2-handed and all the time was how she ate. I, Snorkel Bob, suspect she had baleen in a former life. It made her mean, all that eating. And the television hours on end didn't help. She wasn't anything like her daughter, my ex-#1 main mermaid, who was sweet and pretty as you can imagine. Until...it happened.

The visit started off innocent enough—I, Snorkel Bob, hardly thought twice about it. What's wrong with a sweet young thing—a skinny drink of water at that—relaxing for an afternoon on the sofa with her mom and The Young and the Restless? And maybe a Twinkie or 2 and a couple bonbons and some soda pop for the dry mouth and maybe some chips to cut the sugar?

By the 2nd day I, Snorkel Bob, feared the worst, and at sunrise, Day 3 (Good Morning America, waffles, Portagee sausage), I, Snorkel Bob, faced it...

The horror, the horror, the horror...

## WHALES!

Now I, Snorkel Bob, take solitary strolls along the south coast, January through April, and remember how it used to be.

# WATER SKI HAWAII

**KAUAI WATER SKI & SURF CO.**
Kinipopo Shopping Village
Wailua, Kauai
(808) 822-3574

This is the only water ski outfit on Kauai and I, Snorkel Bob, rate it ☆☆☆☆ in the bang-for-your-buck category.

Conditions are perfect. Most water ski outfits in the tropics run off the beach near daybreak to beat the trades and subsequent chop—even little 1-2 footers will reach up, pull your toes under and mess witcho rhydm. But this 1 is different.

It's on the Wailua River, which is more than just a river. It's a wide, smooth stream in the country. It could be PagoPago or Arkansas. It's beautiful and stays that way all day.

Kathy and Kenny pull you with a Mastercraft scaled right to the conditions. I.e.; most boat people tend to associate waterline length and horsepower with personal development, station in life, relative connection to the Big Skier, etc. But this is a specialized ski boat that 1) minimizes intimidation and 2) won't yank your chain on liftoff.

Most important, Kathy asserts, is the pricing. It's $45 per half-hour, $85 per hour. But that's not per person, it's for the boat. 2 or 3 people can ski in 1/2 an hour, cutting cost to reasonable levels. And if you book 3+hours with Kathy and Kenny, you get another 10% off.

The ski run is 2 miles up river, and other toys include wakeboards, kneeboards, the ski tube, trick skis and ski torpedos.

High achievers can take lessons, basic to advanced, slalom optional. Crass consumers can achieve acquisition in the Hawaiian style bamboo and grass surf shop where Kathy and Kenny like to sell skis & accessories, swim suits and of course much much more. Idle talkers can shoot the breeze on the wrap-around deck, drink beer and/or wine with a samich from the deli.

Kathy and Kenny also rent a studio cottage down the street for $65/night. The cottage sleeps 2 but in a pinch will eat 4. YOU GET a fruit basket, guava jelly, Kona coffee and 20% off the rides. Now is that an amazing freaking deal? Kathy and Kenny also rent kayaks on the Wailua River—no shore break, current or wind. $25/single, $50/double.

# WINDSURFING

Windsurfers get bad press anywhere if they stay long enough, like dustbowl Oakies or other subcultural groups with deviant tastes that I, Snorkel Bob, would'ruther not mention au'jourd hui. Windsurfers are not famous for stimulating local economies, nor are they known for loquacious elocution or gracious articulation, except, of course, out there. Out there or in here, the best of the lot keep it down to a grunt and throw their clothing in the drier at least twice a week.

HOOKIPA BEACH, on Maui, attracts windsurfers from the USA, Europe and Japan. They come for the wavejumping.

Many places claim to be the Windsurf Capital of the World. Like that lake in Switzerland, or that creekbed up in Washington. But those people are sorely confused, and I, Snorkel Bob, can promise you: Hookipa is the Windsurf Capital of the World. It's on the way to Haiku, Pauwela and Hana, just past Paia, a mile or so before Maliko Gulch. And on any given (windy) day, if the waves are pumping, you'll see 70 or 80 world-class athletes running and jumping waves. It makes me, Snorkel Bob, need an ice-cold beverage just looking at them.

What makes this the windsurf capital of the world are optimal conditions for the 3 primary skills:

1) Open water for high-speed sailing.

2) Strong, steady wind for figure-8 sailing round the buoys.

3) Big waves for wave jumping.

Windsurfers ride waves like surfers then spin on a dime and head back out, into the waves. I, Snorkel Bob, mean big waves. They shoot the faces and keep going. It was historical a few years ago when the 1st guy did a 360. Then 1 did a 720! I, Snorkel Bob, ponder a 1295. Beverage and shade are recommended for the bleachers at Hookipa.

# FISHING

KONA is 1 of the top 3 fishing areas in the world. The other 2 are off the coast of Mexico near Acapulco, and off the coast of Australia near New South Cucamonga.

The biggest fish are black marlin off Australia. But they're rare and hard to catch, often weighing 2,000 lbs. I, Snorkel Bob, saw a home movie shot on a boat there that had just hooked a very big fish. The fish sounded, ran up for slack, then jumped straight up at the transom. His head was big as a Volkswagon, and his body just kept coming. Up, up he went and at 30' up he fell away from the boat. 3,000 pounds was consensus on board, but that came later. Sooner, you only saw the skipper flying off the flying bridge to C-cc-ccc-cu-cu-cut her loose.

Meanwhile, back in Hawaii, billfish are big. Some say they're plentiful, but I, Snorkel Bob, deny any animal count from humans who can't even keep themselves accountable. Sailfish, spearfish, striped marlin, a rare black marlin and Pacific blue marlin are the draw. The record blue was 1,300 pounds. It was killed so it could be weighed.

Heavy season on Kona is Summer, tournament time, which is Status Quo Vadis, if you get my drift. I, Snorkel Bob, mean these guys got microwave Big Macs, health spas, roller rinks, mini-twin cinemas and shoe shine parlors on board now. 1 guy had a bowling alley below deck, only 2 lanes, but still. And the worst conflagellation I, Snorkel Bob, ever saw, was a fishing boat with a swimming pool on board, when over the rail is right there. I mean really. The Old Man and the Sea this ain't.

The 2 popular spots are Double D, 1.5 miles straight out from Kailua, and The Grounds, 2 miles straight off Keahole—Kona Airport.

The fleet is big. A boat runs about $300 for all day and $200 for a half day. A share boat carries up to 6 anglers.

Kauai, on the other hand, is famous for honeymoons. So you might think: Ah ha! I fish Kona, go bumpety squish on Kauai. But don't forget Grant's Law of Proximity. Heavy action peaks in the 2nd concentrice from the center.

What do I, Snorkel Bob, mean? That you may have greater luck playing this 1 off-center—seek the deep spot on Kauai, the G spot on Kona.

Why that is? Because fame is a function of 1-dimensional data. Kona gets the fishing press on account of marlin. But far more fish are caught off Kauai—tuna, mahi mahi, ono, bonita.

This leaves Kona for romance under a relentless sun, with the heat, the sweat, the naked abandon.

Kauai fishing is close at hand—10 minutes to the drop. These boats are 6-packs with variable sideflies (groceries, sodas, beer).

**GENT LEE**
Nawiliwili Harbor in Lihue, Kauai
(808) 245-7504

The Gent Lee is 1 of 2, 32' Radoncraft Sportfishermans available for $90/person for 4 hours, $120/for 6 hours. Private charters available. Your catch can be eaten up at the boat owner's restaurant, Fisherman's Galley (246-4700) at no charge.

**SEA BREEZE**
Anini Beach in Kalihiwai, Kauai
(808) 828-1285

Sea Breeze runs off Anini Beach on the north shore near Princeville in Summer and sometimes in Winter from Port Allen near Hanapepe on the south shore. After 18 years as a 26' Custom Sport Cruiser, Sea Breeze is now a brand new (no smudge, sludge, grease, grime, bilge swill, fonky bottom, rotten cotton nor bilious fumes from tired gaskets). It's a 33' twin volvo diesel now, still only $85/person for a half day, 6-pack. You may keep part of your catch. You must ask.

If any boat does not release bill fish, don't go.

# 2
# Dry Fun

# SIGHTS TO SEE

No dryness can approach the warm and wet, yet we must let the wrinkles subside. Snorkeling is like life; we dry today so that tomorrow will be the greater when wetness doth again prevail.

Hail Atlantis!

# KAUAI

Kauai is thickest with postmodern plantations. Why? Because the plantation era, with its estates, cane fields and quaint, camp poverty, not only seems close at hand on Kauai; it is. Sugar still rules here. Call it a lifestyle. See it up close at:

**OLU PUA BOTANICAL GARDENS AND PLANTATION**
Hwy 50 in Kalaheo, Kauai
(808) 332-8182
9:30-3:30 Daily. $12/Adults & $6/Children 5-12

Ola Pua reopened after assault and battery by the hurricane in '92. (The estate is a few miles inland from the beach). This may be the best stroll in Hawaii for scent, color, deep sighing and the beauteous beauty of it all.

This place was put together by the Alexanders of Alexander, Bishop, Baldwin, Castle and Cooke fame—the initial missionary families who came with the Golden Rule for the heathen and ended up with all the land in Hawaii; Thank ya Jaizus! But being good missionaries they capitalized some labor-intensive industry so the heathen could have jobs (by God) and company stores that actually gave credit now on the entire $8 a day unearned until clean into next month. Hallelujah.

But don't get me, Snorkel Bob, started on justice. It's the beauteous beauty we came to peruse, and the pretty smells too.

The Irvine family now runs Olu Pua and knows how to trim a hedge. We're talking flowers, and I, Snorkel Bob, mean big sumbitches that damn near blot the horizon with color and make you weak in the knees with so much beauteous beauty. If you could O.D. on beauteous beauty, I, Snorkel Bob, suspect this place would be the focal point of catastrophe.

The plantation house was designed by C.W. Dickey, who created the peaked-roof, rambling style common to old money Hawaii. You are allowed a guided tour through the house, past the Irvines still living there and on through the grounds. Here again the hand-wrought detail, celestial views and heart-thumping Asian art is enough to make a water rat like me, Snorkel Bob, crave some tea and crumpets, you know, them big squishy goobers with gooey inside and chocolate on top and fancy sprinkles and a couple beers, because it does get hot in the afternoon, even up next to all this old dough.

The friendly guides lead tours each hour from 9:30 to 1:30 and insist on accompanying your stroll, but it's not like they think you might steal their stuff or anything, not really. If you're in a big group, call ahead for reservations. Major mosquitos here, but ain't that the way it goes way down south?

## GROVE FARM HOMESTEAD
Nawiliwili Rd. Lihue, Kauai
(808) 245-3202
Mon, Wed, Thurs 10 & 1
$5 Adults, $2 kids 12 & under

Grove Farm, in the National Register of Historic Places, is 80 acres of orchards, gardens and cattle pasture surrounded by the town of Lihue. Here in the oldest standing plantation buildings in Hawaii is a research library with reams o' historical documents. You, my friends, might think this is heavy sledding for a guy like me, Snorkel Bob, who knows how far from wet this kind of dry can get. It was. It is. It will be. But that doesn't mean *you* can't go soak some history and tingle in the dust. Guided tours at 10 and 1. Reservations in advance, said the gate guard, though I, Snorkel Bob, never heard of reservations in arrears, except maybe in San Francisco. Now is that nice? No, but you must remember that life is like snorkeling; some days are just plain choppy, murky, overcast. I, Snorkel Bob, usually go anyway, because what else can you do?

## KILOHANA
Hwy 50 in Lihue, Kauai
(808) 245-5608
9:30-9:30 Mon-Sat, 9:30-5:00 Sun
No admission charge

Just west of Lihue on the main highway, Kilohana is old Hawaii via Rodeo Drive. Is it beauteous? Yes. Is it historical? Yes. Is it authentic? Like a reacher's mall with carriages pulled by Clydesdales (in Hawaii?) and an overpriced, ass-kissing restaurant. Still I, Snorkel Bob, loved the lunch repartee.

**KILAUEA POINT NATIONAL WILDLIFE REFUGE**
Kilauea, Kauai

This 31-acre forest preserve on a volcanic bluff faces the deep blue sea. The preserve was closed to foot traffic for a long time after the hurricane, but even the view from the parking lot is so solitary, vast, epic and inaccessible to tour buses that it's worth a look, especially with a full cooler on your way to the north shore for some real fun. Turn off Hwy 56 at Kilauea town and follow the signs for a few miles to land's end. You are here.

# BIG ISLAND

The Big Island gotta lotta untrammeled territory left, where you may have social intercourse with people less keen on parting fools from their money. Not that T-shirts and shell necklaces don't have their place, but it's not here. Best among Big Island singularities are coffee country, cowboy country (Parker Ranch area) and Puna, remnant stronghold of the Revolution and home of the infamous lolo, Puna Butter, ranked highest by those most high. Some say Puna Butter be better than Kauai Electric or Maui Wowie, but I, Snorkel Bob, suspect they're stockholders.

Terrain, climate and ambience vary dramatically on the Big Island. Wide, smooth, roads lead to outbacks where tourism is but a blur on a fringe. Good roads come from the State Highway Department's foresight that the Big Island would be the next focus for tourism after Waikiki. But Kona has practically no beaches, and tourists want beaches, so they chose Maui next because of all the beaches, leaving the Big Island with excellent roads and thin traffic and Maui in endless jam. But don't get me, Snorkel Bob, started on foresight at state level. At least the Big Island is good for cruising.

THE COFFEE HIGHWAY, for example, refers to a stretch of State Rte 180 along the flank of Hualalai Mountain about 10 minutes uphill from the Kona Coast. The road runs through little towns separated by coffee groves, and at 1,800' the cool breeze and epic overview is a perfect backdrop for a coffee jag. A cloud bank prevails by afternoon, but you're so jacked by then your irises may burn through the haze, which must turn purple now and then, judging from your average pedestrians here running coffee houses, art galleries and farms.

This stretch ain't for everybody. Architecture is early Appalachian Baroque, but with excellent jo and local color, it's worth a cruise.

HOLUALOA is the nearest town to Kailua Kona, a 10-minute drive, but 50 light years from Cleveburg, what with the altitude, the country pace and tropical flavor (see Coffee and Art). The State Tourist Council declared Holualoa an official arts district. I, Snorkel Bob, think the State Tourist Council is in the same building as the State Highway Department, but the art galleries in Holualoa show no mo junk than the high-ticket schlock galleries down in the hubbub, and the little galleries up the hill do unveil some rare talent. More fun than the Goodwill before the Goodwill was cool, this 1.

KEALAKEKUA is a few miles south of Holualoa, beyond the point. Rte 180 rejoins Hwy 11, the main north-south road on the Kona Coast. Kealakekua has its old hippies too, crafts galleries and coffee. Community theater still plays in a cavernous wooden theatre here.

KAMUELA (also called Waimea) is cattle country and gateway to 2 lush, unspoiled areas of windward Hawaii, the Kohala Peninsula and the Hamakua Coast. Kamuela, about an hour's drive north of the Kona resorts on Rte 190, looks like what you imagined the Hawaiian countryside to look like—vibrant green pastures rolling under cloudy skies. The Parker Ranch HQ is Kamuela. Steakhouses rule, and a custom butcher can chop your cow to specs. Kamuela wants to be a cowboy town but like so many wannabe's, it came out a shopping mall. Big dough walks these streets, through these saloons and boutiques. The Parker Ranch is the biggest spread around, but the biggest view is through the high-tech telescopes on nearby Mauna Kea (offices in Kamuela).

Hawaii Prep Academy and the Parker School, 2 of Hawaii's most expensive private schools, are here too.

Kamuela's vintage wooden theatre is renovated and active with professional theatre, ballet, concerts, and community theatre. A few museums on local history, chachka shops that call themselves art galleries and a decent European art collection make Kamuela a must for you who like to walk around, feel the fabric, watch the traffic.

**HISTORIC PARKER RANCH HOMES**
Rte. 190 in Kamuela, Hawaii
(808) 885-5433
Open Daily
$7.50 for Adults, $3.75 kids 12 and under

Set back from the road in a landscape that makes Bonanza look like Dogpatch, this housing cluster includes a replica of the original New England-style cottage built by ranch founder John Palmer Parker. The main attraction is the 8,000-square-foot home built by Samuel Parker, among the more flamboyant of J.P.'s heirs. J.P.'s last descendent, Richard Smart, filled the big house with art from his travels abroad. I, Snorkel

Bob, have seen no finer collection of Chinese carving or minor pieces by major French impressionists anywhere from Kamuela to Booneville. My, Snorkel Bob's, favorite is a scene of Venice by Jean Dufy (1888-1964) apparently rendered under the jazz influence. Smart died recently after an on-and-off-Broadway career in musical comedy, and his voice still drifts through the house when the staff remembers to flip the record. Tours of the homes are from 10-4:15 daily. At 9 the visitor center opens, where you can view a 22-minute film of the working ranch.

WAIPIO VALLEY on the Hamakua Coast northeast of Kamuela is an hour north of Hilo on Rte. 19, and from Kona it's maybe 1-1/2 hours. Once in Kamuela you go east to Honokaa, then left on Rte 240 and follow the signs through dense tropical rainforest on the weather side of the island. Waipio lookout is a definite pull over, smell the view over a tropical valley and sea cliffs. The road to the beach from there cuts down along the southern wall of the valley. It's bad, about a mile, 4WD only! Continuing along the south wall, oceanside, for maybe another 2 miles, the road cuts across the valley for a great shot of a south wall waterfall.

Those who continue will arrive at a Water Department gate and a sign that says Keep Out. Obey all signs. If you don't, you cross a river and go waaay back in the valley where some spectaculacular water falls.

Option 2 is a hairpin turn at the bottom of the road, which goes about a mile to the beach. Big ironwoods carpet the forest floor with pine straw, making this a comfortable camp spot. If you go north along the beach toward the north wall of the valley, you will cross a river that will fill your waders. On the far side you may find a trail heading along the north wall through heavy foliage (jungle), past a small waterfall and some houses. This trail ends in about 1.5 miles.

Option 3 is hiking the switchback up the north wall. This tough, 8-mile hike drops into the next valley. It's jungle—deep bush. Some of you will make it. Some won't. You should know by now who you are.

It's 16 miles round trip if you follow the switchback trail up the opposite face, over to the next valley and return to Go, which some of you, my middle management friends, may have trouble doing, considering the work load, low pay, no respect and other baggage dragged so far already. A trail like this 1 may be too much. Remember: "Kapu" means Keep Out, or, more to the point: The horticulturalists back there might take you for a revenuer and open fire.

HILO is a 2 to 2-1/2 hour drive from Kona—more if you stop to drink or ditch beer. Sights along the way will add 30-45 minutes per and will also add tonight in beautiful downtown Hilo and tomorrow too, for the trip back.

Those of you with rental cars were told, Don't take this rental car on the Saddle Road, because if you do, you'll get stuck! And we'll take everything you have or hope to have for the rest of your life. This speech usually precedes: Would you like the insurance? Or would you care to risk your life and assets and those of your heirs and/or assigns?

Not so bad, the Saddle Road. Little bit bumpy maybe, but what the hey—it's a rental! Worse than the bumps are the bleak and the boring and, believe it or not, the frequent gridlock in this outback fringe on the empty side of a rock in the center of the biggest ocean in the world. I, Snorkel Bob, suspect the end is near, but what do I, Snorkel Bob, know?

Better is to come down the Hamakua Coast on Rte. 19 after leaving Waipio Valley.

AKAKA FALLS, about 20 miles south of Waipio Falls on the rain coast, is the longest unbroken waterfall in the Hawaiian Islands—442', freefall. It always makes me, Snorkel Bob, want to drink a beer and shishi at the same time, maybe from a subliminal urge to fit in. Anyway, go down Rte 19 to Honomu, turn toward the mountain on Rte 220, then go left to Akaka Falls State Park.

An asphalt trail to the lookout takes 10 minutes. A mud or dirt footpath goes about 500' behind the falls.

HAWAII TROPICAL BOTANICAL GARDENS (808) 964-5233 is midway between Honomu and Hilo on Hwy 19. The flower show is $15 a head, ages 16 and under go free. It's a fair deal, and they do have you where they want you.

RAINBOW FALLS is easy by car once you're in Hilo. Follow Waianuenue Avenue (Rte 200) about 1.2 miles through town. Then fork right on what is also Waianuenue Avenue. Go 3/4 mile to the sign, Rainbow Falls, which is part of Wailuku River State Park—this is not the same Wailuku as on Maui. Rainbows live and breed in the mist here.

Higher up the river are Boiling Pots; leave the falls and head uphill, away from town, about 1.2 miles. Turn right at Peepee Falls Street and go 1/4 mile to Boiling Pots.

Some of you, my friends, might think the name implies hot springs and a nice soak. Wrong! The boil describes the action of the water. It's frigid and swirling with undercurrent, bottom tow and nasty flagellations. Campers like you who hadn't the guidance, nay the forbearance of my, Snorkel Bob's, Guide, have taken the plunge at Boiling Pots, and now plunge no more.

KAUMANA CAVES, formed by rushing lava in 1881, are now part of a county park with picnic tables and shishoirs. Steps lead down into the cave, where 2 flashlights are best, i.e., 1 primary, 1 secondary. It's sooo dark you'll feel like a lump o' charcoal in the closet at night. Closed-toe shoes will reduce stubs, and an Ace Bandage will assist ankle twists. The cave goes 3/4 mile back and is only for the physically fit.

Take Waianuenue Avenue (Rte 200) west out of Hilo about 1.2 miles. Fork left onto Kaumana Avenue (look for Saddle Road signs) and go 2 more miles to Kaumana Caves County Park.

After all that fun, you drive farther down the coast to:

PUNA Local amazements include orchids growing roadside and a thick forest growing out of relatively young lava. As if that ain't enough, the capitol city (Pahoa) looks at night like where Bogie met Bacall and learned to whistle.

On the map the Puna District is a tight grid with no aesthetic highlight. Maybe that's why so few people come here. In fact the roads are 2-lane and unpaved and wander off the main road every mile or so to deep penetration of inscrutable greenery within 50 yards. Red dirt roads are part of the Homestead Program that offers a country alternative to native Hawaiians. Most Homestead land has no electricity, running water or cable TV, just like in the days of the heathen.

Along the coast, the lava has eroded into a series of shallow pools protected from the surf. (see Snorkel, Where to) These pools are a mix of seawater and spring water, warm from the lava flow underlying Puna, surrounded by palm jungle. They never scuz no matter how many people use them because of incessant circulation, and this could be the far-from-home you dreamed of.

Used to be you could cruise Puna on the circle road, but then Pele awoke and flowed over miles of road and a town and Kamoamoa Campground. Visitors to Puna are fewer now.

Puna has its own circle road, which is more of a triangle, but it passes the pools. I, Snorkel Bob, like to stop in Pahoa, have a bite (see Eateries), secure shelter (see B&B) and seek the groove.

PAHOA is a groove. Its cavernous wooden theatre was built in 1917. Most places stay open until 9 or 10, and though the honkytonk factor is low, the New Agers are thicker n' swamp flies. I, Snorkel Bob, used a few Q-tips there, they talk so soft. And stink? Well, they weren't so bad, mostofum. Puna can be a memorable stop, including but not limited to:

## HAWAIIAN HEMP COMPANY
Rte 130 in Pahoa, Hawaii
(808) 882-7778
10-6 Mon-Sat, 10-4 Sun

HHC has a storefront on the main drag and sells hemp-based clothing, food, paper, literature and art, but no smokeables. "Our planetary woes need a green solution yet Earth's most useful plant is illegal to grow in the U.S.!" HHC declares. I, Snorkel Bob, admire a merchant with a mission.

LAVA TREE STATE MONUMENT is just off Rte 132, the main highway south out of Pahoa, named for rock formations created when lava hit living trees and froze into shapes outlining the trunks. All these years later, eroded and moss-covered, the formations now look in the eerie green mist like the unfinished work of Michelangelo or Harry T. McSwain. Spooky, this place, with hobgoblins in the lava stumps. At sundown the stumps grow nubs, the nubs get fuzz, the fuzz breathes and reaches out... But so nice, the short loop trail.

ISAAC HALE BEACH PARK is a couple miles south of Kapoho tidepools (see Snorkel, Where to) on Rte 137 and has a big lava pool for swimming. Lifeguard Michael used to be a surfer but now he mostly thinks. He'll talk some too. Grass, coco palms, shishoirs, make this a park to relax in.

KILAUEA—THE VOLCANO I, Snorkel Bob, most love the night action, with the red hot, the steam and sizzle, the crackling flow that will ooze anything in its path. Yet I, Snorkel Bob, also worry for my less-than-cautious friends who may not fully grasp the meaning of QUICK DEATH by lava or asphyxiation. I.e., the crust gets thin, and though the gruel is only knee deep, no 1 has yet waded out. The sulphur smoke will make you sick and kill you too, but gently, after it lays you down and melts you. These things are trickier at night, if you don't know your way around.

Kilauea is easy to reach from Hilo (1/2 hour) or Kona (about 2 hours) on Hwy 11. The volcano is a caldera that erupted on the flank of Mauna Loa, a much older and larger volcano. Kilauea is easier to get to and not nearly so cold (4,000' up compared with 13,679'). From the Park Visitor Center, it's another 1/2 hour down the Chain of Craters Road to the drama, where Pele speaks, where you emerge from the bush on the far side of Uranus.

I, Snorkel Bob, enjoy the Volcanoes of Hawaii video with my darts and beer at Volcano House, especially the part where Pele rolls across the

Wahaula and Kilauea National Park Visitor Centers. Something about lava anarchy makes me, Snorkel Bob, feel good, kind of like when Joe Montana and the World Champion San Francisco 49ers took apart the Rams or Cleveburg or just about anyone, piece by piece. Those were the days.

If you like that video, you can check out Past Eruptions of Kilauea and Mauna Loa, playing across the street at the visitor center every hour for 10 minutes. You can get a map and basic orientation there too.

Volcano House is a cozy lodge and restaurant, but at 4,000' it can get cold outside—take a jacket with floppy sleeves you can tie around your belly if you're hot but won't be without in the event of dramatic temperature fluctuation.

And bear in mind a probability greater than zero that you will arrive at Pele's nap time—sleeping lava, little action beyond the steam vents. If you please Pele, she will show you her A'a, the slow-flowing, bright-red lava; and those of you whom Pele wants to entertain may see her spout the high red 1, Pahoehoe.

Among the hikes is the Halemaumau trail, 2.9 miles over the caldera. Leave a car at trail's end or it's another 2.9 miles back to the visitor's center. Or you can hike the rainforest on the Kilauea Iki trail, about a 2-hour loop. No slouch stroll, this 1, and shorter trails await those of you past cardiovascular prime.

Thurston's Lava Tube is a classic example of tube formation, where the sauce gets crusty on top but still flows underground, like my, SB's, Reality Guide. The lava cools but the tube stays. Thurston's is a walk-through with permanent lights for visibility. Unless you want to share the tube with the teeming refuse yearning to be free, hit it early or late in the day.

Again, I, Snorkel Bob, respect lava exploration the same as Mama O. That is, no amusement park, this 1. Take a flashlight and note the return route, since any ingress can pass acutely-angled tributaries that will fool you on the way out. I, Snorkel Bob, go with a buddy and always mark the trail with breadcrumbs.

And don't forget your raison d'être when your flashlights fail, your buddy splits, the birds ate the breadcrumbs; attain calmness and see the way.

NOTE: The hot lava is about 30 miles down Chain of Craters Road to the water. The park rangers stationed near the flow will tell you don't do this, don't do that. Those of you with college degrees will find this an excellent opportunity for practical application. Sometimes you can hike down to the ocean for enhanced proximity to Pahoehoe. If not, you may see some A'a roadside or through the crust cracks.

If you go at night (no rangers) take a flashlight for each person. An illustration of reality here will best make the point. I.e., a veteran nature photographer last year went in close for a tight shot and the crust collapsed. The end. His friends say he would've wanted to go that way. I, Snorkel Bob, encourage self-interrogatory on your way of choice.

Oceanside, by the flow, black-sand beaches evolve daily as the molten sauce hits the water and explodes into glass particles. The beaches, like Pele, are beautiful but dangerous. Black sand is recently formed glass striata. (Striata?) The glass particles are unbuffed, still sharp. Barefoots shred. And these beaches are exposed to severe ocean swells.

See Hiking for more info on campsites and cabins, and Places to Stay for leads on reservations at Volcano House and nearby B&Bs. The park service report on lava activity is (808) 967-7311. Weather is (808) 961-5582.

# MAUI

HANA I, Snorkel Bob, hate to be a party pooper, but you ought to know that 1.7 zillion hairpin turns in 60 miles is enough to wear out a Snorkel Bob barf bag. If you suffer the go-for-it burden, then you're in for a kidney pounding on the far stretch around that feels like Ali/Foreman in the 14th (rope-a-dope).

Hana pegs the meter for humans standing still and sighing. Ah, the beauty of it all. Don't get me wrong again, it's beautiful, what a Hawaiian town ought to be. My cosmic friends say Hana has a strong vibration, peaceful and healing, elixir to the soul, and I, Snorkel Bob, don't doubt it for a single heartbeat, not 1.

But out to Hana and back in 1 day is a bad push; 2 days ain't much better. Hana is for lovers and meditators; it's 1-on-1 in Hana, you and your honey pie, or you and your own self. Beyond K-Y, vitamins and the Void, goings-on in Hana are slooow. Many people don't know this, so crowds form and wonder what. Reservations recommended for overnight.

I, Snorkel Bob, most often get it for less than at the HOTEL HANA MAUI @ $395 to $795 per night. Or the Sea Ranch Cottages apart from the main hotel each @ $525, or $795 for a de Luxe suite. In case you're wondering, I, Snorkel Bob, already rolled the numbers for you: $290,175 a year if you really like it, and of course a few bucks for tax and tip. What a place, and what a lobby, (800) 321-4262. (See Places to Stay for cheaper digs.)

You got a bunch of beautiful, remote tropical beaches in and around Hana, but you must take care since the Hana coast is exposed to huge ocean swells. When they're up, they can permanently alter your rhythm. (See Beach Awareness.)

Hana has some good adventures, like the bamboo forest, Oheo Gulch and Wainapanapa State Park, with its cabins for those who call ahead (984-8109) @ $45 per night, and its tent spaces where you might get rained on but will likely have a good time, even wet.

Best of all: You can snorkel Hana anywhere with local guidance. Just ask. Hana Bay is great (see Snorkel, Where to).

Just remember that I, Snorkel Bob, wouldn't go to Hana for only a day, and a 2-day visit could only happen if I, Snorkel Bob, was in love, I mean really.

IAO VALLEY  If love for you requires less fervor, fewer miles and not as much sound insulation as you get in Hana, then you must ask yourself: What Hana got what Iao Valley no got?

Iao Valley is no secret, but I, Snorkel Bob, am amazed at those who spend 7 hours (1-2-3-4-5-6-7) in a car, contorting to the far side for a brief interlude of sighing and wandering around, when the same prospect awaits at Iao (.14 hours): rainforest, hiking trails and mountain stream.

How to get there: Find it on the map and go. It's above Wailuku.

I, Snorkel Bob, love Iao most in Summer heat. 1 personal favorite is 3 warm beers followed by a stop at War Memorial Stadium in Kahului to kick a soccer ball up and down the field, followed by Iao Valley. Park in the lot at the end of the road, cross the foot bridge and follow the steps down to the path by the stream. Go up the stream a short way to the big round smooth rocks and ease on in...Sssssss. I, Snorkel Bob, get so hot that the ice water in the stream is only a cool, distant quenching lapping playfully at the molten core.

Coming down Iao Valley Road is a place called President Kennedy's Profile. Somebody sunk a post in concrete and welded a short metal pipe onto it like a peepsite. You bend over, peep the peepsite, and the edge of a hillock is supposed to look like President Kennedy's profile, so they call the place: President Kennedy's Profile.

I, Snorkel Bob, will not give you, my friends, exact directions to the place because I, Snorkel Bob, consider President Kennedy's Profile hokum. If you still want to go, don't worry, you'll find plenty people in line at the peep site oohing, aahing, crying, "Oh yes I see it!" Who cares? You can see it far easier on a half dollar.

My friend Matt Roving ran a controlled experiment to prove President Kennedy's Profile is hokum. For scientific purposes only, he smoked 1 sample da kine lolo weed, spun around 6 times, stood on his head and looked down, which was of course by then up. "All I saw, horizon to horizon," he said, "was all these clouds that looked exactly like Ross Perot."

That Matt Roving has no sense of political delicacy at all. And I, Snorkel Bob, mean none.

HALEAKALA The problem with places like Haleakala or Hana, or rather the problem with the info, is that guidance is usually mindless and reactive, i.e.; "Oh! Yes! You've got to go there!"

Trust me, the Snorkel 1; you, my friends, no got go nowhere. All these people drive bumper to bumper in the middle of the night up this hill forever for a view of the world, which isn't a bad thing to do. And make no mistake, Haleakala is 1 ono place. But now teeming masses yearning to be free go up the hill because some bimbo commission hound at the corner booking table said yeah you got to do that.

It's a commitment—2 hours from Kihei, Wailea, Makena; more from Kaanapali, Napili, Kapalua. That's 1 way. So if you go the sunrise route you got to fill your tank, pack your winter clothing (often freezing or below at the summit), find out sunrise time at the crater and back off 2 hours travel time, 30 minutes get lost time and 30 minutes goof-off time, find out who gots da joe at 3 a.m. (or 2) and go.

Don't worry about feeling foolish on the final ascent, when you find yourself on a tiny dot in the middle of the biggest ocean in the world at 9,000' in a traffic jam. The ranger station gets a little crowded too. Nevermind, the world is overpopulated and so is the summit at sunrise.

I, Snorkel Bob, went up 1 time for sunrise and wedged into the jam at the ranger station and got situated for the show and finally old Sol came up and everyone was fairly awed, and then they all yawned and mumbled breakfast, and this guy with long hair and earrings and genre clothing from 1969 starts yelling, "More! More!" He was yelling at Sol.

I, Snorkel Bob'm not saying it's a bad thing to do. When the sun rises and thrusts you into another day you can head on down the hill, relaxed now since Haleakala is checked off your list.

But you don't need another guide to give you the knee-jerk stuff like you got to got to got to go to Haleakala and sunrise is the time. Better idea is to go after brunch, when you get to see all the stuff on the way too. The crowds are gone, and by then you can check the weather just like a real weatherman: look up. (Those of you on the West side must call the weatherman; those of you planning deep penetration into the crater can call the rangers at 572-9306 for conditions).

If you do hit the summit for sunrise, Kula Lodge serves breakfast on the descent and nearly makes up in convenience what it lacks in culinary delicacy—and sometimes it's way crowded. (See Eateries.)

And as for bicycle rides down Haleakala, see Bicycles Rides.

**KULA BOTANICAL GARDENS**
Rte 377 (Kekaulike Rd.) in Kula, Maui
(808) 878-1715
9-4 Daily
$4 Adults, $1 Kids 6-12

Variety, maturity, and a strong vibration make this place my, Snorkel Bob's, flower garden of choice. It's private on 5 sloping acres with 25 years of TLC, resulting in rare and beautiful flora. Orchids, bromeliads, protea and epic succulents from another planet thrive in a Kula climate some call...perfect. Begonias big as wide-screen TVs and hydrangeas (hydrangii?) big as basketballs meander the paths and terraces. Benches allow sitdown absorption of this most beauteous beauty at perhaps its most beauteous. The deck and picnic tables near the entrance/gift shop allow another sitdown where you may eat.

# OAHU

Oahu is a unique blend of urban sophistication and tropical atmosphere with another unique ingredient—tropical sleaze. It's not as bad as, say, L.A. or Miami. It's cleaner, with more Aloha. I, Snorkel Bob, am compelled to say, however, more caution, more doubt, more disgruntle reside in these pages than in those for other islands.

Honolulu comes 1st in touristic history. It's a mature market, more developed, more degenerate. Many places here enjoy false must see/must do reputations arising neither from fair value nor real adventure but rather paid promotion. This is the city. The seasoned traveler will relax in a different mode in Oahu by instinct. Be aware, be alert, use your 3rd eye, and keep 1 of the 1st 2 on your wallet. Fleecing flatlanders can be sport here in H-town.

Speaking of wallets, Oahu is the shopping capital of the Pacific, its islands, confederacies, principalities and suburbs. You got Ala Moana Center, Waikiki Plaza, Royal Hawaiian Shopping Center, The International Market Place, Kahala Mall, Ward Warehouse, Ward Center and many more.

Some are gross-tonnage displays of beads and trinkets, like The International Market Place in Waikiki, where vendors hawk chachkas from Thailand, the Philippines, Macao, China, Malaysia and of course Timbuktu—flashy stuff worth twice the price, considering overhead. (Scientific Fact: Many shops on Wakiwaki's main drag pay $10-15,000 a month in rent, and a percentage of gross on top of that. That makes for jade, hustle, quick approach, hard close.)

Other places have real stuff, but it's all stuff, more stuff than could fit on a fleet of freighters. For easy access the malls have garages: subterranean cement plains with low ceilings and enough carbon smoke to make you long for Jersey, Houston or L.A.

But Oahu can be good for urban stimulation and night life. For day life, guess what I, Snorkel Bob, do?

FYI: Oahu snorkel and boogie are excellent.

If you want whale watching, go to Maui. But, beware of whale sharks; those sincere guys calling themselves scientists, researchers, nonprofit. "Will you adopt a whale? It's only a few bucks, and the dough benefits the whales, honest! How about er, uh...that 1, right there on the horizon, yes, I think he's available. We'll call him Cloey, just for you, isn't he cute? And aren't you something! Bless you." The latest is OFFICIAL GREENPEACE SPONSOR. Not.

If fishing lures you, go to Kona or Kauai.

Oahu is hazardous. The careless may spend their days far from the reef. As your friend in the tropics I, Snorkel Bob, encourage you to stay atuned to the magic of the tropics, where all talk floats away in bubbles.

## POLYNESIAN CULTURAL CENTER
Rte 83 in Laie, Oahu
(808) 293-3333 or (800) 367-7060 from the mainland
12:30-9:30 Mon-Sat (Closed Sun)

"This is probably the very best, all-out, touristy, bogus thing to do."—Matt Roving

$27, this 1, and that's for the bleachers. Shuttle pickup can be arranged from Waikiki for $15 round trip.

Many people will say that you Must See the Poly Cult Center. I, Snorkel Bob, assure you, it's not necessary. In fact, compared to getting wet with mask, fins and snorkel, it's like having another cupcake before bedtime compared to getting up at 5 a.m. to take a leak. 1 is whimsical gluttony while the other is spiritual transmutation.

In reality—and I, Snorkel Bob, use the phrase loosely—the Poly Cult Center is what Jim 'n Tammy Faye's Heritage Heaven or Paradise Park or whatever the hell it was called in the Carolina outback always wanted to be. I.e., a theme park to control your mind, generating million$ for Jeeezus, less a modicum of administrative moolah off the top in the Spirit of non-profit.

That is, what many people won't say is that the Poly Cult Center is owned and operated by the Mormon Church, the most aggressive recruiters in the Known Universe. They're smart enough not to proselytize in your face but the more observant among you will note the pervasive influence, from cherubic cashiers in cages with computer monitors, to the all-Vegas showgirl revue called This Is Polynesia. I, Snorkel Bob, have been to Polynesia. I, Snorkel Bob, know Polynesia. Polynesia is a friend of mine. This ain't Polynesia.

Nowhere—and I, Snorkel Bob, mean No Where—in Polynesia is a showbiz pavilion, restaurant, theatre, snack bar, retail shop and A Mission Compound in perfect manicure right there in the village. Polynesia is dirt floors mostly; no cashiers, no retail and, in certain blessed parts of it, no missionaries.

I, Snorkel Bob, mean to say this is another perfect display of what the mission promised; another architectural rendering of applied Christianity that, alas and alack, got stuck 2 places: 1) the drawing board, and 2) The Poly Cult Center.

Some of the culture captured in the center is authentic, some is not. It's all incidental to a guy like me, Snorkel Bob, who cannot fathom the lie. These few Polynesian cultural exhibits are formatted in what I, Snorkel Bob, call 2nd person condescending, the voice of the mission.

For example, in the Samoan exhibit, "learn the arts of coconut husking, firemaking, rope braiding and mat weaving from the experts." In New Zealand, "try twirling a poi ball or the Maori stick game." In Tahiti, "you're in Tahiti now...sample Tahitian cuisine," and so on down the line through Fiji, Hawaii, The Marquesas and Tonga.

Did you, my friends, know that Koa wood—the dramatic reddish, swirled-grain hardwood, 1 of the most beautiful woods in the world and once thick in Hawaii—is now virtually extinct? The missionaries planted kiawe trees, because kiawe spreads like brush fire, displacing every other species and dropping thorns like 8-penny nails—this to force the Hawaiians to wear shoes, since God shunned the sight of bare feet. You will not see this exhibit in the Poly Cult Center.

Nor will you learn that the muu muu came from the mission to hide natural feminine curvature, since God didn't like that either (although I, Snorkel Bob, suspect a mission in denial).

Nor will you learn in the Fiji exhibit that Fiji is a rare place where the mission never took hold, because missionary M.O. is to convert from the top down—get the chief, the rest will follow. Fiji never consolidated but rather remained confederated, so that even when 1 chief buckled, the rest retained the old way. To this day, Fiji is owned by native Fijians and not the dominant missionary families and/or their sugar companies, which is the case in Hawaii.

But I, Snorkel Bob, have a bad habit of laying too much blame on a small spot. Even if the Poly Cult Center makes a museum of what its sponsors made disappear, it does a fair job.

Why, my, Snorkel Bob's, Aunt Beebee visited from Nebraska and thought the Poly Cult Center was just about the greatest thing since automatic transmissions. She said they have nothing like this in

Nebraska, nothing a'tall. She loved the luau and the show. She danced her ass off with a really real grass skirt. She loved the buffet, except for the soggy pigmeat. And she said the very best thing that ever happened to her in her whole, entire life may be the Special Ambassador Passport VIP Service, in which she got a souvenir lei greeting, a guided tour through 7 villages, her choice of an Alii Luau/Gateway Restaurant Buffet, VIP seating for This is Polynesia and the Admission-Buffet-Show Package.

This is the place where they paved paradise and put up a parking lot, put all the trees in a tree museum, and now charge a dollar and a half just to seeum.

But like I, Snorkel Bob, say; Aunt Beebee loved it, and she's for real. "Hey, they put on a nice show" is what she said about the missionaries at Poly Cult. Why, she'd visit Polynesia anytime, now that she knows what it's all about. It's just like when she didn't used to like fishing. Then she went to The Boat Show and caught a whole mess o' trout, and now she understands. "You, Snorkel Bob, got to keep a open mind", is what she said.

CHINATOWN is a patch of downtown Honolulu that could be Hong Kong—restaurants, Oahu Market (open-air fish and vegetable market), restaurants, many guys hanging out, and more restaurants. It's smaller than most other C-towns I, Snorkel Bob, have seen. It's also home to China Sea Tattoo parlor (see Eclectic Sampler). The Chinese Chamber of Commerce, 533-3181, runs walking tours on Tuesdays from 9-noon to help you understand what you're seeing, hearing, smelling, tasting.

### WAIKIKI AQUARIUM
2777 Kalakaua Ave. in Honolulu, Oahu
(808) 923-9741
9-5 Daily
$6 Adults, Under 12 Free, Student and Senior discounts

Here's a little sample of the other-world spectacle so accessible in the tropics. This place cannot begin to compare to snorkeling. But it can get you up close in your civvies to most of the fish on your fish I.D. card.

I, Snorkel Bob, grant high marks on 2 tanks, the cleaner shrimp and cup coral tank and the anemone tank, mostly because invertebrates don't require as much elbow room as pelagics. Habitat in these tanks fairly duplicated the filter feeding process naturally occurring on the reef out front. The leaf scorpion fish tank is good too, except for overcrowding.

The Hawaiian monk seal here is a lively pup, and the tidepool habitat is accessible to juvenile vertebrates. The shark tank is long and thin, with viewing from 1 end only, of baby white-tip and black-tip reef sharks. It's a fair mix and a good example of what you may see if you're lucky and get way off the beach. These guys cruise the bottom and skeedaddle at the mere thought of tourists. My, Snorkel Bob's, overgrown shark buddy, Oscar, the 1 who went prima donna ever since I, Snorkel Bob, put him on a t-shirt, says, "White tip reef shark. Bah!"

The mahi mahi exhibit is worth a look, little babies on up to special-of-the-day size. And the giant deepwater clams from New Zealand are the only such specimens kept successfully in captivity on all of Planet E.

This place ain't in the same league as, say, Steinhart or Scripps Institute or the Seattle Aquarium or Miami or Bermuda or New England or Chicago—this is primarily a series of 300-gallon tanks. Still it's clean and if you're decrepit or very small or for any reason unable to shuck your civvies for mask, fins and snorkel and some real Communion, or if you want the Communion but feel uncertain, this is the best place to begin.

## SEA LIFE PARK
Rte 72, Makapuu Point
(808) 259-7933
9:30-5 Daily, 9:30-10 p.m. Fri
$19.95 Adults, $9.95 Kids 4-12

This is an amusement park with no correlation to the tropics other than what you see beyond the guardrail, through the window. I.e., they packum in and processum, filling them with that popcorn and soda feeling along the way, hollering hoopla, look at this!

This is a tourist shrine, with credos like "fun for the whole family," or "welcome to Hawaii's ocean world," or "don't miss it!" My, Snorkel Bob's, very favorite is: "You'll discover things you never knew about these much-feared predators of the sea!" Maybe they never expected a guy like me, Snorkel Bob, to show up. It's a tour de force, this place; bells and whistles, hoops and leashes, damn the reality, full speed ahead.

The place is crowded with captive animals on both sides of the guardrail, with a retail shop on 1 side. And I, Snorkel Bob, must stop and ask at times like this, when that old urban nausea comes burbling to the surface, if the place is better than nothing. I, Snorkel Bob, think not, but then I, Snorkel Bob, love nothing better than almost anything, especially the watery kind—ooh! How about the watery kind at night?

Maybe if Sea Life Park was on the bottom and it was night I, Snorkel Bob, would like it better. Maybe not. At least it would be quieter and not so hot.

You should not be surprised to hear that this is not my, Snorkel Bob's, cup of tea. Snorkeling is a feeling from the C.G., down low. Sea Life Park is to me, Snorkel Bob, without apparent benefit, like a dark speck with fibrous tendrils showing its carcinogenic eye on the hitherto unblemished bosom of this, the land that I, Snorkel Bob, love.

## USS ARIZONA NATIONAL MEMORIAL
Pearl Harbor
Honolulu, Oahu
(808) 422-0561
8-3 Daily, closed holidays
Admission Free

Strange and unusual place, this 1. Current controversy in Hawaii's 2nd biggest industry, tourism (pakalolo is still #1—see Chapter VI, How to Speak Pidgin) surrounds the "deal" heavily promoted by some tour companies for a free visit to the Arizona Memorial. In fact, the Arizona Memorial is free and easy to find. You don't even need a rental car, since its a stop for 5 local bus routes, including those serving Waikiki, the north shore and Makaha (leeward) side.

The critical point, however, is not that a bunch of tour companies are fleecing flatlanders but that the Arizona Memorial is a cemetery, a grave yard, burial site of over 1500 sailors who drowned when the USS Arizona and Oklahoma sank. Now it's a walkway/deck over the shallow grave of the sunken ship.

I, Snorkel Bob, am not drawn to graveyards, however unique and ghastly, whatever the size of the dead crowd or the mode of passage from this life happens to have been. I, Snorkel Bob, once passed within 3 miles of Belsen and Auschwitz and didn't stop in for a visit. Of course, that comparison isn't parallel except for the historical fact and focal point of massive, instant death. Maybe a closer comparison is Arlington National Cemetery or the Viet Nam Wall. But most visitors there are families or friends of the deceased or ex-service people.

The reality at the Arizona is, however, that gazing down into the water is hard to do without sensing the moment of drowning for those sailors. The sensing is also difficult and therein is the draw—it's a kind of masochistic media/tourist event. But then again, that's my, Snorkel Bob's, opinion.

A guy died a couple years ago who'd been aboard the Arizona and whose wish was burial there along with his shipmates. Whether that man carried an emotional attachment to a thing and an event for the rest of his life is incidental; his burial at the Arizona Memorial was his prerogative.

It was carried on all the local news stations. The Arizona stimulates the media and its fixation on death and disaster.

The solution and the point? The dead are gone, let them go. I, Snorkel Bob, cannot take credit for that, since teachers for thousands of years have taught their students the same thing my teacher taught me, Snorkel Bob: Let the dead go.

But, if you just must go too, the Navy launch runs from shore out to the memorial everyday but holidays, 8-3. Or you can get a good deal on a tour.

If you like museums, you will like these. Exhibits at the Academy are dynamic; displays at the Palace and the Museum are extravagant; and art at the Contemporary shall make you free, kind of.

### THE BISHOP MUSEUM
1525 Bernice St.
Honolulu, Oahu
(808) 847-3511
9-5 Daily
$14.95 Adults, $11.95 Kids 6-17

The Bishops were missionaries who garnered considerable land and power here and 1 of them, Charles Reed, married a Hawaiian princess, Bernice Pauahi, in 1850. She looks much younger than he in the renderings but she died 1st, after a lifetime of collecting Hawaiian artifacts. Charles Reed Bishop set up the museum and it expanded to a little bit of everything, more or less a natural and cultural history with birds, fish, insects, plants, sea shells and so on. None of this stuff is alive.

Now a planetarium, library, hula and folk arts and Polynesian history areas are added. The 3-tier Hawaiian Hall surrounds a central room, extravagantly arched and pillared with ironwork, koa wood and tiles. If you like museums, you will like this 1. If you don't, your head will nod and fill with dreams of clear water, sunshine, fish who live and breathe and swim the most graceful reality.

To get there go west on H-1 (from Waikiki area) to the Likelike Exit (20 A, 63 North) and follow signs to the museum.

### THE HONOLULU ACADEMY OF ARTS
900 Beretania St.
Honolulu, Oahu
(808) 532-8701
10-4:30 Tues-Sat, 1-5 Sun
$5 Admission

This small art museum is just the right size, i.e., cruisable through the medieval religion section in an hour or 2 with a cafe for a break in aesthetic intake. Vincent van Gogh was here, and so was Georgia O'Keefe with her Paintings of Hawaii show, which was all flowers, up close. But they were good flowers, colorful and suggestive as only O'Keefe can make them, the labiatic orchids, the excited anthuria. I, Snorkel Bob, think this 1 could be banned in Cincinnati. The museum is on the corner of Beretania Street and Ward Avenue, a few blocks east of the State Capitol and downtown areas.

## IOLANI PALACE
State Capitol Grounds
Honolulu, Oahu
(808) 538-1471
9-2:15 Wed-Sat

Reservations required for the 45-min tour @ $8 unless you're under 12. Then it's $2 unless you're under 5. Then you can't come in—nothing personal, it's just that your parents probably can't control you or your grubby little hands smudging everything, breaking stuff and trashing the place after we worked so hard to restore it, not that we're finished, we're not. There's so much more to do. But oh! isn't it lovely and just the way it was, when the Hawaiian Monarchy ruled, ante 1893. Spectaculacular is what I, Snorkel Bob, call it.

## THE CONTEMPORARY MUSEUM
2411 Makiki Heights Dr.
Honolulu, Oahu
(808) 526-0232
10-4 Tu-Sat, 12-4 Sun, Closed Mon & major holidays
$5 Adults 13 & Over, $3 Seniors and Students
Free admission 3rd Thursday of every month

Begun in 1961 for the works of artists living in Hawaii, the Contemporary Museum emphasizes art of the last 4 decades. Housed in the unhumble home of another missionary family, the Contemporary is attached to a 3.5-acre Japanese garden of international renown. I, Snorkel Bob, cannot understand why anyone would build a garden rather than a reef, but this garden is worth seeing. It's at the top of Makiki Heights—hotsy-totsy—and some of the best art is in the garden. The exhibits change, but not the outdoor sculpture or the garden. The gift shop scores high in art book selection, and lunch at the Contemporary Cafe is most tolerable. Art tours are 3 times a day and garden tours are by special arrangement (526-1322), or you can tour solo.

THE BUS will get you anywhere on Oahu. I, Snorkel Bob, cannot guarantee punctuality, but the bus is often less hectic than the auto crush of Honolulu. The Hawaii Bus and Travel Guide was not written by me,

Snorkel Bob, but it works. It's by Milly Singletary, author of Finding Fabulous Phoenix.

It's $1 for adults, 50¢ for kids and less for monthly pass holders.

## WAIMEA FALLS PARK
59-864 Kamehameha Hwy
Haleiwa, Oahu
(808) 638-8511
10-5:30 Daily
$19.95 Adults; $9.95 Juniors 6-12; Free for Kids 5 & under

A better place, this, for history in a lower key, more authentic, north shore. 1,800 acres of botanical beauty and cultural exhibits laid out along a mile or 2 of stream lead to a small (50') waterfall. Local candidates for steroid testing jump the falls. It's billed as the sport of Hawaiian kings, but I Snorkel Bob think the kings only relaxed with a few cold 1s in the shade and watched, like me, Snorkel Bob.

The Park has guided tours and a tram for the infirm and/or lazy and a restaurant/giftshop. This garden grows in conjunction with the Honolulu Botanical Garden, with an impressive greenhouse and garden-plot propagation of endangered native species.

And across the highway is Waimea Bay, famed for surf.

# THE FAT STIFF AND THE LAND SHARK

*—A story with a moral brought to you as a special service and caution about real life off the reef in balmy Waikiki.*

Once upon a time there was this fat stiff. He wasn't always fat, not until he figured out that 1 of life's rare joys is eating, and a most-favored feeling is that satisfied stupor after eating too much. Nor was he always stiff, until he began fattening and became more aware of all-you-can-eat specials. He knew when the feedbag was honest—no bottom—and when it was just a come-on, like those fried shrimp places where the shrimp look like skinny grubs and the tempura batter looks like Nanook of the North's insulated blizzard coat. Or how about those rib places that advertise all-you-can-eat, and then after the 2nd or 3rd go-round they start bringing you more and more potatoes and insisting that you have to eat the potatoes too, to get more ribs?

That's when he got a gallon of mayo in a plastic container and ate it all in a week which wasn't that difficult even though it made his calves swell up and caused him to hurt across his chest like he didn't have enough worries, but it was worth it, he was so excited about his plan to have the wife carry the empty container to this all-you-can-eat rib place. Then when they started bringing more potatoes, he shoveled them into the plastic jar—good with a couple 3 eggs and bacon in the morning all week, thanks to the rib place that had done him this favor.

When he and the wife walked out, her purse weighed over 12 pounds, and he heard a waiter say, "What a stiff." But he knew he wasn't a stiff. He was keeping things honest, the way they ought to be, the way a guy who works hard for his money has a right to expect them to be. The fat stiff worked 8 hours a day for $12.50 per hour. He lived in the industrial outback called Orange County and he was used to it, even though he had trouble with his breathing. This is a true story.

Meanwhile, across the ocean in an unlikely little burg called Wakiwaki by those who live there, an enterprising fellow knew instinctively that the best margins on a deal are had by the middle man. He figured quick enough that 2 prime products here are drugs and sex. And he could dispense his wares most effectively from a pedicab—called a rickshaw in Hong Kong but even more exotic here, with a white guy pedaling.

Anyway, this guy did okay because he was no dummy and he always took care of the kids when he thought they were too young for drugs—sold them basil and oregano balled up in rubber glue, but at a decent price. The pimping part was infrequent since most local hookers were badder than him, but every now and then he could make a referral and cop a few bucks.

Things were good, until they got so good with all these white guys on rickshaws with all the da kine and puhehe for sale, they got out of hand. It got worse than real estate agents, if you can believe that. And sure enough, the local media got wind of it. Then you had the noise and pressure and the heat came down. It wasn't so bad—attrition can be good; only the strong survive. Our guy survived. This is a true story.

The stiff and the shark met 1 breezy tropical Saturday morning in Waikiki, just in front of the Holiday Inn. The fat stiff and the wife had arrived a couple days earlier and the balm of the place was beginning to set in, even though they took him good on the airfare, the taxicab, the room, the tax, the tax on the tax and then the other tax. Still, walking out front he felt good, he felt relaxed and untight in the chest, even after a couple eggs, Portuguese sausage, hash browns, rice, and what the hey a Loco Moco just to try it out, and some fruit to ease things along and some jo to hurry it up.

Don't you know the sight of a young fellow on a rickshaw made perfect sense, especially since the cabby took him for a real ride coming up. The fat stiff and the wife were staying 4 miles down the coast at the Kahala Hilton. Oh sure, it was rich but he liked the sound of it, and it wasn't so bad if you came into Waikiki for cheap breakfast, especially now, with this rickshaw service. Sheesh, with a white guy pedaling too.

The white guy was good, maybe great. He did nothing. He sat there in his white shirt and half smile and let the fat stiff come on. He didn't even care when the fat stiff grunted on board and bottomed out the shocks. So what. Plenty fats before, plenty ahead. Nor did the white guy blink when the fat stiff said, "Kahala Hilton." The fat stiff liked how it rolled off his tongue.

And off they rolled, nice and easy down the road. The fat stiff liked rolling up the driveway too. It was stick-it-up-your-nose to the parking valets. It was sheer opulence, with a white guy pedaling. So they come up nice and slow and they stop and the wife gets out and the fat stiff gets out and rubs his belly with 2 hands and scratches his ass and wonders if a 10 spot isn't a bit much since the cab was twelve but it could insure good service next time and everyone was looking. And the white guy, soft as a kitten, purrs, "Hundred and fifty."

"Wha...!" exclaimed the fat stiff. "Hundred fifty! For a bicycle ride?"

"You rode. I worked. Hey!"—the white guy hunkered low now, just the way Oscar, the shark, drops his pectoral fins before making a hit—"I had to pedal up the hill! All the way!"

"So I should pay you $150? That I had to work 12 hours for?" Everybody shook their heads. Guys who make $12.50 an hour shouldn't hire slave labor, even if they really want to.

"Have a little class!" the white guy implored. His voice was low and urgent, as if the fat stiff didn't get what was happening here. "You said 'Kahala Hilton.' I thought you were loaded. People with money stay here." He shrugged and looked miffed. "I thought it would be a buck seventy, with the tip!"

"Call the cops!" The fat stiff yelled at the wife.

"Call the cops?" The white guy couldn't believe his ears. "This is the Kahala Hilton! You don't call the cops at a place like this just because you can't afford cab fare!"

The white guy was yelling now. He was very good. Everybody stared at the fat stiff, wondering if the hundred fifty was available. "Look! Look!" the white guy gesticulated. "Right here! The fare is right here! Right here for you to read! Look!"

The fare was in fine print on 1 of those little bicycle license plates strung to the seat back below 4 other little license plates advertising hot, sizzling luaus and dinner cruises you'd never forget. It was plain to see; the rickshaw fare hung far below the fat stiff's belly, down periscope.

The fat stiff rushed the wife, grabbed her purse and pulled out a wad of dough—10s and 20s. He spun quick, fisting it in the white guy's face. "I can afford anything!"

It was sad. The crowd turned away. The white guy was very good, standing still and silent in his King's X. The fat stiff counted to 150. Damn if he'd pay a tip. He didn't even think about how many ribs he'd just blown down the rat hole, or the tickle in his chest.

He turned and strode into the hotel, crummy goddamn joint that it was. The white guy shrugged again. "I thought he was loaded. Guy can't afford cab fare."

And he pedaled off, back toward Waikiki, and it wasn't even lunch.

 The End

*Moral: Use your street smarts. Stay alert. And if you think smart means asking, How much is this going to cost me?, be ready for the comeback interrogatory: How much you got?*

# GOLF

(G-o-l-f) n. 1) a game in which a small hard ball is struck with clubs toward a series of holes. 2) sedentary men in strange pants, walking.

The resort golf here runs about a buck 10 a stroke on Oahu, Kona and Kauai; 2 bucks a stroke on Maui, unless you triple bogie the back 17. Then it's a much better deal.

NOTE: Have lively feet, shift your weight from left foot to right foot then back to the left, take the club back slow and easy, stop at the top, start back down with your left foot, don't try to hit the ball but swing right through it. Don't muscle, stay elastic, watch your breathing, keep your head still and swing your body around it (your head).

Don't break your clubs or throw them into the ponds when they miss an easy shot. Don't forget your course etiquette and remember: It's only a game.

So this guy finally meets this girl he can relate to and sure enough they date and fall in love and before too long they're planning the wedding. So it's the night before the wedding and they're not supposed to see each other but the guy comes over anyway and he says, Look, I think going into something like this it's important that we're completely honest with each other and...well...I'd like to get something off my chest. He mopes around a little bit and kicks the rug and says, I'm a golf addict. I can't get enough. I live for golf. I've tried to control it, but every now and then I'll disappear for a binge—72 holes maybe, maybe more.

So the girl gets all sheepish too and blushes and says she loves him, she really does and she too would like to offload her chest and she says, On weekends I'm a hooker.

That's okay! he says. Just keep your head down and your left arm straight.

# KAUAI

Kauai greens fees wobbled worse than a jellyfish frappé after the hurricane with promotions and specials. And though I, Snorkel Bob, could grasp the joy of teeing off on 300 yards of devastation, ruins, rubble like downtown Beirut, I, SB, cannot vouch for sustained accuracy here. The mess is cleaned up for better or worse, which is better for most golfers, you are such a tidy group.

**KUKUIOLONO GOLF COURSE**
Kalaheo, Kauai
(808) 332-9151

This is a 9-hole course with a spectaculacular view at $5 a day, plus $5 for the cart and $6 for the clubs, which translates to Aloha Nui Loa, Bubba, for a duffer like me, Snorkel Bob. However, if you need the clubs, get them before 2:30.

## PRINCEVILLE GOLF COURSES
Princeville, Kauai
(808) 826-2727

Princeville has 27 holes on the Makai Course, 18 on the Prince Course. Hotel guests pay $85 for the Makai 18, $100 for the Prince 18. $115 and $150 respectively for non-guests to play 18 on each course. 9-holes on the Makai Course is $48. Prices include green fees and a cart. Clubs are $15 for 9 holes, $30 if you play 18. Call for a tee time, this 1.

## POIPU BAY COURSE
Hyatt Hotel in Poipu, Kauai
(808) 742-8711

Every November the Mastercard Grand Slam Pro Tour is hosted on this course. The proshop opens 6:00 a.m. 1st tee is 7, last tee is 2:45. Hyatt guests $90, non guests $135, sometimes lower depending on where you're staying. After 12, prices drop to $80 for 18 (includes cart) and down to $45 after 3:00–play till dark (twilight fee).

## THE MARRIOTT
Lihue, Kauai
(808) 245-5050

The Marriott has 2 golf courses. The Lagoons Course is $100 for Westin guests, $110 for interlopers, flatlanders, pedestrians et al. The Kiele Course is $110 for Westin guests, and $145 for civilians. This includes a shared cart. I, Snorkel Bob, think this 1 is nice, and if 18 holes takes 4 hours, we're only talking $36.25 an hour.

From me, Snorkel Bob, $9 a week gets you mask, fins, snorkel, netbag, snorkel map n' tips, and *The Legend of Me, Snorkel Bob*. And now I throw in the No-Fog Goop, and a Free Fish I.D., not to mention 24-hour express and interisland gearback. So let's say you snorkel 3 hours a day–we'll keep it conservative so no 1 can say the numbers were pushed. That's 21 hours at 43¢ per!

And does the Kiele course at the Marriott throw in the Fish I.D.? Hell, no! Enough said, except for maybe a brief reminder that nobody in the History of the World has even considered breaking her clubs while snorkeling.

# BIG ISLAND

### KONA SURF COUNTRY CLUB
78-7000 Alii Dr. in Kailua-Kona
(808) 322-2595

12 miles south of the Kona airport on Keauhou Bay, this place, with plenty variety in 36 holes. $60 for guests of the Kona Surf Hotel or Keauhou Beach Hotel, $100 for walk-ins, unless you're staying on the west side, making it $80 before 1:00, $55 after. All 36 holes is only $10 more.

### MAUNA KEA GOLF COURSE
Mauna Kea Beach Hotel on the Kohala Coast
(808) 882-5400

Moonscape on lava with a deep blue sea back makes this 1 most dramatic. 18 holes run $90 for guests, $150 for visitors.

### MAUNA LANI GOLF COURSE
Mauna Lani Resort on the Kohala Coast
(808) 885-6655

Like the Mauna Kea, this 1 rolls around the ritzy end of the Kona Coast; narrow greens twist around lava berms with a new and improved design. $85 for resort guests to play 18 holes on the North Course, $90 for the South Course. Visitors pay $160 for North, $170 for South. Fee includes cart.

### WAIKOALOA VILLAGE GOLF COURSE
Waikoloa, Hawaii
(808) 883-9621

Everybody pays $55 per round. This course meanders through the village, sometimes breezy but what a view. On a clear day you can see Haleakala 90 miles away on Maui, across Alanuihaha. Plenty challenges here in the golfer mode.

### WAIKOLOA BEACH GOLF CLUB
Waikoloa, Hawaii
(808) 885-6060

Archeological history in your divots on this 1. Like the 2 above, designed by Trent Jones Jr., and better yet, chilled water and towels in a cooler on the carts here. I, Snorkel Bob, do like that kind of attention to detail in personal service, especially when the personal is me, Snorkel Bob. Guests of the Waikoloa Hotels pay $85, everybody else pays $125.

## SEA MOUNTAIN AT PUNALUU
Pahala, Hawaii
(808) 928-6222

18 holes of green on what looks like the plains of Jupiter is far from what you played before. Volcanic lava to the horizon here, and a 6th fairway aimed dead upwind across a lava canyon. $25 for 9 holes. $40 for the whole 18.

## VOLCANO GOLF AND COUNTRY CLUB
Volcanoes National Park, Hawaii
(808) 967-7331

Inside the park and mere miles from Kilauea's eruption, but cool and crisp up there on the mountain, like Scotland, kind of. $60 for 18 holes for everyone.

## HILO MUNICIPAL GOLF COURSE
340 Haihai St. in Hilo
(808) 959-7711

Flat, this 1, and sometimes soggy, like Hilo, but with beautiful views of the bay, big trees and flowering plants throughout the course. $20 weekdays; $25 weekends. Carts are $14.50.

## NANILOA COUNTRY CLUB
120 Banyan Dr. in Hilo
(808) 935-3000

18 holes on a tiny finger of terra firma seeking penetration into Hilo bay, 18 holes runs $30 on weekdays, $40 on weekends. Carts are $7 per 9 holes.

## HAMAKUA COUNTRY CLUB
Honokaa, Hawaii
(808) 775-7244

9 holes like many mainland urban courses—rectangular and tightly laid, except that here it's surrounded by lush tropics in a sugarcane town

with the Pacific out front. $10 a round, BYO cart or else go the old fashioned way.

**DISCOVERY HARBOR GOLF AND COUNTRY CLUB**
Naalehu, Hawaii
(808) 929-7353

A good place to practice where nobody you want to see you will—lumpy greens, dogie traffic, in the heart of the heart of nowhere (67 miles south of the Kona airport near the southern tip of the United States of America) $28, includes cart.

# MAUI

### WAILEA GOLF COURSE
120 Kaukahi St. in Wailea, Maui
(808) 875-5111 Gold, Emerald; 875-5155 Blue

3 courses here, Gold, Emerald, and Blue, with plenty challenges, even for experts. Guests of Wailea pay $95-$100 a round for all 3 courses, $125-$130 if you're not.

### MAKENA GOLF COURSE
9415 Makena Alanui in Makena, Maui
(808) 879-3344

A true beauty, this 1, but only while it's way out there past the development juggernaut. This course is famous for its care and grooming and 64 sand traps. Duffers beware. Guests of the Maui Prince Resort pay $80 per round, non-guests pay $125.

### SILVERSWORD GOLF COURSE
1345 Piilani Hwy in Kihei, Maui
(808) 874-0777

This is the bargain public course with a high-end view and generous layout. Best in the morning before the sun hits you like Bakersfield in July and the wind affects yo rhydm. $70 for everyone.

## PUKALANI GOLF COURSE
360 Pukalani St. in Pukalani, Maui
(808) 572-1314

Up on the mountain with the neighborhood crowd, this 1. Much cooler than Kihei because it's 1,100' higher. The course is fairly open, so it's good for all skill levels. $55 includes the cart, $42 after 12.

## SANDALWOOD GOLF COURSE
2500 Honoapiilani Hwy. in Waikapu, Maui
(808) 242-4653

A well-kept, challenging course with sloping, tight fairways and vast views of Maui. 18 holes is $75 and includes the cart. Reservations taken up to 6 days ahead.

## ROYAL KAANAPALI GOLF COURSES
Kaanapali Beach Resort
(808) 661-3691

The North Course is memorable and well-laid with an ocean front and mountain back. $100 for resort guests, $120 for others. The South Course is the same but shorter and easier but not by much. Same prices for this 1. Rates drop some after 2 p.m.

## KAPALUA GOLF COURSE
300 Kapalua Dr. in Kapalua, Maui
(808) 669-8044

3 courses here, Village, Bay, and Plantation, with the Plantation rated most difficult. Arnold Palmer designed 2 of these courses, and some holes here are legendary (among golfers). $70-$75 for guests of the hotel, condos or houses; $130-$140 for non-guests. Here too rates drop after 2. Epic views here of the Pailolo Channel and Molokai.

# OAHU

## MID-PACIFIC COUNTRY CLUB
266 Kaelepulu in Honolulu, Oahu
(808) 261-9765

This private club sets aside "non-restricted tee times" for non-members. The course is over the pali from the hubbub, exposing it to more weather and more beauty too. 1 of the longest courses in Hawaii. $125 a round, cart included.

## ALA WAI GOLF COURSE
404 Kapahulu Ave. in Honolulu, Oahu
(808)733-7387

Guinness books this as the busiest course in the world. Is that good? It's a tight rectangle between Waikiki and the rest of Honolulu. $40 a round for visitors, $14 for the cart. Call a week ahead for tee times, and call early—6:30 a.m. Hawaii time.

## MOANALUA GOLF CLUB
1250 Ala Aolani in Honolulu, Oahu
(808) 839-2411

The 1st golf course built in Hawaii (by a Scotsman too) is only 9 holes, but they'll dog your dreams with blind greens, wind, narrow fairways and water hazards. It's enough to make you think the guy liked whips and chains with his plaid pants and logo shirt. It's semi-private now; $20 for 18 holes on weekdays, $15 after 4:00. $14 for the cart, if you can get a tee time. Thursdays and weekends are reserved for members until 2:00.

## HAWAII KAI GOLF COURSE
8902 Kalanianaole Hwy in Honolulu, Oahu
(808) 395-2358

About 12 miles east of downtown, this 18 in a great setting has a few surprises. $100 on weekdays and weekends with a "Par 3 Executive Course" at about half price. Early tees reserved for members, with non-member tees starting at 10:30 on weekdays and 2:00 on weekends.

## TURTLE BAY HILTON
Kahuku, Oahu
(808) 293-8811

Near Haleiwa on Oahu's north shore. Next to the Turtle Bay Hilton, this course got a revamp in '92 by Arnold Palmer and Ed Seay, and new rates to match. Everyone pays $25 for 9 holes or $50 if you want to go around twice. 18 holes on the Links at Kuuli Course is $75 for resort guests, $125 for others.

### KAHUKU GOLF COURSE
Kahuku, Oahu
(808) 293-5842

At $40/18 holes with quality and ambience, this 1 justifies the trip to the north shore. Call ahead for the weather report. You push the cart, and maybe bring your own clubs.

NOTE: Avant-funk kudos to Kahuku Golf Club—play 9 holes for even le$$. This is what I, Snorkel Bob, call the greatness what is America. Oh, say, can you see?

### MAKAHA VALLEY COUNTRY CLUB
84-627 Makaha Valley Rd. in Makaha, Oahu
(808) 695-7111

18 great holes with plenty ocean on the lee side here. $55 a round on weekdays for outlanders, $65 on weekends, includes the cart. Reservations more easier on weekdays.

### MILILANI GOLF CLUB
95-176 Kuahelani Ave. in Mililani, Oahu
(808) 623-2222

In a suburb, this, with tricky doglegs and plenty big trees. This 18-hole public course is popular but not too crowded. $84 a round weekdays before 11:00, $62 after 11:00, $92 weekends.

### OLOMANA GOLF LINKS
41-1801 Kalanianaole in Waimanalo, Oahu
(808) 259-7926

Another lush and windswept links on Oahu's weather shore. Clever challenges and water hazards make this 1 great. $80/round for Canadians or U.S.ians, $90 for the rest. ("Mexicans, Albanians; they're all the same!"—Walter Mathau, Candy)

### PEARL COUNTRY CLUB
98-535 Kaonohi in Aiea, Oahu
(808) 487-3802

This 1 starts easy but gets tough, like life. But with Pearl Harbor in the offing, the sun, the light breeze, how tough can it be? $75 a round on weekdays, $80 on weekends, unless you're a furner. Then it's $110 and $120. Don't ask me, Snorkel Bob.

**SHERATON MAKAHA**
84-626 Makaha Valley Rd. in Makaha, Oahu
(808) 695-9544

This spectacular resort course is lined with flowers, sculpted hazards and memorable views. Opulence is not for everyone at $160 a round, cart included. But after 12 the price drops to $90, $80 if you're staying at the hotel.

**TED MAKALENA GOLF COURSE**
Waipio Point Access Rd. in Waipahu, Oahu
(808) 296-7888 or 675-6052 for the direct starter line

This municipal course close to the city is in fair shape and is real busy, especially weekends. Pearl Harbor battle ships line the horizon. At $40/18 holes, $20/9 holes, it's still an honest pour, so help me Bob, even w/the cart a la carte at $14.

# HIKING & CAMPING

I, Snorkel Bob, wistfully recall the lean and hungry days of youth on the road, close to the ground with no plan, no schedule, no choreography. Now I, Snorkel Bob'm fond of taxis and room service. Every now and then a mermaid will allure me once again to the bush, but it takes me, Snorkel Bob, longer now to stop grumbling about the cold, hard ground, the mosquitoes, wet matches, soggy groceries, aches, blisters, endless paraphernalia, mosquitoes and the cold, hard ground...
Where was I, Snorkel Bob? Oh yes, the beauty of nature/the nature of beauty. Listen to this, Campers:
Mosquitoes rule! They love hiking trails most of all. I, Snorkel Bob, prefer Pest-Off, widely unsold here, except of course by me, SB.

## KAUAI

Kauai also rules, with world-class hikes at all levels of difficulty; the stroll, the trek, the purge, human sacrifice.

THE NA PALI COAST is known for the Kalalau Trail, inaccessible from any other part of the island. From the Kee Beach trailhead at the N.W. corner of Kauai, it's 11 miles and a hard go, up and down, down and up, just like the elevator in the Empire State Building but with beaches, waterfalls and whales!

Ambient reality is hot and muggy, with each beauteous bloom doubling as a visual highlight and a mosquito condo. Lather up. Relather liberally as necessary.

Most Important: Stay on the trail. Severe gravity hazard here is proven by humans falling to forevermore. Marginal consolation derives from prevailing dysfunction at the moment of transcendence; i.e. most fatalities result from bad judgment—short-cutting the trail, traversing when wet, all the usual go-for-it stuff so easily avoided with calmness and common sense.

1 or 2 die here each year. So the Division of State Parks tracks who goes in, who comes out. Permits are free and required, with only so many out at 1 time, so plan ahead. The permit allows 5 days on the trail. Call or write the Division of State Parks, 3060 Eiwa St., Rm. 306, Lihue, Kauai, HI 96766 (808) 274-3444. If you're here and want a permit, the parks division office is in the State Building, room 306, in Lihue. My, Snorkel Bob's, favorite map is Earthwalk Press' Recreation Map of Northwestern Kauai, from the Kokee State Park museum shop.

The Kalalau Trail has 3 campsites with restrictions. The beaches look inviting but can kill you quick. Take your dips in the side streams, stay out of the ocean. Also note tsunami markers on the beaches and camp above them.

Hanakapiai Camp is 2 miles in. You get more daytripper company here. You can stay 1 night going in and a 2nd night coming out but not 2 nights in a row. An excellent side trail goes 2 miles upstream to Hanakapiai Falls, 200' & pool below.

Hanakoa Camp is 6 miles in with the same rules and a nice little (1/2-mile) trail up the west fork of Hanakoa Stream to the falls—cool water direct from Kokee Plateau, 3,000' up, and a deep, wide pool to swim in, in solitude.

Last stop is Kalalau Beach Camp, 11 miles in. The stretch from Hanakoa to Kalalau is arid and hot (southward kink in coastline makes for rain shadow, no mo mosquito). At Kalalau Camp you get 3 days max, or you can hang forever if you play in the sea caves at the west end of the beach.

If sheer punishment turns you on, you can hike up Kalalau Stream 2 miles to Big Pool. You must still walk 11 miles out, a push, possibly a grind, maybe down to bare metal.

You may also see Big Pool by taking a boat to Kalalau Beach. Both Captain Zodiac and Hanalei Sea Tours are licensed to drop you off and pick you up, May through September, if you have your state permit. The boats are also licensed to land at 2 additional beaches, Nualolo Kai and Milolii, south of Kalalau, that are inaccessible by land. (See Das Boats)

Streams at all 3 Kalalau campsites run cool, fresh water that must be treated for drinking. Warning: Na Pali is called the fastest-eroding coastline in the world. The rock is rotten. No off-trail climbing or bushwhacking anywhere on this coast.

KOKEE STATE PARK is due south of Na Pali. It overlooks the cliffs from a misty plateau 4,000' up. Tour buses swarm the faaabulous overlooks worse than skeeters on white meat. After 10 a.m. it socks in for romantical interlude, moody, warm and moist. Great hikes are here too with few mosquitoes (altitude).

Awaawapuhi and Nualolo Trails overlook the Na Pali Coast, but you must work. Awaawapuhi is 3.1 miles 1 way, starting at a marked trailhead on Rte 550, 1.6 miles past the Kokee State Park HQ. The trail hooks up with Nualolo Cliff Trail near its end, which runs into Nualolo Bench Trail, which connects to Nualolo Trail, which gets you back to the park HQ eventually. The terrain is native dry-land forest, a rare and exotic sight.

I, Snorkel Bob, actually saw large groves of mature Koa trees in this mist. These native Hawaiian hardwoods were decimated by cattle, Kiawe encroachment and poachers. Kiawe was encouraged by the missionaries so that its big thorns would discourage the heathen from bare feet, since bare feet can lead directly to Polaroid spread shots, or something. Cattle and goats also claimed everything in their path. 3rd hit came from hardwood poachers. Koa is now rare in extremis.

East is wet on the plateau, all the way to Alakai Swamp, which absorbs the runoff, kind of, from Mt. Waialeale, the wettest spot in world, so they say. You can hike in the swamp without a permit, just as you can eat dukey and bang your head on a wall without a permit (Sheesh). Pluff mud (low grade quick sand) here will sink you quick to your knees. No 1 ever complained of sinking deeper.

I, Snorkel Bob, also like a short hike, Kaluapuhi Trail (under 1 mile), and a longer 1, Pihea Trail (nearly 4 miles 1 way) that explore the rainforest, where rare native birds live and the flowers glow like Roman candles. A rain poncho here is good. Both trails start just off Rte 550, so you don't need 4WD to reach the trailhead, unlike some other favorites, like Kawaikoi Stream Trail, Sugi Grove Camp and Kawaikoi Camp.

Trust the "4WD Only" signs in Kokee; the back roads get slicker'n snot on a door knob after a heavy mist, let alone rain.

The Kokee Museum, next to the lodge at HQ, has maps and info on the trails and of course, much much more.

A flat, grassy area near the Lodge is for tent and trailer camping. You need a permit from the State Parks Division in Lihue (see Na Pali, and bring your patience). The same goes for back-country camping, Kawaikoi and Sugi Grove, most beauteous when wet, but then wouldn't a water rat like me, Snorkel Bob, think that? Groceries are in Waimea or Kekaha, not in the park.

The park also rents cabins for $35-45 per night. Some sleep 2, some sleep 3 and some sleep 6, but in a pinch they can all eat 11. The wood stoves fend off the mild arctic chill and at $9 a bundle for the wood, I, Snorkel Bob, would budget $18 for warmth. Pots, pans, silverware, showers and blankets are there. For reservations call Kokee Lodge, (808) 335-6061. 6 months ahead is not too soon. Then again, sometimes you can walk right in, sit right down, baby let your mind roll on.

Get to Kokee on Hwy 50 west from Lihue to Kekaha. Turn right on Kokee Road (Rte 550) and go uphill for about 20 miles to Kokee Lodge. You can get breakfast and lunch at:

**THE KOKEE LODGE**
Kokee State Park Headquarters
(808) 335-6061
9-4 Daily (Breakfast and Lunch served 9-3:30)

The restaurant has a limited menu and no dinner but it works and it's warm.

WAIMEA–THE CANYON is a beauteous work of nature and is among the 7 Wonders of Kauai. You may traverse from 4 different angles. A detailed map is at the Division of Forestry and Wildlife in the State Office Building in Lihue (808) 274-3433, where you can also get your permit if overnight camping is on the agenda—not required for day hikes. Free, the permit. 4 campsites to choose from, 4 nights max in the canyon.

Hot and dry prevail with little shade on the trail, so sunscreen and water are key to comfort; stream water is potable if treated. Waimea Canyon is often called the Grand Canyon of the Pacific. I, SB, wonder who often calls the Grand Canyon the Waimea Canyon of Arizona, yet spectaculacular is what it is.

The main trail in is Kukui Trail, 2.5 miles long, dropping 2,300'. The ascent feels more like 12,000', and 1 alternative is the Illiau Nature Loop, a 1-mile stroll at the top of the canyon past native plants with I.D. tags and benches. The trailhead is right off Rte 550 and well marked. No parking lot here, but the road has shoulders.

Kukui Trail is steep with switchbacks down to the Waimea River and an alternate reality. Kukui Trail ends at Wiliwili Camp at the river. From there you can hike upriver on Waimea Canyon Trail, branching onto Koaie Canyon Trail about 3/4 mile from the junction with Kukui Trail. Koaie Canyon Trail goes about 3 miles into a side canyon and achieves deep penetration.

Helicopter traffic was bad along these trails. Then it was very bad. Now, alas, the monster gnats can cause even a peace-loving snorkel executive like me, Snorkel Bob, to wish upon a star for a ground-to-air

Sidewinder missile. There oughta be a law, and I, Snorkel Bob, urge resistance to this further degradation of our Natural Trust.

Call the Lodge at Kokee for weather. High water, heavy rain or flash floods should cancel your trip.

THE SLEEPING GIANT (Nounou Ridge) is just behind Wailua and Kapaa on Kauai's east shore. Turn off Hwy 56 onto Haleilio Road (by the Sizzler), pass through a neighborhood until the houses thin. Look for a trailhead sign on the right side of the road. A small parking lot is just beyond, also on the right side. The trail is about 1.5 miles ending at a nice spot on top. It's a little steep for nappy poo, but acceptable for sitdown groceries and a couple brewskies. Mosquitoes here.

# BIG ISLAND

HAWAII VOLCANOES NATIONAL PARK on Mauna Loa has most of the best hiking trails on the Big Island and many campgrounds too.

Mauna Loa Summit Trail is for macho guys with hairy chests and independent women who know how to pick up a check without flinching or hike 19 miles for 3 days with nary a whimper. Hairy and independent must both check in and get a permit. The 1st ascent is 7 miles, 3,400' to Red Hill Cabin (no cable, no phone, no room service, pool, spa or bar). The 2nd ascent is 11 miles, 3,650' to Summit Cabin, which is comparably void. The cabins have bunks, blankets, white-gas stoves and lanterns. Bring your own white gas. Ask the rangers about water. It's cold. Bring warm stuff and a good sleeping bag.

You must register at park HQ with the rangers, then take Hwy 11 west a couple miles, turn on Mauna Loa Road and go 11 miles to the end. The trailhead is here. No mosquitoes.

Kipahu Puaulu Trail is an easy 1.1-mile hike on the way to the Mauna Loa Summit trailhead. It circles a hillock crowned with unique forest and surrounded by lava flow. Early morning and evening, rare birds may appear, may sing, may dance. The trailhead and parking lot are 1.6 miles up Mauna Loa Road.

Halemaumau Trail traverses the Kilauea Caldera on Mauna Loa's southeastern flank and descends through rainforest from the park visitor center, then crosses the Martian landscape of the caldera floor. It's 3.2 miles, 2 hours, 1 way. Leave a car at the far end or plan to loop back on intersecting trails.

Kilauea Iki means "Little Kilauea" and is just east of Big Kilauea. "Iki" is a relative term—in '59 Kilauea Iki spewed lava 1900' high. In 36 days it filled the crater with the hot broth. Kilauea Iki Trail is a 3-mile loop passing steaming vents and rising to a heavy fern and ohia forest. 2-1/2 hours, this 1.

The Kau Desert section of the park is barren lava with many interconnecting trails. Many lead to oceanfront campgrounds with shelters, but you need a permit from the rangers.

CAMPING requires no permit for established campgrounds, but the feds require 1 to make camp anywhere else in the park. Enforcement is sincere. If you fail to check in, you may return to find your campsite vanished.

Campgrounds accessible by car are free on a 1st-come basis, with a 7-day limit. All park cabins are rented by reservation through the Volcano House, (808) 967-7321, where rooms run $79 to $131, depending on wing and view.

Namakani Paio Camp is 3 miles west of the visitor center in a eucalyptus grove. Tent and trailer camping and cabins here. Restrooms have running water but showers are in a separate shared cabin. The camp is dry but 4,000' up, so it gets cold. The cabins have 1 double bed, and 2 bunks, with grill & picnic table outside. $32/night, $10 key deposit, $5 linen deposit.

Kipuka Nene Camp is 11 miles from the visitor center and closer to sea level. Descend Chain of Craters Road, then turn right on Hilina Road. It's more primitive here, with water from a tank and pit toilets.

Kamoamoa Camp, at the beach 30 miles below the visitor center, is, alas, no mo; swallowed by lava in '93.

Good hikes outside the national park include:

THE KONA COAST and Captain Cook Monument, where the snorkel barges dump their live cargo at $59 a head. Hwy 11 goes into Captain Cook. Take the jeep trail just north of the Kealakekua turnoff (across the highway from Shiraki Cleaners).

It's a 2.5-mile hike, 3 hours round trip down to the shore and back. You will pass excellent snorkel grounds on this 1, but ingress and egress is advanced and tricky, unless you scope it, meditate, relax completely, slither like a fish.

Puuuhonua-o-Honaunau National Park, a few miles south of Captain Cook, has a 1.6-mile loop trail, G rated.

MORE CAMPING (Outside Volcanoes National Park) is available in several state beach parks. Make cabin reservations through the Division of State Parks, P.O. Box 936, Hilo, HI 96721 (808) 933-4200.

Hapuna Beach State Recreation Area, 7 miles north of Waikoloa, is dry and warm. Screened A-frames run $20/night and can sleep up to 4 people. Reservations taken up to a year in advance. No tent or trailer camping allowed.

Kalopa State Park, on the Hamakua Coast, is maybe 3 miles south of Honokaa on Highway 19. It's cool (about 2,000' up) and green. Tent camping is allowed. 4 "housekeeping" cabins share 1 kitchen. Spartan motif is offset by comfy bunks, heat, lights, electric cooking, 1 blanket per camper and a fireplace in the mess hall. You must bring your own firewood. 1-8 campers runs around $55, plus $5 for each additional camper. Bunkhouse facility available also.

Mauna Kea State Recreation Facility, in the center of the island, is dry and mild. Single cabins run $45/night for 1-4 people, and group unit "bunkhouses" are the same as Kalopa with common mess hall, electricity, etc. It's 2 miles east of the military camp on Saddle Road.

Manuka State Natural Area Reserve, on Hwy 11 south of Kailua, is a beautiful stop midway between vacationland and volcanoland. The state parks allow sleeping bags in the wayside pavilions, avec permit. Picnic tables and restrooms.

# MAUI

Haleakala covers 2/3 of Maui and most of Maui's most excellent hikes are in the volcanic, midlin and tropical ranges.

At Volcanic level (cold, often dry, way high) is the best known and most amazing trail down to the dormant crater, which is actually an erosional valley; the crater was hundreds feet higher before returning to dust.

Sliding Sands Trail goes in and Switchback (Halemauu Trail) comes out (about 12 miles total). Between the 2 is the crater floor. Sliding Sands descends 2500' to the basin floor, and Switchback is a cliffside footpath that looks like a scene from Shangri La. You can do this hike in a day, but it's more fun as an overnighter. A sincere humdinger, this 1.

Holoa cabin at the bottom takes a few months' advance reservations. (Haleakala National Park, P.O. Box 369 Makawao, HI 96768 (808) 572-9306). It can sleep 12 in 4 bunks, 3 tiers each. With a wood-burning stove, a sink, 4 walls and a ceiling, it feels like The Ritz after the hike in. Those without reservations tent camp outside, which can be cold, wet and lumpy. Bring your own sleeping bag, candles (no electricity), groceries, wine, aspirin et al. The cabin is $40 a night for 1-6 people, $80 a night for 7-12 people. This includes the firewood. The rangers will know if drinking water is scarce and fill you in on details.

I, Snorkel Bob, can fill you in on this inside tip: If you call the rangers a day or 2 or 3 before you want the cabin, you have about a 30 percent chance of getting it, because whoever reserved it months ago isn't coming. This is an excellent outing.

Or, on a full moon or close to it, hike the whole thing straight through. You'll need the moonlight for footing. I, Snorkel Bob, head up around 4 or 5 p.m., hit the trail about 6 or 7 and climb out around midnight or 1, about the time all the poor stiffs who got to got to got to see sunrise at the crater are rolling around trying to sleep because they only got 1 more hour. (Staying over at Holoa Cabin is good either way; on the full moon, for the light, or with no moon, for the stars).

This hike is not a loop, and the trail ends a few miles from the start, so stash a car at the Halemauu trailhead, off the main road (Rte 378) 4.6 miles inside the park boundary. Then drive to the summit, where Sliding Sands starts. All hikers must register at this park (look for a box near the visitor center at the summit).

A more zealous jaunt follows Sliding Sands to the crater floor, about 5 miles, and continues straight another mile or 2 to the cabin at Paliku. The following day calls for 13 miles down the backside of the mountain through Kaupo Gap. It's mostly downhill, rocky and scenic as a low-budget sci-fi movie. Here too, arrange for pick up at trail's end in Kaupo on Rte 31. These logistical problems are formidable, but cost/benefit analysis by me, Snorkel Bob, results in a resounding Yes.

Another most excellent hike is through Oheo Gulch, about 7 miles southeast of Hana on the main road (Rte 31). The park ranger should know conditions, flash flood hazards and so on. The trail leads to Waimoku Falls, 2 miles in. I, Snorkel Bob, rate these falls in the spectaculacular zone with no hesitation. If you want guidance, the rangers lead a hike back there every Saturday at 9 a.m. starting at the parking lot.

**The Nature Conservancy of Hawaii** runs a guided hike in its Waikamoi Preserve, a 5,230-acre mid-altitude rainforest on Haleakala's northern (rainy) flank. The Conservancy protects natural habitat the old-fashioned American way: they buy it. I, Snorkel Bob, approve and donate when possible and hope that you will too. The Waikamoi hike occurs on the 2nd Saturday of each month, from 9 to noon. You will pay a $4 vehicle entry fee into the park and donate $15 per person for the hike. Come with layered clothing, rain-gear, sturdy shoes, water, and food. Call TNC's Maui Project Office in Makawao, (808) 572-7849, to register and get details.

ALSO ON MAUI is the expedition expediter:

**HIKE MAUI**
P.O. Box 330969
Kahului, Maui 96733
(808) 879-5270

Ken Schmidt has led hikes ranging from the Teddy Bear's Picnic to Pork Chop Hill since 1983. Ken is an intrepid leader and a treasure trove of flora/fauna info—eat this, don't eat that; this will bind you, this will set you free, this is lunch.

For example, you can hike Haleakala alone. Hiking with Ken Schmidt lets you know what you're looking at when you're looking at it, like lava tubes and caves invisible to the tourist eye.

Hikes like the falls at Hanawi depart radically from the beaten path—a tough blaze if you don't know the trail. I, Snorkel Bob, mean you can get waaay back there and lost, like in life but more pressed by dark and hunger.

Ken Schmidt hikes the West Maui Mountains, coastlines, forests and Haleakala, half day or whole day. He arranges transportation and supplies chow, day packs, bottled water, and rain gear for $75 half-day (5 hours) or $110 full-day (10 hours.).

On your half-day coastwise promenade, you get 3 stretches of coast with dramatic rocks, blowholes and a magic shrine.

The Oheo Gulch trip is 10-12 hours past numerous pools in the stream (still shown as 7 Sacred Pools on most maps.) and penetrates 60' bamboo forests to 400' falls.

Swimming is optional on most of these hikes but alas...

## You Must Schnorkel!

# OAHU

Oahu is so intense that hiking should be a required course here, along with English.

I, Snorkel Bob, head for the mountains behind Honolulu and hike to Manoa Falls, or up Mt. Tantalus, or the Makiki Valley loop. The south side of the Koolau range is rife with trails. Most trailheads mentioned here are on city bus routes, and you can get a good trail map and info at:

## THE HAWAII NATURE CENTER
2131 Makiki Heights Dr. in Honolulu, Oahu
(808) 955-0100
8-4:30 Daily

The non-profit Nature Center operates in a funky but quaint building at the foot of Mt. Tantalus. Its focus is educating local kids on the rare (and disappearing) Hawaiian ecosystem. The center trains teachers and organizes hikes on weekends—$7/person, reservations required. Call for a schedule. The Nature Center is not touristic, has nothing to buy and no hula girls in coconut bras. It has family hikes and advanced hikes for the physically fit, and it's a great place to start a hike:

The Makiki Valley loop starts with the Maunalaha Trail, 1 mile along Makiki Stream, behind the Nature Center and up the hill through lush, low-altitude jungle. Plenty mosquitoes here, but it's beautiful, serene and silent. Most important on this trail is a large canteen filled at the Nature Center.

The trail hits an intersection with several other trails. The left-hand route is the Makiki Valley Trail, which dips to the streambed and back up again. It joins the Kanealole Trail, which goes about 3/4 mile downhill and ends at the State Division of Forestry and Wildlife baseyard, next to the Nature Center. The loop in reverse is a gentler climb, starting on the Kanealole Trail.

Manoa Falls Trail, at the head of neighboring Manoa Valley, is another short (0.8 mile) hike. Follow Manoa Road up the valley to Paradise Park and Lyon Arboretum (or take the #5 bus).

The trail starts beyond the arboretum, where it crosses the stream then meanders muddily through eucalyptus, African tulip trees and native hau. The pool at the base of the falls is good for wading, except when it's high. Don't confuse this hike with the Manoa Cliffs Trail, which is longer, higher and more difficult.

Don't climb up behind the falls. If you want more exercise, the Aihualama Trail veers left just before the falls, then zigzags uphill for a little over a mile, where it joins the Pauoa Flats Trail. You can go right on the Pauoa Flats Trail and go uphill another quarter-mile to its end, or left for a half-mile and pick up Manoa Cliff Trail, which goes for a couple miles and ends at Tantalus Drive next to a Hawaiian Telephone Company facility. The sights along this trail, which crowns the mountain, are most beauteous. The city bus doesn't go up this far, so leave a car here unless you want to turn around and go back the way you came.

The Manoa Cliffs Trail, by itself, makes a nice 3-mile hike around the north side of Tantalus, ending at Round Top Drive. Start at the telephone company and go until you hit blacktop again. This is Round Top Drive.

Turn right and follow the road (minimal traffic here) for 1.5 miles to get back to your car.

If you want to hike with somebody, you can call:

**THE SIERRA CLUB**
Honolulu, Oahu
(808) 538-6616

This Sierra Club schedules events like weekend hikes and clean-ups. Bring your own gear, snacks, water and a $3 donation, unless you're a member, then it's $1. Slideshows are offered once each quarter. Reservations are required.

**THE HAWAIIAN TRAIL AND MOUNTAIN CLUB**
P.O. Box 2238
Honolulu, Oahu, HI 96804
(808) 262-2845

This group hikes on Sunday—call ahead for a schedule. Relaxed, unstructured, and only a $2 donation, this 1.

Oahu also has a branch of the Audubon Society, (808) 528-1432. I, Snorkel Bob, condone bird-watching because they used to be fish, kind of. Didn't they? I, Snorkel Bob, recommend camping on the outer islands. Legal campsites on Oahu are few and mostly taken by homeless humans.

# TENNIS EVERYONE

## MAUI

**KALAMA PARK**
Across from Foodland and close to me, Snorkel Bob, in Kihei, Maui

4 public courts with lights and usually a wait, especially a.m. and late afternoons. It's free and reasonably maintained but not like a tennis club, where you wouldn't be surrounded by the little rascals playing baseball and basketball. Good for a pick-up game with a heavy hitter.

## MAUI SUNSET
1032 S. Kihei Rd. in Kihei, Maui

6 public courts by the ocean, sometimes with sagging nets and court puddles, but usually 1 is open (except weekend mornings). Shorts and T-shirt.

## MAKENA TENNIS CLUB
5415 Makena Alanui Dr. in Makena, Maui
(808) 879-8777

6 beauteous courts with a pro shop and perfectly manicured surroundings. $18 reserves 1 hour of court time, after which you may play on any available courts. Tennis whites only here, though I, Snorkel Bob, wonder how they get away with that.

# OAHU

Tennis is more important on Oahu because an urban hub needs ventilation, lest the citizens buckle under. (That's my spot, you sonofabitch!) Aggression & hostility are more acceptable within bounds, either side of the net. Public courts range from free to a few bucks and are usually accessible.

## ILIKAI SPORTS CENTER
1777 Ala Moana Blvd. in Honolulu, Oahu
(808) 949-3811

5 courts, this 1, at $5/hour for guests; $7.50 for visitors. That's 7 to 7. Add $2/hour after 7 p.m. and play to 10, if you got the 1 court with lights. 1 day maximum lead on reservations here. Private lessons with the pro go for $44/hour. Racket rent is $3/day.

## DIAMOND HEAD TENNIS CENTER
Paki St. in Honolulu, Oahu
No Phone

No snack bar, chachka shop, balls, string, restring—no nothing clutters the pure tennis here. Go toward Diamond Head on Kalakaua Avenue until it ends near the big round green fountain. Go left and you will swing around and be coming back the same direction you came from. This is Paki Street. Go 200 yards and stop. You are here.

This could be my, Snorkel Bob's, favorite courts anywhere. 10 courts with good surface means good turnover. It's free–city and county maintained—and it's in a good park. No reservations here. Each court is represented by a little fake clock in the waiting area. When you take a court, you turn the hands of the appropriate clock to your start time. You get 45 minutes. If nobody is waiting, you get another 45. You almost always get a court right away and if it's full, you wait only 45 minutes, in the shade, usually with some interesting urban chit chat, check out, do you come here often?

This 1 has a water fountain. And off to 1 side at quasi-oblique angulature are the Kapiolani Courts, also city and county, also free, where you can continue play past dark. The lights are on a 1-hour timer, hand operated. Court rotation and waiting areas should be fairly easy for those of you with degrees to figure out. Those of you without degrees can go ahead and begin play.

# BICYCLE RIDES

You should know by now that communion is elemental, comprised of water, dirt, wind, fire. It is removed from promo, glitz, plastic wrappers. Nothing attains the void like snorkeling, yet I, Snorkel Bob, will herein serve up the down and dirty on some honest also-rans:

DOWNHILL BICYCLE RIDES—Is it worth it? Is it safe? Is it fun?

Here is the straight poop you've come to expect by now. The downhill phenomenon started years ago when an avid cyclist rolled 10,000' from the summit of Haleakala to the ocean—30 miles of blacktop, downhill. His friends thought he was nuts, but isn't that usually the case?

He went again and somebody asked to go along and the guy said well okay and 1 thing led to another and he was taking people down regular, tourists even, for money. Years ago it was about $30 a head. At 1 point 10 different outfits competed. They attritioned down to 3 as the fare rose to $100. Business was good, and today competition is again keen with 9 outfits, or 10. Most people appear pleased with the value, yet I, Snorkel Bob, am compelled to address another delicate consideration.

They dress you up like a geek—Darth Vader racing helmet, Batman gloves, Nanook of the North rain gear. Then they require single file and otherwise assume you're a blithering idiot and don't know how to let a bicycle roll down a hill. It's another constraint of the adventure-for-sale industry.

But this ride is no cakewalk. Here too, safety requires that the rider not blither but must be aware that Haleakala Highway can clog with traffic thick as a New York arterial these days. Few people fall on the commercial downhill rides, but too much speed in the tight turns can quickly flux your rider/injury ratio. This is still safer than driving a car, having sex with a stranger or fixing a flat in Florida.

I, Snorkel Bob, wince from time to time at the fleets of vans, walkie talkies, bicycles with expensive brakes, crash helmets, spacesuits, payroll, advertising, utilities, rent, groceries, alimony—10 outfits running 6 trips a day so herds of molasses-assed 2-wheelers block the highway from dawn to dusk, like the whole place was a frigging amusement park, which it is. And bicycles are better than cars, and most people who do this are satisfied, or gratified, or possibly fulfilled. If you want to go, I, Snorkel Bob, can fix you up.

Or you can go solo on a decent road not yet "discovered" or marketed. Alternate roads cross Haleakala's slopes through the countryside way up where it looks like southern England and the air is crisp and cool for miles and miles. Bike routes on Kauai, Oahu and the Big Island offer diversity and beauty, and bicycle outfitters deliver in all these places.

Most tours start at parks or other pretty spots where you meet the outfitter—they bring the bikes. Sometimes they bring eats, depending on the deal.

Critically significant to bicycling in Hawaii is that the State Highway Department never heard of designated bike lanes or bike paths, or maybe they heard but couldn't understand. Roads with shoulders are few and the shoulders are often covered with pinestraw and sticks. Most roads are too narrow, and many local drivers still yell at bicyclists to get out of the road. It's not as bad as it used to be, but it ain't good.

Ask questions. The outfitters listed here are hip to the situation, and some of them factor reality into their trips:

# BIG ISLAND

### MAUNA KEA MOUNTAIN BIKES
Kamuela, Hawaii
(808) 885-2091
Toll Free (888) MTB-TOUR

Mauna Kea Mountain Bikes has 2 mottos: "Good Clean Fun" and "Ride the Newest Place on Earth". This outfit runs 4 tours deep in cattle country. Beginning to intermediate riders can try the Kohala downhill, the "Kamakazi" ride down Mauna Kea (the highest peak in Hawaii—13,796'), or Mana Road, 8-15 miles up and down. Generation

X'ers (Xtremely advanced) may want to lunge onto the single-track "Mud Lane Tour" through the rainforest. Tours are customized to fit your needs, providing your needs can fit on a bicycle. Tours run $55-$115/person and include snacks, and sometimes lunch, depending on the trip. Rentals run $20/24 hrs. or $130/week, and they'll bring the bikes to you between 8:00-3:00.

### HAWAIIAN PEDALS
Kailua, Hawaii (in the Kona Inn Shopping Village)
(808) 329-2294

The retail outlet here has all the helmets, gloves, water bottles, patch kits and other stuff you didn't know you needed. Bikes rent for $20/day, or $25 if you want a performance bike.

# MAUI

### CHRIS' ADVENTURES BIKE OR HIKE
Kona: (808) 326-4600
Maui: (808) 871-2453

Chris' has morning and afternoon bike tours at $89 or $59. On Maui, the Haleakala Wine Trek begins at the top of Haleakala with a short hike and view of the crater, followed by a bike ride down the front side of the volcano to Tedeschi Winery, ending at La Perouse Bay. Includes picnic breakfast and lunch.

The Big Island mega ride is called the Kohala Mountain Adventure. This volcanic-mountain ride traverses pastureland over to the tropical side of the Kohala Coast and continues oceanside to Pololu Lookout (secluded black sand beach). Includes breakfast and a picnic lunch.

Chris' also offers a Coastal bike/hike to remote waterfalls around the West Maui Mountains and off-road tours once a week. Average 4-6 people per tour.

### MAUI DOWNHILL
199 Dairy Rd. in Kahului, Maui
(808) 871-2155 (all hours)

Does what the name says. Free pickup/custom bikes with drum brakes/big buffet/beverage/sunrise & day tours/gear et al. Sunrise tour begins at 3:15 a.m. and ends with breakfast at a restaurant. $93 with 24-hr. minimum cancellation.

While you, my friends, got your choice of bicycles to rent on the outer islands; on Oahu you got your choice of mopeds.

# HORSEBACK RIDES

HORSEBACK RIDES Some people love horses. Some people find them friendly. Some like to talk or sing to them or make goo goo with them. Some people find them agreeable, even at the apex of the equine flatulence curve.

I, Snorkel Bob, ever game, want to understand these things. So I, Snorkel Bob, ride them. Some of these places are booked days in advance, especially in peak periods. None will let you ride in flops. Boots are best, but any closed-toe shoes will do.

All these places limit group size and provide good horses—youthful, well-mannered and hardy. So you only need to decide where you want to ride.

Kauai has rides in the Hanalei area (beauteous but rainy) and the Poipu area (need sunscreen).

# KAUAI

### POOKU STABLES
Princeville, Kauai
(808) 826-6777 or (eve.) 246-6585

Between the Princeville Airport and the condomania, this stable's rides cross neighboring ranchland overlooking Hanalei Valley and Bay with a mountain backdrop. Optional is a 4-hour picnic/waterfall ride, $110 per person, max 6 riders. 1-1/2 hour country ride is $57/person. Call at least 2 days ahead.

### CJM COUNTRY STABLES
Poipu, Kauai (on the main road, west of the resort-golf thicket)
(808) 742-6096

The highlight is the 8:30 a.m. beach ride for 3 hours that includes breakfast and occasional monk seal sightings at $71. Other rides go 2 hours to beaches and ranches @ $56. Must call ahead for reserves.

# BIG ISLAND

Big Island rides vary as you might suspect, with variable terrain and conditions. Cattle country has optimal climate for equine and bovine happiness (for now).

## MAUNA KEA STABLES
Mauna Kea Beach Dr. (20 minutes up from the coast in Kamuela, 1/2 mile behind K.M. Seed & Tractor Co. on Hwy 19)
Kohala Coast, Hawaii
(808) 885-4288

This is the only stable on Parker Ranch. Morning or afternoon rides cross rolling pastures with (maybe) clear views of Mauna Loa, Mauna Kea, Hualalai and the Kohala Range. A 1-hour ride is $40; 2 hours is $70. Special rides and picnics arranged on request, and you must be over 8 and under 210.

## DAHANA ROUGHRIDERS
Kamuela, Hawaii (5 miles east of Kamuela on Hwy 19)
(808) 885-0057 or (808) 885-0000 (reservations)

These guided rides follow no particular trail, and you can jog, canter or walk your horse. 4-5 rides, 1-1/2 hours each, occur daily. $55/person. Speak with the owner, Meestah Nakoa, for custom range rides for large groups.

## KING'S TRAIL RIDES O'KONA
Kealakekua, Hawaii
(808) 323-2388

Bones and his wranglers highlight a 4-hr. Captain Cook Monument ride, starting with a gradual descent of monument trail through the Ekoa forest to the Monument for snorkeling and a picnic at Kealakekua Bay Marine Preserve. Then Bones takes you to "Queen's Bath" for a fresh water swim before the ride back up the trail. Departs daily at 9 a.m., $95/person, age 7 and up. 24-hr. advance reservation and deposit required.

## WAIPIO NAALAPA TRAIL RIDES
Honokaa, Hawaii
(808) 775-0419 or (808) 329-7700 (reservations only)

Waipio Valley is on the wet side so it's maximum lush. Flora of the jungle (Ah, Flora) abounds with waterfalls, historic and spiritual matrices the guide can show you. Then of course is the rain, the possibility of rain, the aftermath of rain. Call 2 hours before your scheduled ride for a rain update.

You meet in Kukuihaele on Rte 240 near the Waipio Valley lookout and get taken to the horses. The 2-hour ride is twice daily but not on Sunday. $75/adults, $65/kids (8 or better), which is cheaper than 2 hours with your shrink and maybe as rewarding.

# MAUI

Good trails in all corners and in the crater. Some are:

## THOMPSON RANCH RIDING STABLES
Kula, Maui
(808) 878-1910 or 244-7412 (answer service to 9 p.m. HST)

Established 1902 on the flanks of Haleakala, this 1 overlooks the isthmus and West Maui Mountains. Take Hwy 37 to Kula and go to Ching store and Fong store on your right. Turn left toward Kula San, then left on Thompson Road. Rides range from $45 for 1-1/2 hours, $55 with picnic, or $50 for a 2-hour ride. Small children can ride double for $25. Reservations required a few days in advance. Stables close after Labor Day for 2 months.

## MAKENA STABLES
7299 S. Makena Rd. in Makena, Maui
(808) 879-0244

This is a long (minimum 3-hour) morning or sunset ride from sea level through scrub forest up into the pastures of Ulupalakua Ranch. I.e., if you saw Alan Ladd saunter the West Texas plains on old Slowpoke with nary a pulse to the horizon except for a tumbling tumbleweed or 2 and a tongue flick and a burp in a shadow from some gila monster engorging some crud, you'll deja vu the 1st 1/2 of this 1. No gila monsters here but this 1 gets lively on account of the lava flows not settling flat like West Texas before congealment but rather freezing in their tracks, leaving a 3D reverberation of molten flow, even if hardly a gnat scratches his ass in this still and spartan terrain. Besides the vibratory flow (flowing vibe?) you get to break on through to the other side, which is green and lush in this case. I, Snorkel Bob, like this 1, slunked low in the saddle, running short on water and jerky, just thinking about them painted ladies back in Abilene.

No kids under 12. Take Makena Alanui Road past all the resorts; the stable is 2 miles past the Maui Prince Resort. The Morning ride is $115. Sunset is $130 on Friday and Saturday only. Special 2-hour intro ride on Wednesday is $99.

## SEAHORSE RANCH
Wailuku, Hawaii (about 9 miles north of Wailuku on Rte 340)
(808) 244-9862

This ranch in a remote corner of the island takes 7 riders max for 3 hours everyday but Sunday. This countryside reminds me, Snorkel Bob, of Big Sur before the cults. The 3-1/2-hour ride goes into the West Maui Mountains with lunch for $99. Ask about the 5-hour adventure with a barbecue by a waterfall ($130). Call 2 hours before the ride to check the weather.

## OHEO STABLES
Kipahulu, Maui
(808) 667-2222

Who'd a thunk a guy like Ray Fuqua—who could go all lucid and emotional on your interior decor, your color scheme and design motif, your lavish denial of post-modern techno-chachkas in favor of your arrogantly subtle eclecticism—could make hay as a cowboy? Not that old Ray has cows or doesn't like girls; he doesn't, and he does. It's just that I, Snorkel Bob, see so many shirts come to Hawaii and swear up'n down they're going to ditch their dull, gray lives and really LIVE! And dagnabbit, Ray Fuqua did it. He's 2" shorter now on account of all the trail humping, and he's on his 2nd honeymoon on account of the first 1 ended on account of all the horses and dirt and ranch stuff. He still pisses me, Snorkel Bob, off for advertising on the TV channel where the floppy-jowled fellow tells you about all the chef's specials he was able to stuff down his gob. Cheez-its, that makes me, Snorkel Bob, want to puke, if you catch my drift.

But back to Rancher Ray Fuqua (foo-kway), what a ride. Maximum lush to salt air, rainforest to ocean view, this 1 has Hana pegged and may be the first real entertainment here beyond luuuv and sighing. 2 rides daily with breakfast at the ranchhouse or picnic lunch on the trail. $119 and $139, and kids must be 12. Some exceptions with an interview. Career counseling available

# SKI HAWAII

If you brought your flannel skivvies, turtlenecks, socks, mittens, gloves, sweaters, hats, scarves, goggles, bun warmers, powder shirts, wind pants, buckle boots, etc, et al, ad nauseum, then a drive up the road between December and April to Mauna Kea might be just the thing.

The snow cap on Mauna Kea in Winter is nice dry powder above 13,000'. It's similar to Chile or Argentina without so much Español and shorter runs—2 to 2-1/2 minutes.

You need 4-wheel drive and your own ski gear. 1 person drives, the other skis, then vice versa.

# 3

# Eclectic Sampler

# DRINKERIES & DANCERIES

Where to go for fun after dark? I, Snorkel Bob, most often opt for eyelid movies, starring a newly discovered reef and sweetly innocent fish. Because I, Snorkel Bob'm, up 'n at 'em at sunrise, which is THE BEST TIME FOR SNORKELING, which is the very most fun of all.

Yet I, Snorkel Bob, understand that some of you are not ready for the life of a snorkel ascetic. Sometimes I, Snorkel Bob, also need to get out and shake loose. I, SB, am no bar hound, but I see what there is to see and herein report those sightings to you.

People often view drinkeries in terms of atmosphere, action, view, service, alternate sexual preference and a host of qualifiers. But I, Snorkel Bob, think there is only 1 reason to visit a bar: to have drink. I, Snorkel Bob, have had a drink at these places and would gladly consider stopping in for another.

# KAUAI

### BRENNECKE'S BEACH BROILER
Poipu, Kauai
(808) 742-7588
11:30-10 Daily

Happy hour all day, overlooking Poipu Beach Park.

### KEOKI'S PARADISE
2360 Kiahuna Plantation Rd. in Poipu, Kauai
(808) 742-7534

Mixed crowd of locals and tourists. Live music some nights. Wraparound bar, open-air, garden setting.

### DUKE'S CANOE CLUB
Lihue, Kauai (in the Marriott)
(808) 246-9599
Open 11:30 a.m

Steak and seafood kind of place.

## THE HIDEAWAY
2975 Ewalu St. in Lihue, Kauai
(808) 245-3473
11-2 (a.m. to a.m.) Daily

Cheap drinks, this 1, and winner (1st Place, Blue Ribbon, Peu Peu) of my, Snorkel Bob's, Special Award For Funk:
Total immersion in Naugahyde and Formica with Philosophy 404 at the bar and a most excellent collection of beer neon, beer lamps, beer mirrors, back-lit beer wall mounts, beer clocks and cheesecake posters. All this and draft beer for a buck 75, ice cold and an honest 12 ozs. Hunger here is slayed quick with an array of chips, pretzels, pork rinds, cheese curls. The juke box spans history, and $5 will get you 25 tunes—an entire disc, while you're playing video games or watching T.V. on the new satellite. I, Snorkel Bob, have a hard time leaving this kind of honesty, this kind of truth. Next to the Toyota dealer on Ewalu.

## TRADEWINDS
Coconut Plantation Market Place in Kapaa, Kauai
(808) 822-1621
10-2 (a.m. to a.m.) Daily

## ZELO'S BEACH HOUSE
Princeville Center in Princeville, Kauai
(808) 826-9700

Lunch from 11:00 a.m., dinner at 5:30, Happy hour 3:30-5:30, everyday. No live music.

## GILLIGAN'S DISCO
Outrigger Kauai Beach in Hanamaulu, Kauai
(808) 245-1955

Thursday, Friday, and Saturday nights. Country line-dancing on Thursday, 8-1, no cover. Top 40 Friday and Saturday, 9:30-2, $5 cover.

## KUHIO'S NIGHTCLUB
1571 Poipu Rd. in Poipu, Kauai
(808) 742-2582

Friday and Saturday nights only. Kuhio's has a 70's swingers format (Hey, baby. I like yo thighs.) Pop tunes and tourists doing the latest from American Bandstand. $5 cover.

# BIG ISLAND

### HUGGO'S
75-5828 Kahakai St. in Kailua, Hawaii
(808) 329-1493

Next to the Royal Kona Resort with a non-stop view of the water, which it hangs out over. ☆☆☆☆☆ sunsets, good grill fare and a lunch rib special on Tuesday and Thursday, if you eat that sort of thing. If not, but you still seek visceral fulfillment, you can SHUFFLE OUT OF HUGGO'S, BEAR EAST SOUTHEAST FOR HARDLY A STEP 'N A STUMBLE AND END UP YOU-KNOW-WHERE—in the humble abode of me, Snorkel Bob, which also happens to be the SNORKEL VORTEX OF THE UNIVERSE, and I, SB, mean ALL OF IT!

Drinks at Huggo's start at $3 and flow till 12:30 a.m. weekdays, 1:00 a.m weekends. Live music after 9, 5 days a week, karaoke 3 days a week. No cover.

### THE KONA INN BAR
The Kona Inn Shopping Village
75-5744 Alii Dr. in Kailua, Hawaii
(808) 329-4455

Open for lunch 11:30 daily, dinner at 5:30, drinks are $3.50 and up, no live music.

### THE CHART HOUSE
75-5770 Alii Dr. in Kailua, Hawaii
(808) 329-2451

This Chart House is right on the water. The bar is open to 9:30 or 10 on weekdays, 10:30 on weekends.

### DRYSDALE'S & DRYSDALE'S II
Kona Inn Shopping Center in Kailua, Hawaii (808) 329-6651
and: Keahou Shopping Village in Keahou, Hawaii (808) 322-0070

Standard menu, sports bar with big screen TV's. The bar serves til 11:30, until later if busy, both places.

## JOLLY ROGER
75-5776 Alii Dr. in Kailua, Kona
(808) 329-1344

Drinks start @ $2.50 and flow to 10 weekdays, midnight on weekends. Live music Friday and Saturday from 8-midnight.

## THE OTHER SIDE
74-5484 Kaiwi (Old Industrial) in Kailua-Kona
(808) 329-7226

Remember the Bette Davis movie where she walks in, looks around and says, "Whadda Dump." That's not this by a longshot, no sirree. It's pool and darts and other light industrial recreation in a warehouse with Bass Ale and Steiny on tap. No charm nor color, but what dramatic potential.

Go up (north) Alii Dr. to the end. Go Left on Hualalai and Right on Kaiwi and up on the left.

## ECLIPSE
75-5711 Kuakini Hwy in Kailua, Hawaii
(808) 329-4686

Open to 1:30 with a $2 cover Friday and Saturday. Maybe dancing, maybe not.

## KORNER POCKET
Hwy 11 in Kealakekua, Hawaii
(808) 322-2994

Sports bar with darts and pool tables. Open 7 days. Live music on Friday nights.

## MERRIMAN'S
Opelo Plaza on Kawaihae Rd. in Kamuela, Hawaii
(808) 885-6822

This is a good place for a drink because it's 1 of only a few places in Kamulea. Open 7 days. Last seating for dinner at 9.

**SOUTH POINT BAR**
Hwy 11 in South Point, Hawaii
(808) 929-9343

Live music once a month. Bar open Mon-TH from 11-10, Fri to 11, Sat 11-10 again and Sun 8-8.

**VOLCANO HOUSE**
Hwy 11 in Volcano, Hawaii
(808) 967-7321

Bar and restaurant open to 9. Make reservations for dinner.

**HARRINGTON'S**
135 Kalanianaole St. in Hilo, Hawaii
(808) 961-4966

Live music Friday and Saturday. Slack key guitar and contemporary with some Hawaiian.

**FIASCO'S**
200 Kanoelehoa Ave. in Hilo, Hawaii
(808) 935-7666

Reasonable margaritas. Thursday is country night to midnight. Live music Friday and Saturday to 1, no cover.

# MAUI

**MAKAI BAR**
Marriott Hotel in Kaanapali, Maui
(808) 667-1200

Live music every night. Excellent pupus, good sunsets. Drinks poured 4:30-midnight Sun to Thursday and to 12:30 on Friday and Saturday.

**KIMO'S**
845 Front St. in Lahaina, Maui
(808) 661-4811

Popular Aloha Friday spot with the local (and younger) crowd. On the water for prime sunset. Dinner served to 10:30, bar open to 2. Live music Friday and Saturday.

## KOBE
136 Dickenson St. in Lahaina, Maui
(808) 667-5555

Excellent liberation from audio overload here, allowing conversation and relaxation more than in most Lahaina bars.

## MOOSE MCGILLICUDDY'S
844 Front St. in Lahaina, Maui
(808) 667-7758

Live music Wednesday, Friday, and Saturday, $3 cover. Cheap margaritas and dacquiris all-day, but I, Snorkel Bob, seldom trust low-end blender drinks. The big dance floor, good barkeeps and waithelp with sex-object physiognomy makes this the kind of place I, Snorkel Bob, would choose for optimal odds on sexual relations, if not for the Dreaded Disease, and if I, Snorkel Bob, didn't long for monkish purity (Yes!).

## THE SLY MONGOOSE
1036 Limahana Pl. (behind Pizza Hut) in Lahaina, Maui
(808) 661-8097

*He garnered a following for a seek-and-destroy designed to drive the Legion bankrupt. By invading at happy hour when drinks were fifteen hundred each, the new patriots could score an upset bigger than the guns of Navarone. It was three thousand to the dollar then and an honest pour. The Legion's arsenal stockpiled in the back room was enough sauce to down a battalion of special forces who could stand up to a five-dollar buzz or a humdinger for a few bucks more. The Legionnaires understood soldiers of fortune in need like themselves on limited income. The doors were open.*

*Charles harrumphed to a head of steam, exhorting the oppressed to take a stand against conspiracy and exclusion, to face duty with honor, honor with duty—"Are we going to just sit here with our heads in the sand? Are we going to turn our backs on justice?"*

*He worked it up to a whistle and hooted down the bar—"Do you think David Niven gave two shits about a bunch of Nazis and steep cliffs and waves! Are you going to tell me it doesn't make a difference if the Nazis are blowing our boys to smithereens! Are you just gonna sit there?" Between his lines another lazy afternoon seeped with blessed silence. A few heads turned. The loud one had erupted a few hours ahead of schedule.*

*Some chuckled. Some dozed. Most dazed. Some shooed the invisible mosquito. "Wait! You men wait here!" Charles ran to the back and came out with a coat hanger. He hunched over it, untwisting and straightening then poking it through two corners of a dollar bill. He tore that off and replaced it with a hundred dollar bill. He raised the flag. "You can't fight without a war chest! I pledge the honor of this flag to duty! I pledge that together we will take back the Alamo! Now come on men! And women! Are you with me?" So the volunteer army enlisted after all. It was fun.*

*The Legionnaires weren't surprised, hadn't been surprised in twenty years. The battalion was down to survivors, a few regulars meeting for cocktails. The long march had led south of the border where a body needing a drink and a body pouring a drink comprised a community, an American contingent at large. The Legionnaires welcomed the invasion, joining the spirit of a campaign rife with honor and duty. Nobody believed the Legion could be bankrupted, not by a frontal assault on the bar.*

*The Legion was shored up and defended by a single Legionnaire with a gut like a globe. Cuddy Dingham was called Cuddy Atlas for bearing the weight of the world on his belly, or Dingy Cuddy when he drank too much, or Dingfuck the Cudball just because. Cuddy Atlas stood at attention, hands on the bar. "State your business, boys. And ladies."*

*Charles stuck the flag in an empty bottle. "Whiskey for my troops and quick about it." Cuddy Atlas asked if turncoats could join. The old vets moved in from the flank and victory was hailed; we have met the enemy and he is us and so on and so forth with drinks all around. The Legionnaires took a hundred-dollar commitment as gratitude and respect, an act of contrition if not patriotism. Cuddy Atlas poured freely from the heart. In an hour alliances were sealed, in two they slurred and by three they were mush: "Eezsh guys... ey... ffff..."*

*Not Charles. He stood on a chair. "We will fight on the land. We will fight on the sea. We will fight in the cantinas..."*

*That was long ago, when happy hour at the Legion was an event on its way to tradition, before relapse, before it came round again to a sullen group drinking cheap under a moth-eaten flag in faint recollection of the rocket's red glare. The real old guys remembered Iwo Jima, the medium old guys recalled LSD and Phnom Penh or Toronto. Charles called it historical, the differing factions drinking their way to peace.*

*"Charles is on leave of absence," came a voice from a foxhole as happy hour faded to dusk, as another night settled on the no man's land ahead.*

*"Leave from what?" someone asked.*

*"You don't need leave anymore!" a Legionnaire corrected.*

*"Maybe he's absent without leave," the first guy said. The Legionnaire grumbled; insubordination to a superior officer could land your ass in the stockade.*

*"Oh, boy," somebody else said, and Cuddy Atlas moved like a medic at the front.*

*Yours truly,*

*Homunculus*

It could have been the Mongoose, 2nd oldest drinkery in Lahaina (Pioneer Inn is 1st) serving canned beer @ 2.75 and well drinks @ 4 bits more. Big Deb runs a tight bar and plays mostly blues tapes and sometimes brings snacks from home. It's mostly veterans in the morning, open at 9, rolling by 11, mostly colonels and up but riff raff is tolerated. Rootbeer Schnapps from the freezer is $2 a crack and every now and then, impromptu, as it were, you can "Show your tits and get a FREE T-shirt." This is 1 of the more honest offers I, Snorkel Bob, observed in Lahaina, but when I, SB, hiked up my tutu I got nada but goose bumps. So what? What? 2nd hand smoke is a doozy here. But Professor Dave DeBow got a job at Snorkel Bob's Lahaina because his resume showed 2 years behind the bar at the Mongoose. Prof. Dave said he never, not once in his Mongoose phase, saw a fight inside. Cash only. A slice of the old flavor.

## LONGHI'S

888 Front St. in Lahaina, Maui
(808) 667-2288

Hip to make you sick, this place, unless you have a few drinks and relax for a change. Then it's only sleek, trendy and chic with not a hair out of place and only slightly nauseating.

## OLD LAHAINA CAFE

505 Front St. in Lahaina, Maui
(808) 661-3303

A legend in the luau biz—what local used to be, and still oughta. They even got guys from the local high school to paddle Hawaiian canoes up to the beach to start the luau, and if that ain't authentic, then what? On the water for optimal Lanai sunset.

## BUZZ'S WHARF
Maalaea Harbor in Maalaea, Maui
(808) 244-5426

The harbor is out of the hubbub with some okay boats to look at. Great views, decent bar. Mainly an eaterie; closes at 9.

## MAUI ONION
Renaissance Wailea
3550 Wailea Alanui Dr. in Wailea, Maui
(808) 879-4900

By the pool and an excellent spot for beer and (famous) onion rings.

## THE CHART HOUSE BAR
100 Wailea Iki Dr. in Wailea, Maui
(808) 879-2875

Across the street from the Wailea Shopping Village. The fountain patio and ocean view are fresh and receptive to sighful reflection over a stiff drink.

## INU INU LOUNGE
Aston Wailea Resort
3700 Wailea Alanui Dr. in Wailea, Maui
(808) 879-1922

Live music and dancing Thursday, Friday, Saturday, attract a younger crowd. $5 cover. Sexual potential is raw and energetic here, what with the physically-fit boys and girls on vacation and mostly undiddled this week. Over 21, the kids.

## TSUNAMI LOUNGE & DISCO
Grand Wailea Resort Hotel & Spa
3850 Wailea Alanui Dr. in Wailea, Maui
(808) 825-1234

Discotheque and hip hop, lasers, fog machines, big video screens make this place as attractive to me, Snorkel Bob, as Penn Station at rush hour. But some people love love love this level of bells and whistles, this brand of anarchy. 70's and 80's music to 1:30 on Friday. Top 40 on Saturday to 4 (four) a.m. All this and pricey drinks make Tsunami anomaly for me, Snorkel Bob. And oh, arrival must be practically premature if it's a table you'd like.

## PRINCE COURT
Maui Prince Resort
5400 Makena Alanui Dr. in Makena, Maui
(808) 874-1111

Expensive drinks make more sense at a place like this, where high prices help keep the riff raff to a minimum. Pupus here are ☆☆☆☆. Sunday brunch @ 32 clams with unlimited bubbly was voted best on Maui, but I, Snorkel Bob, abstained, because 32 clams is too much to pay for anybody's eggs, and anyone who drinks too much bubbly will sure enough be stuck on the throne with regrets when she could be snorkeling and (who knows?) perhaps finding the goddess within. Hey, you want to stuff your gob with 2 hands, have at it, but don't say I, Snorkel Bob, did not advise the lean and clean.

## CASANOVA ITALIAN RESTAURANT & DELI
1188 Makawao Ave. in Makawao, Maui
(808) 572-0220

Sometimes well-known bands play rock, reggae, country-western, and eclectic here. Music from 9:45-1 with a $5 cover, unless you're a diner; then it's free.

## SHARK TOOTH BREWERY STEAK HOUSE
Kaahumanu Shopping Center in Kahului, Maui
(808) 871-6689

A pleasant enough idle, this 1, with a single amusing flavor, the Whale's Tale Ale, but hardly worth time in a MALL, of all places in PPParadise.

# OAHU

Most outer-island bars, music and dance spots have a small town flavor, i.e., honkytonk, or fancy honkytonk with colored lights, or extra-fancy discotheque honkytonk. Honolulu has some too, but with a much stronger pulse than the outer islands. What you want, you can get. These places are a mere smattering; even I, Snorkel Bob, would not attempt deep penetration.

Some places are dumb, like waitpeople dressed as cheerleaders. What's the point, if not to encourage misguided fantasy, traveling-salesman mentality? And why should anybody be subjugated to that kind of packaging? I, Snorkel Bob, for 1, have an easier time engaging a woman at a nude beach rather than 1 who's dolled up like a cheerleader so she can earn a living. Oh sure, they dress the guys up too, but that's gratuitous, equal-time rah rah, sisboombah. Give me a break—and some low light and dark jazz while you're at it.

Decent music is here in Honolulu too, in bars with big city views and uptown anonymity where you can be invisible, be somebody else, or become who you really are, at last; where you can sample a wider range of aesthetic than many other places in Hawaii.

## SHIPLEY'S ALE HOUSE
Manoa, Oahu
(808) 988-5555

Many favorite beers in bottles here include Oatmeal Porter, Rogue 'n Berry, Espresso Stout, Honey Cream Ale and many more, which may be no big deal if you're from Seattle, but equals Ponce de Leon's discovery of the Fountain of Youth if you're not. **FUTHAMO**, on tap: Nut Brown Ale, Wild Irish Rogue and Pyramid Hefeweizen. Yet an ambitious menu does not a successful tap make, because these delicate beauties can so easily be left on a dock in the blazing sun for hours and hours hence wrecking the flavor, as if somebody didn't care. So I, Snorkel Bob, conducted the freshness/flavor test. And the winner, in Manoa, is Shipley's. They and I, SB, do care.

Downside is the price, $4.25 for a draft, accompanied by the claim, "Handcrafted," as if we were all 3rd worlders who believe what we're told. But hey, they got you this far and you must be thirsty. And it's A-1 Hawaiian music here Sunday nights, the real kind most suitable for notation in a Reality Guide. Other nights it's standard pop and ballad groups.

Okay, from my, Snorkel Bob's, place on Kapahulu, take Date to University (the 3rd light). Go right on University past the U of Hawaii. University becomes Oahu Avenue (at the 7th light, I, SB, think). Go right onto East Manoa. Go through 1 light and into the Safeway Parking Lot. Look up and side to side. Hone in. Go.

## THE MAI TAI BAR
Royal Hawaiian Hotel
2259 Kalakaua Ave. in Honolulu, Oahu
(808) 931-7194

Monday is luau night; Thursday, Friday and Saturday are live music nights with no cover to 12:30. What kind of live music is what I, Snorkel Bob, don't know, because whodaguy on da phone say, Oh, you know, da kine. I, Snorkel Bob, suspect he no speaka too gooda de English, like maybe he 1 lawdy lawdy cumma summa matriculator from da kine, you know, public school.

## MAHARAJA HAWAII
2255 Kuhio Ave. in Honolulu, Oahu
(808) 922-3030

Maharaja, in the Waikiki Trade Center on Kuhio & Seaside is a modern uptown swinging discotheque with a bar and restaurant. (Modern discotheque?) Pervasive boom shackalacka with obtrusive lighting and rampant eye contact with a Top 40 score make this place unattainable for me, Snorkel Bob. Oh, these kids today. What will they think to bring back next? An extreme dress code here—no sneakers, T-shirts, shorts or slippers—suggests the management would like to have good taste. Open to 4 with a $5 cover. Free to 11 on Wednesday, and only $1 after 11.

## NICHOLAS NICKOLAS
410 Atkinson Dr. in Honolulu, Oahu
(808) 955-4466

NN is generic top drawer with a VistaVision view of the city and easy elbow rubbing with upwardly mobile uptowners. Or at least you get checked out to see if you're anybody who is anybody or if you might share a sexual need. Top 40 here too (what is it with these people?). Open to 3 weekdays. Friday and Saturday, dance to 4, then go home.

## ANNA BANNANAS
2440 S. Beretania St. in Honolulu, Oahu
(808) 946-5190
11 a.m.-2 a.m. Daily

Funky but groovy, a mixed platter of darts, avant junk and rock out like no tomorrow. Live music Tuesday through Sunday with bands like World Reggae Night, Surf, Cycle, Sex, and, as always, much much more. I, Snorkel Bob, commend this place, because a beer is your basic price hydrometer, and $2.25 is more real than $3.50, which is somewhere between a nick and a gouge.

## WAVE WAIKIKI
1877 Kalakaua Ave. in Honolulu, Oahu
(808) 941-0424

This place can pop your brain quicker than hot grease can spring the little yellow kernel. Loud Mufah Rock Wednesday through Sunday with the Wave's own hothouse band, 9-4. Tuesday it's another local band from 8-4, and Monday is DJ night. This place can cure the drowzies, and crowd wank varies directly with the hour. No conversation allowed. Introductions must be yelled. $5 cover starts at 10. No dress code.

## RUMOURS
Ala Moana Hotel
410 Atkinson Dr. in Honolulu, Oahu
(808) 955-4811

Rumors is your average '70's discotheque every night except Thursday and Friday, when it's "Big Chill Night." I, Snorkel Bob, think that's terribly original, since they could have called it something dumb like "Old Timer's Night."

It's for those who lost that lovin' feeling in 1972 and got jobs with insurance companies, banks, mutual fund managers, leverage consolidators, acquisition holding groups, affiliated amalgamated trusts and/or annuities, debenturated high rise guaranty brokerages—you know, the guys who begin with, "What we do is, we..." They hit Rumors on Thursday and/or Friday nights and hark back as the needle hits the groove, Oh God, was life great then. I, Snorkel Bob, can't wait to go back and listen to Heard it Through the Grapevine 1 Mo Time!

Pupu buffet is Thursday night, 5-8 with a $3 cover.

SPECIAL NOTE: At this juncture of Reality Guide's of the past, I, Snorkel Bob, was pleased to list those places in the jazz groove. Alas and alack, the world is changing southward. Only 1 of 3 places remains and it has the dreaded Top 40. Arrrrghh!!

## ESPRIT LOUNGE
Sheraton Waikiki Hotel
2255 Kalakaua Ave. in Honolulu, Oahu
(808) 922-4422

Live music Tuesday through Saturday NOW features "Sold Out" (Top 40), and occasionally the Hawaiian band Kapena. 8:30-12:30 weekdays, to 1:30 weekends. No cover.

# COMEDY

Okay, how do I, Snorkel Bob, save a stiff from drowning?
I, Snorkel Bob, take my foot off his, the stiff's, head.

HA!

Hey, what's green and hops from bed to bed?
A prostitoad.

HA!

Okay, so this (*) carpenter goes to a lumber yard and tells the lumber yard guy, "Hey, I need a load of 2 x 4s."
The lumber yard guy says, "Okay, how long do you want them?"
And the (*) carpenter says, "Oh, for a long time. I'm building a house."

HA!

1) Hey how many people from (*) does it take to eat a mongoose?
2) How can you tell if someone from (*) has been working at your computer?
3) Hey what do you call a guy from (*) with a knife?
4) What do you call the same guy in a brand new Lincoln Continental Mark XVI?
5) How many Denver Broncos does it takes to fix a flat?

(*) Fill in your favorite ethnic target here. Some popular choices are Poland, Portugal, Israel, Africa, Albania, Mexico, Southern California, Iran, Texas and of course, Canada.

ANSWERS:

1) It takes 2—1 to eat and 1 to watch for traffic.
2) You can tell by the white-out all over your monitor.
3) Sir.
4) A thief.
5) Only 1, unless it's a blowout. Then it takes the whole team.

HA!

Okay, okay—so this guy goes into the confessional and tells the priest, "Father, I'm 75 years old. I'm a civic leader, a pillar of the community. 40 years I'm in business. Thousands of dollars I give to charitable causes. 50 years I'm married to the same woman, always faithful, until last weekend, when I met these 2 gorgeous women, 25-year-olds. So we go to this hotel and it's 2 days and 2 nights, non-stop you name it, the works, over and under, head to toe, 2 on 1, 1 on 2, around the clock and around the world, upside down and inside out, every nook and cranny to the point of total saturation.

"Hmm," the priest says. " I think I see. For your penance you must..."

"But Father, I can't do penance. I'm Jewish."

"Well, what are you telling me for?"

"Father, I'm telling everyone!"

HA!

Okay, so this guy goes to the dermatologist with a nasty rash all over his body. So the dermatologist gives him some miracle ointment and sends him home. 2 weeks later the guy comes back with the same problem. So the doctor says, "Tell me something. What do you do for a living?"

"Well, doctor," the guy says, "I work for a circus. I give enemas to the elephants before they perform so they won't make a mess in the arena."

So the doctor says, "I'm going to tell you 2 things to do, and if you follow my advice, you'll never have this rash again. The 1st is that you must continue to use this cream. The 2nd is that you should find a new job."

"What?" the guy gasps. "And give up show biz?"

HA!

Hey what do a walrus and I, Snorkel Bob, have in common?
We both like a tight seal.

HA!

Okay why did the punk cross the road?
Because he had a chicken stapled to his chest.

HA!

Here's where to go for more swell comedy:

## THE COMEDY COW
1777 Ala Moana Blvd. (Ilikai Hotel)
Honolulu, Oahu
(808) 926-2269

1) Hey did you hear about the new TV sitcom about gays?
2) What's the difference between a dead skunk and a dead lawyer lying on the side of the road?
3) Why will a shark never attack a lawyer?
4) Hey what has 2 eyes but can't see, 2 legs but can't walk, 2 wings but can't fly?

Answers:
1) Leave it. It's Beaver.
2) There's skid marks in front of the skunk.
3) Professional courtesy.
4) A dead bird.

HA!

Okay, so this building gets built and it's all brand new and this guy who really likes new buildings goes to see it, and this other guy just inside the door says he's the architect and this is the 1st suicide-proof building in New York.

So the 1st guy says, Go on, you're pulling my leg. And the architect says, No, no kidding. Come on. I'll show you. It's got special windows.

So they ride up to the 12th floor and the architect says, Watch this. And he jumps out the window and whoosh, he's sucked right back up and inside.

Unbelievable, the 1st guy says. The architect says, okay, you don't believe it? Watch this. And they ride up to the 27th floor and the architect jumps out the window and whoosh, he gets sucked right back up and inside.

So the 1st guy who really likes buildings says, Gee whiz, Can I try? Sure! the architect says, and the guy jumps out the window and whoooooooooosh ... SPLATTT!

The architect kind of sluffs it off and straightens his tie and rides on up to the penthouse and takes a seat at the bar, and the bartender says, "Boy, Superman, you sure are an asshole when you're drunk."

HA!

Okay, this farmer is driving down the road in his truck and he comes to a state cop in the middle of the road with the blue light flashing, and the farmer asks, What's the problem, Officer?

The cop looks worried and nods at this pig sitting in the middle of the road—big damn pig—and the cop says, We got a problem with this pig in the road. So the farmer says, Hmmm. And the cop says, Hey, I got a idea. Why don't we load this pig into your truck and then you take him to the zoo? And the farmer says, Well, I reckon we could do that. So they load the pig into the truck and off the farmer drives and that's that.

So the next day the cop is out there again because that's his usual speed trap, and who drives by? The farmer—and sitting next to him in the cab is the pig. And the pig's wearing a baseball hat! They cruise on by.

So the cop fires up the flashers and the siren and tears out and catches up and pulls the farmer over and walks up to the truck. The farmer says, Yessir.

The cop says, Hey, I told you to take that pig to the zoo!

And the farmer says, I did! We had a good time too, so today I thought we'd go to the ball game.

HA! HA! HA!

# ART

(Whaddah we widdout aht?)

I, Snorkel Bob, hope that by now you have arrived at the heart of your Reality Guide and have arrived as well at an understanding of what in the tropics is real—and what ain't.

Damn near 99.44 percent of the heavily-marketed, highly-advertised "art" ain't. In a word, it's trash, especially if it shows the sky above the water and the little fishes below the water, along with smiling whales, thoughtful turtles, galloping sea horses and dolphins rollicking playfully among the planets.

Planets? Like I, Snorkel Bob, said: Trash.

Or if it was painted by a movie star, look out. And if you are among the fools who paid what? 2, 3 grand (Yes!) for a comic-book illustration of some meaningful looking fish or clowns or other hokum, then my, Snorkel Bob's, advice is to gift wrap it and send it to someone you don't like and chalk it up as a very expensive practical joke.

Vacation art is what the industry is called locally, and it's a scam, in the aesthetic sense.

I, Snorkel Bob, don't want to kick a dead horse, but sometimes it must be kicked, the horse. Some of these guys—mostly the ones with 3 names—are getting hundreds of thousands of dollars for this pap. They got warehouses and factories and corporate headquarters and good for them, but this stuff ain't no more art than the white powder you get at the airport for your coffee is cow juice. I mean really.

It's like John Madden said when the '90 World Champion San Francisco 49ers (Joe Montana, Jerry Rice, Ronnie Lott, Bret Jones) disassembled the LA Rams in the conference playoffs—"You got a lot of stuff here. You got some mud and some rain. You got wind. You got cold air and hot tempers. You got bruises and sprains. You got blood and bones. And it's not just stuff. This is all good stuff. This is football."

Okay. You get it? You want art? You need some rain and wind and maybe some cold air like you'd get in a garret. Throw in some sawdust and spartan furniture—no clutter, no fluff, only the beholder, and the color and line applied by the artist, free and clear of the set director and the promo man. This is art.

On the other hand, you are close to some rare talent here in Hawaii, but you must use the Bible system to get up next to it, i.e., seek and ye shall find.

# MAUI

### GALLERY MAUI
1156 Makawao Ave. in Makawao, Maui
(808) 572-8092
10-7 Mon thru Sat, 11-3 Sun

A rare find, this, in the spirit of less is more. No art scammers here, those comix painters hailing themselves as beloved or ingenious. This 1, owned by the Zaleskis, Deborah and Robert, covers multi-media better than any triple-matted, over-lit, price-gouging hotel gallery in Paradise. Raku, Koa bowls, mango tables and exotic chairs are here. Oil paintings include still-life and landscape by Robert Zaleski. Paper wall sculpture, photography and so on, presented in a well-lit, unencumbered cleanliness with no heavy close. An excellent gallery.

**VIEWPOINTS GALLERY**
Makawao, Maui
(808) 572-5979
10-6 Mon thru Sat, 11-5 Sun

Viewpoints is a co-op of Maui artists who run the gallery. Talent and imagination are common here, like bronze sculpture by Ilene Kratka and airbrush art by Peter & Maddy Powell.

**HUI NOEAU VISUAL ARTS CENTER**
2841 Baldwin Ave. in Makawao, Maui
(808) 572-6560
10-4 Mon thru Sat

Local artists show here with regular changes. Some of it's bad, most of it's good. Nearly all is honest effort, unlike the heavily promoted manufactured illustrations you will see advertised ad nauseam on TV. ("Whales are my life."—Bah!)

**THE MAUI CRAFTS GUILD**
Hwy 36 (Hana Hwy.) in Paia, Maui
(808) 579-9697
9-6 Daily

This little co-op on the main drag into town also shows some extremely talented, unhyped local artists.

# OAHU

**ROBYN BUNTIN GALLERIES**
848 S.Beretania in Honolulu, Oahu
(808) 523-5913
9-5 Mon thru Sat

This isn't the only decent commercial gallery in Honolulu but is the only decent 1 found by me, Snorkel Bob. RB shows Ho Hung Wong and Guy Buffet (who live here) and the Tollman Collection of modern Japanese lithographs and woodblock prints. The gallery focuses on Oriental art and antiques and Hawaiian art with other prints and oils also available.

# MASSAGE

It's a tricky business these days, hands on bodies. I, Snorkel Bob, perfectly understand all you traveling salesmen who might want outcall love, or at least outcall friction. But this ain't it. Look in the Yellow Pages under "O" for ooh-la-la, or maybe under "P" or "F" or "BJ" for that stuff.

This stuff is the real thing, what vacation and snorkeling are all about; relaxation, healing, tuning in to what ails you and letting it go away. The massage therapists listed here are among the most talented in Hawaii. Each has passed the knots/aches/injury test as judged by me, Snorkel Bob.

And though I, Snorkel Bob, draw a line in the sand on advising anyone on any behavior other than snorkeling, a massage on arrival is the exception. It will change your mind, then your body, and then you can honestly feel that you are here.

If you are sensitive to massage technique, you should experience lomi lomi. Lomi lomi means massage, although the word is mostly used in Hawaiian cooking—lomi lomi salmon or any kind of fish that's been tenderized by hand.

Lomi lomi massage relies on the technician's feel for what's going on through surface rub, joint adjustment and easing the knots out. The lomi lomists regard the knots as fluid build-up; deep pressure dissipates the fluids through the lymph network.

Foo-foo maybe, except for 1 iotum: It works.

# KAUAI

### MANA MASSAGE
Kauai Athletic Club in Lihue, Kauai
(808) 822-4746

Being part of an athletic club means it has steam, sauna and spa too. Leslee (Manima) Dancosse and Laurel Pettersen practice Hawaiian lomi lomi (deep strokes with elbows and forearms), trigger point release, energy balancing and unblocking, deep tissue therapy for injury, chronic pain and old patterns, myo-fascial relief (not facial but fascial—releases the tissue around the muscle), and craniosacral therapy. Aromatherapy uses essential oils to relax and rejuvenate. I, Snorkel Bob, got so relaxed under the golden touch of Ms. Leslie (Manima), she could have asked for anything. Man oh Manima.

Experience spans decades and includes training in Hawaiian lomi lomi with Auntie Margaret on the Big Island. Rates begin at $60/hour,

Monday through Friday. Reserve at least 1/2 day ahead. Outcall is a definite maybe, depending on where and when. Unequivocal merit on this 1.

# BIG ISLAND

**KONA RUB-A-DUB**
75-5894 Alii Dr. in Kailua, Hawaii
(808) 329-1002
9-7 Mon thru Sat

Hawaiian Lomi Lomi, Shiatsu, Swedish and sport massage in a screened room on the beach with sand, palms and surf can be pleasing. Right on the main road but easy to miss because the sign is tiny. 1/2 hour is $25, 1 hour is $40, 1-1/2 hours is $55.

**EAST-WEST CLINIC**
16-590 B Old Volcano Rd. in Keaau, Hawaii (Hilo)
(808) 966-7441
8-4:30 everyday but Sat, closed 12-2 Daily for Lunch

Several techniques under 1 roof here with an emphasis on Chinese medicine, herbs and acupuncture. Chiropractic facilities on site. 1/2 hour massage is $20, 1 hour is $37.

# MAUI

**CAROL KATO**
Wailuku, Maui
(808) 244-8238

Carol Kato can come to you if you call ahead—but why would she come if you didn't call, unless she's psychic, which she is, combining psychic healing and energy work with lomi lomi in what she calls release massage. Cranial-sacral, zero balancing, orthobionomy and neuro-muscular therapy round out the menu. "Soul to spirit integrative body work is what I do. I 'listen' on different levels—physical, emotional, psychic, and energetic, then help contact and release what is being held onto. If you want 'grind 'em out' massage don't come to me. I go deep with energy, not physical strength. Nothing I do hurts. Hurt compounds trauma. I want to help you release trauma, not add to it. I usually take 1-1/2 to 2 hours." $60/hr.

**JEANNE SIELEN**
Keokea, Maui
(808) 877-9380

Jeanne Sielen specializes in Jin Shin Do (acupressure), orthobionomy (release), and Hawaiian lomi lomi. She mixes her own massage oils from roots she grows. Jeanne Sielen has eased the ripples on my, Snorkel Bob's, pond more than once and is eminently qualified to do so once again. $60/hr.

**LAHAINA ACUPUNCTURE & MASSAGE CENTER**
180 Dickenson St. Suite 205 in Lahaina, Maui
(808) 667-6260
8-5 weekdays, 8-12 Sat

Swedish, shiatsu, reflexology, acupressure, acupuncture and chiropractic under 1 roof. No take out—you go to them. Prices range $30-80. This outfit comes to me, Snorkel Bob, with high recommendations from Un Im Peachable sources (to the best of my knowledge, at this point in time.) And I'm not kidding!

# OAHU

SPECIAL NOTE ON OAHU: I, Snorkel Bob, checked it out for research purposes—any kink, perversity, strange taste, off-taste, bad taste that tickles your fancy or whips it till it bleeds or maybe drip by drip trickles water on it, or shishi, or maybe lays big old logjam turds on it from above a glass-top coffee table maybe—any of that disgusting stuff (and of course much much more) is in the OAHU YELLOW PAGES, delivered even, for a few scones more. But like I, Snorkel Bob, say, this elaboration ain't on that topic. I, SB, only spew because Oahu may be the hardest spot on Planet E to find a legit massage—some relief where the therapy doesn't hone to the bone with some da kine lomi lomi. I mean really. But the real thing, as in healing, relaxation, tuning in and letting go, does exist on Oahu. Doesn't it?

# SNAKE OIL, ELIXIRS, POTIONS, HERBS, ROOTS and PILLS

And if you're 1 of those foo foo magic powder, secret potion, snake oil, hoo-doo herb, Chinese medicine kind of people who think you're a long way from anybody who understands your particular idiosyncrasy (idiosynchronicity?) then I, Snorkel Bob, got news for you: You ain't.

# KAUAI

### HANALEI HEALTH AND NATURAL FOODS, INC.
Ching Young Village in Hanalei, Kauai
(808) 826-6990
9-7 Daily

This place is natural as it gets, or as my friend, Matt Roving, said years ago when he was on his health and nature kick—If they don't have it at Hanalei Health Foods, I don't need it. They got your full range of samiches and gooeys including guacamole, salsa, pesto, tahini, Alfredo, humus, au gratin, basmati and tabouli (gooey with lumps.)

They got your elixirs, grains and brans in all grit sizes, your vitamins, minerals and trace elements, decoctions, pastes, muds, puddings, gruels and potions striving for the all elusive...

## *IMMORTALITY!*

### AMBROSE'S KAPUNA NATURAL FOODS
Kuhio Hwy in Kapaa, Kauai
(808) 822-7112
Open to 6 everyday except Sun

Ambrose is on Kuhio Highway across from Waipouli Shopping Center with your full range of stuff, and it's 2 doors down from my, Snorkel Bob's, new snorkeldome! If closed is how it looks, look for Ambrose in the backyard, and he'll let you in.

# BIG ISLAND

### OHANA O KA AINA COOP
Hwy 11 in Kainaliu, Hawaii
(808) 322-2425
8-7:30 weekdays, 8:30-6 Sat & Sun

Kainaliu is next to Kealakekua in coffee country, and the co-op is tops on snake oil with the full line of tofus, sprouts and other meretricious edibles for those who know what to eat, what not to eat. Fresh sandwiches here too.

## PAHOA NATURAL GROCERIES
Rte 130 in Pahoa, Hawaii
(808) 965-8322
8-8 Mon thru Sat, 8-6 Sun

1-stop shopping for all your grain and gruel needs when sojourning in Puna. About 30 varieties of grain available here.

# MAUI

## THE DRAGON'S DEN
3681 Baldwin Ave. in Makawao, Maui
(808) 572-2424
9:30-5:30 Mon thru Sat, 11-4 Sun

A most excellent selection here of vitamins, minerals, Chinese elixirs and healing agents, early folk remedies, raw, bulk teas, health books AND herbologists who know their stuff like nobody's bidness make this a must visit for me, Snorkel Bob, for every ache, pain, trauma, rash or kink in the aging process.

## NATURE'S NECTAR
Baldwin Ave. in Makawao, Maui
(808) 572-9122

Although it's often patronized by people who don't bathe, this vitamin-remedy store is on my, Snorkel Bob's, list of favorites for complete inventory of health care products and awful tasting juices that must be good for you. Assorted trinkets for the New Age and home-brewing supplies round out the inventory, and if you ever considered a march to a different drummer, this could be your first step; N's N sells strange little drums too that will surely set you apart.

HAWAIIAN MOONS NATURAL FOODS
2411 S. Kihei Rd. (Next to the Sports Page bar) in Kihei, Maui
(808) 875-4356

Great selection, good produce, grains, oils, lotions, A SMOOTHIE BAR and groceries to sustain life make this a soothing oasis in the vast and epic honkytonk of Kihei.

# OAHU

DOWN TO EARTH NATURAL FOODS
2525 South King St. in Honolulu, Oahu
(808) 947-7678
8-10 Daily

This is Hawaii's largest natural food store and covers a whole city block with a crystal gallery, a beauty boutique and books and toys about clean thinking and clean playing around. They got juicers big enough to juice a pig's head and a deli buffet with fake (tofu) egg salad, tuna, beef stew, BBQ ribs, whole slab or half slab, pork snoot, New York strip, filet mignon, caviar canapes, Alaskan king crab claws, roast suckling pig, laaaamb chops, ham samiches, pork rinds, blood pudding, pig brains, chitterlings, tripe, crayfish gumbo, gator tail, skewered leg of Bambi, fried guinea under glass...Stop!

Amazing stuff, that tofu, but it has its limits. Nevermind, no boring saltines here—it's Ak Mak!—right at the salad bar. They got rice cream with no dairy, 240 bulk herbs including but not limited to organic marshmallow powder, ginger root powder, cut licorice root and gotu kola, cut or powder.

They got juices, pastes, seeds, beans, mixes, flours, grains, nuts—Nuts! Salted pistachios already shelled! Who cares how much they cost? Or if some Iranian had to chew on them 1 time? This is fantasy come true!

Fresh fruit and produce, 200 different chips, 19 different sprouts and colon cleanser—On Special!

Breads, sauces, foul mudammas, toasted sushi nori & seaweed, 28 kinds. Phytoresinoids! And if you need a lift, they got the cocaine of the Cosmos: Ginseng! American, Chinese White, Shiu Chiu, Tang Quai and Hsus Kirin.

It's like my friend, Matt Roving, said years ago at the end of his health and nature kick—I think I got to get out of here.

They got your full range of gooeys too, with and without lumps.

145

Throw in your elixirs and brans in all grit, your vitamins, minerals and essential trace elements, decoctions, pastes, muds, puddings, gruels and potions, and you, my friends, are yet 1 mo giant step closer to the all elusive:

## *IMMORTALITY!*

I, Snorkel Bob, feel in my heart, that it won't be long now.

# TATTOO WHO?

I, Snorkel Bob, ain't saying I likem. And I, Snorkel Bob, ain't saying I don't likem. All's I'm saying is that the land shark wouldn't have moved on the fat stiff if the fat stiff had a few good tattoos. Note the operational adjective here: good. Plenty fat stiffs with red and green blobs on their arms get gobbled by land sharks. I mean a tattoo that would make the guy look like a shopper, a chooser, a connoisseur of skin illustrations.[*]

All's I'm saying is, if you do it, do it right. Stoned drunk is the traditional mind set for a tattoo. The decision-making process, however, should occur in clear light—these comix are for keeps. I, Snorkel Bob, know a woman who got some butterflies arching her pubis and a year later got tired of insects on her crotch. And my longtime snorkel buddy Matt Roving spent 3 grand on surgical removal of a peace symbol on his ankle he got in '69, right after burning his draft card and vowing Hell no, we won't go. The surgery came in '94, after he'd changed his mind about the Commie bastards. 3 grand for 1 little drunk. Sheesh.

**DRAGON TATTOO**
10 Kam Hwy in Wahiawa, Oahu
(808) 622-5924
2-9 Daily
No appointment necessary, 1st come.

Lance McLain, sole proprietor, swears "Me mither is Oirish." I, Snorkel Bob, expressed sincere wishes that she is also well. Lance is a 20-year man with a tattoo parlor in the boonies. He's clean cut and has no plans to grow a beard or change his name to Bear or Gypsy. He regrets the end of romance, when real rebels and misfits wanted a badge or flag to proclaim their beliefs. Now MTV musicians have so many tattoos, it's become trendy and trivial. Lance's message is clear: Beaver Cleaver kids

[*]cf. Rod Steiger, *The Illustrated Man*

and tattoo groupies, this is not the place for you. Lance likes people with unique ideas and a mission.

What tattoos are his favorites? Radical images with impact, like "Wolves with slobber dripping from their mouths, and big black panthers with bloody scratch marks trailing off the claws". His very most favorite tattoo? The writhing woman in trashy lingerie with a dragon wrapped around her—1 that's holding a dagger dripping blood. Then we had tea and crumpets and watched a Doris Day movie.

## CHINA SEA TATTOO
1033 Smith St. in Honolulu, Oahu
(808) 533-1603
9-9 Mon-Sat, or by appointment on Sun

China Sea is Hawaii's oldest shop. Tattooing was as fundamental to Samoa, Polynesia, Tahiti and Hawaii as poi, taro and outrigger canoes. Tattooed faces scared enemies; tattoos were an art form. China Sea is from that tradition.

Mike "Rollo" Malone bemoans modern tattooists attempting detail with a single needle, like a castle with a winding road. Because a tattoo that loses its detail is only a blemish, and single-needle tattoos lose their detail. Mike is old school. He has tattooed soldiers and celebrities, drunk and sober. He is the shop of choice for Yakuza, both initiates and cover-ups.

He says only Texas in the Other States of America has a strong tattoo tradition. They want lone stars, armadillos and cowboy hats mostly—identity stuff. And though Texans talk funny, walk strange and wear those hats, it's a Texan responsible for Malone's most challenging tattoo, possibly his bid for masterpiece. Across the shoulders and down the back, spanning the butt, wrapping the hind thighs and festooned to the knees: Japanese movie monsters in technicolor and micro-detail. Mothra swoops under a shoulder blade. The Spider spins across the lumbars. Rodan demolishes buildings cheek to cheek, and crashing through giant killer surf, undaunted, Godzilla!

This fresco required many visits. Mike Malone says he's never sold an identity tattoo for Illinois or New Jersey.

# 4
# Bill of Fare

# EATERIES

*"We had a miserable freaking lunch, Snorkel Bob. Dinner was only $190, and we didn't gag all that much, but we need to know, Snorkel Bob, is this as good as it gets?"*

Well, my children, the answer is yes and no and yes. I, Snorkel Bob, have known fine restaurants. Fine restaurants are a friend of mine, Snorkel Bob's. These are not fine restaurants. Hey! It's a joke! Yet how quickly the hash slingers lose their sense of humor when it's their skills in question. The crux of the matter is perception. Those on the supply side perceive tourists as eminently forgettable, a 7-day turnover, leaving soon; next. This perception has undermined another perception, the 1 that sees the importance of repeat business.

Now we see in all of Hawaii the phenomenon of the commercial kitchen as show business. I, Snorkel Bob, understand the drama intrinsic to a good kitchen and the gravitational pull of any kitchen, but most expensive restaurants in Hawaii (yes, it's redundant) are happy to charge you $50 per and expect your gratitude for the view, the linen, the gratuitous pampering, the warm air, the beaches, palm trees, reefs, amazing little fishes—wait a minute.

Ever since a few guys gained 400 pounds (each) and scored a little airtime and couldn't even stand up while stirring the saute, not a single cook remains in Hawaii. They're all chefs now. The superstars are executive chefs at 1 resort or another. The buzz cuisine is called Pacific Rim, whatever that means. It reminds me, Snorkel Bob, of a tranquilizing toilet cleaner. I, Snorkel Bob, have circled the Pacific Rim. What we think of as house pets or common nuisances are primary bill of fare on the obtuse majority of the rim's circumference, and it's hardly ever served on a 14" plate with pureed garnish that looks applied by Pablo Picasso. I, Snorkel Bob, can sauté some fresh fish with ginger and garlic, bake a spud and steam some broccoli for about $5 in America or $10 in Hawaii. Or I can order up for about $50 if I want it overcooked in cheap oil, signed, numbered, matted and framed and served by an ever-so-concerned waitperson asking every 3 minutes if everything is okay.

NO! This is not okay. This is a no-brainer, a primary reason why tourism is down in Hawaii and up in Mexico, the Caribbean, Southeast Asia and on around the Pacific Rim. And the floppy-jowled fellow on TV who looks about a 1/2 feed away from coronary thrombosis and won't show you the gut over his belt or the gut under his belt says, "I had the laaamb." But please, don't get me, Snorkel Bob, started.

The question persists: Where is best to eat? And I, Snorkel Bob, understand: You kids just want to have fun. These are places of note, not necessarily a good note or a bad note, but a note that rings true, a note transcendent, a note received in sensory input by me, Snorkel Bob. You will note that most places listed here are either A) off the tourist track or B) the only choice for miles. Some notable places are:

# KAUAI

(Price range for entrees: $ under 10; $$ 10-15; $$$ 15-20; $$$$ 20 and up).

### BRENNECKE'S BEACH BROILER—$$$
Hoone Rd. in Poipu, Kauai
(808) 742-7588

Brennecke's is popular because it's across from Poipu Beach Park, a most excellent snorkel beach, giving rise to the question: Why did the snorkeler cross the road?

Casual with a view here. Happy hour all day long. Lunch 11:30-4, dinner 4-10.

### KEOKI'S PARADISE—$$$$
Poipu Shopping Village in Poipu, Kauai
(808) 742-7534

Keoki's is in the shopping center across Poipu Road from the Kiahuna Plantation Resort in Poipu. It's owned by TS Restaurants, the same outfit that owns Duke's and Sharky's, with simulated Hawaii inside (foliage, a pond, nature) so you can forget that it's 2084 and Shop-O-Rama outside. The cocktail bar is open 4:30-midnight, and so is the seafood/taco bar. Dinner is served 5:30-10 daily with entrees at $12-20, shrimp and lobster at $24, steak and lobster at $26, steak, lobster and personal counseling at $26.05. I, Snorkel Bob, was thoroughly tolerated by the waitpersons, and the local fish was delecto inflagranté, (Latin: muh, good). Children's menu too.

### POIPU BAR and GRILL—$$$
Hyatt golf course and pro shop complex, Poipu, Kauai
(808) 742-8888

A great setting if you like an overview of a golf course and distant mountains. Very good breakfast with high marks (I, SB, am told) on the pig meat in assorted preparations. Also a splendid sandwich buffet and lunch menu. This course hosts the PGA Grand Slam of Golf. It's actually the Mastercard Grand Slam of Golf, but I, Snorkel Bob, feel as queasy about that as the Grand Slammers might feel about calling it the Snorkel Bob Grand Slam of Golf. Hey. It's a game.

And what a game it was back in '96, when PGA Champion Mark Brooks hit 74 & 73 for a 147, Masters Champ Nick Faldo hit 67 & 72 for a 139, U.S. Open Champ Steve Jones hit 70 & 66 for a 136, and British Open Champ Tom Lehman shot 68 & 66 to take the whole shebang with a 134!

Or back in '95, when Elkington, Pavin & Daly hit 141, 141 & 148 only to lose in squeaker to Ben Crenshaw's 140!

The score cards are enlarged and mounted on the walls and go back to '94, but I, Snorkel Bob, was already red-lined.

### PIATTI'S—$$$$
Kiahuna Plantation Resort in Poipu, Kauai
(808) 742-2216

Hey, let's face it: if you have to grind on umpteen zillion restaurants in a place numb to the idea of repeat bidness, then you have to get semi-toasted every now and then just to get it up to go 1 mo time. Call it the luck o' the draw, but Piatti's was the place. It was Friday at the end of a real nutbuster, so I, SB, and a few closest friends hit Piatti's for din. So? We got all pickled up and easy to please. So? It's a great place, I think, especially on the terrace outside, near the stars and up next to a frosty Fire Rock Lager and extra especially with some fresh greens & herbs grown out back by Sherri, the manager's wife. I, Snorkel Bob, found the ahi peu peu most amusing and a vigorous feed. Moreover, repeat bidness may be in the offing.

### BEACH HOUSE RESTAURANT—$$$$
5022 Lawai Rd. in Poipu, Kauai
(808) 742-1424

Mediterranean and Pacific Rim cuisine. Open for dinner 5:30-10. Casual dress. The perfect left out front is a wildly popular break called Centers. It's just over from PK's and down from Acid Drops and way down from Heroine (which may be all that could get me, Snorkel Bob, out there). Besides the sterling action viewable from the bar, a lovely boogie break resides just in from Centers.

But this smorgasboard of action outdoors is mere wavelets lapping next to the wave of a different nature rising from all sides, inside. Suddenly glimpsing the abyss, I, Snorkel Bob, added 2 and 2:

The Beach House Restaurant is owned by The Shell Company (no fooling), and the 46 tables times 3 persons each stack up in the heaviest

153

break of all. The Shell Company also owns the timeshare place across the road—the Beach House is the boiler room. 46 time dogs work the bone on 92 Norm & Normas who like vacations, need vacations, can't afford the whole unit (wouldn't that be crazy anyway?), love this beach, love the trade flexibility, got a C or better in high school math and can easily see that a lifetime of vacations would cost far more than mere thousands and wouldn't even generate a Rolodex card. So! Sign here. And here. And here and here.

Hey! It changes late in the day. It cools down, kind of, but from sunset on it can pump with another heavy break, another ebb and flow of warming gizzards and eyeballs seeking potential.

And oh, by the way, the restaurant serves delectible grinds from Filet Mignon to Grilled Salmon with Ancho Chili Linguine, Julienne Vegetables and Tomato Coulis for 23 clams.

## KOLOA BROILER—$
Koloa, Kauai
(808) 742-9122

11 a.m. to 11:30 p.m., 7 days a week here, lunch and dinner. It's grill your own from 5 selections of cow, chicken, fish. It's casual. It's rustic. It's basic—meat, potatoes, salad bar, tureen baked beans, tureen rice, plenty bread, big grip salt and pepper shakers, ketchup smothering everything like the Red Sea closing over Pharoah's hapless troops. Every gut at the grill cast a shadow to midthigh; i.e., these guys need periscopes to find their pee pees. But they know how to scratch an itch blindfolded, and there they be. Mmuh. Good grub. Koloa is on the way to Poipu.

## KUNJA KOREAN RESTAURANT—$
Rice Street in Lihue, Kauai
(808) 245-6554

The best Korean on Kauai. 4-star funk, no jive, starring Kunja herself and her homemade kim chee. Reasonable with lunch from $4.50-$6.50 and dinner a buck or 2 more. Kunja gets 2 thumbs up from me, Snorkel Bob, myself. Open 8 or 9 a.m. (Kunja is always there cooking) until 8 p.m. Monday through Sat, closed Sun.

## GAYLORDS—$$$$
Rte 50 in Lihue, Kauai
(808) 245-9593

Gaylord's is just south of Lihue on Route 50 in the Kilohana Plantation, in 1 mo Shop-O'-Rama with horse & carriages, dog & ponies, etc, et al, which gives me, Snorkel Bob, the old vertigo, like anywhere USA is now Everywhere USA and closing quick. Arrrgh! The Sunday Brunch is very good with none of that all-you-can-eat nonsense but an elegant repast, a la carte, and well-served. High marks here on dessert and wine selection too, and the surfer-guy waiters appear committed to the clean break, the honest drop with no room for jive, deceit, treachery or impatience. Ask about the daily specials. Lunch 11-3 & dinner from 5-9, Mon-Sat, with brunch on Sunday.

**DUKE'S CANOE CLUB—$$ to $$$$**
Marriott in Lihue, Kauai
(808) 246-9599

In the Marriott, this 1, overlooking Kalapaki Bay the way Kalapaki Bay can't be overlooked anywhere else. Besides that, it marks the approach pattern for Lihue Airport, so you can get that old sphincter pucker like when you were a kid and would sneak through the fence and lay down at the end of the runway because cheating death was what life was all about, if you were lucky. You might get lucky again, relaxing in a chair with a stiff drink as the big tin can rumbles over.

**KIIBO—$ to $$$**
Umi Street in Lihue, Kauai
(808) 245-2650

Kiibo is in the heart of beauteous downtown Lihue, north on Rice Street to Umi Street, go left and look up. Local style this 1, with the best sushi in Lihue, but sometimes da kine talk da kine, so da tourist guys like come eat no can because cannot read da menu or understand da kine. Capiche? 11-1:30 for lunch, dinner served until 9, only dinner served on Sunday.

**TOKYO LOBBY—$$$**
Pacific Ocean Plaza in Lihue, Kauai
(808) 245-8989
11-2 Lunch Mon-Sat,  5-9:30 Dinner Daily

Casual attire. Traditional Japanese menu.

## HANAMAULU CAFE AND ARA'S SUSHI—$ to $$$
Hanamaulu, Kauai
(808) 245-2511

Ocular disparity here between outside and in; in is a beauteous courtyard much bigger than met the eye (out). Good sushi bar and prices. Open daily 10-1 and 4:30-10:30, take-out only on Saturday and Sunday until 10:30 p.m.

## KINTARO JAPANESE RESTAURANT—$$ to $$$$
4-370 Kuhio Hwy in Kapaa, Kauai
(808) 822-3341
5:30-9:30 Mon-Sat, closed Sun

This may be the best sushi bar in Kapaa with formidable tempura, teppanyaki and nabe mono too, all served in traditional style, traditional ambience, with a nice tatami room for private parties. Reservations suggested.

## A PACIFIC CAFE—$$$
Kauai Village in Kapaa
(808) 822-0013

It looks prefab inside, like a franchise, nautical-theme place, but the eats is oh-riginal, maybe the best around. 5:30-9:30, 7 days a week.

## BUBBA BURGERS—$
Kapaa and Hanalei, Kauai
(808) 823-0069 and (808) 826-7839
10:30-8 and 10:30-6, Mon-Sun

I, Snorkel Bob, like any place whose motto is "We will serve no hamburger that costs less than a can of dogfood." And don't forget: "Welfare mothers make better lovers." Welfare or no, a pretty mean burger.

## KAPAA FISH & CHOWDER HOUSE—$$ to $$$$
Hwy 56 in Kapaa, Kauai
(808) 822-7488

In the chowderhouse mode, this place could get hosed down, not to worry, it'd dry out. It's overlit like a chowderhouse or a 24-hour hardware store or a bus station, so that by the salad/entree interval you'll squint in the tungsten glare and feel watched. This is not the place for petty theft, secret touches, stolen moments. But I, Snorkel Bob, do enjoy the shrimp remoulade, and the seafood crepe is amusing. They serve an acceptable seafood kabob broiled over kiawe and the Fish House Platter is a trustworthy cross-section of groceries del mar—i.e., unfrozen, not from Taiwan, which the more savvy among you will know is the case with nearly all Captain's Platters, Neptune's Buffets, Seafood Medleys, All You Can Eats, Engorge Till You Chokes, Special Come On Downs, Feedbag Frenzies, Swine-o-Ramas, Stuff Your Gob with 2 Hands, Shovel Swill Down Your Gullet Til Your Eyes Turn Purples, Hey Take a Swan Dive From the High Board into a Giant Freaking Cesspool Crawling with Dead Animal Parts, Bend Over...

STOP!

...Where was I? Where am I? Oh...yeah...Snorkel Bob. The Kapaa Fish & Chowder House—excellent Fish House Platter. Why wouldn't it be? And I, Snorkel Bob, can tell you why this place gets extra high marks: 1) no atmosphere and 2) zero view. That means the place won't be all jammed with sentimentals sighing and stretching their necks. It's fine cuisine at this place, New Orleans, New England, Hawaiian, French. At the north end of Kapaa on the mountain side of the road. Dinner 5:30-9.

### THE BULL SHED—$$$
Kapaa, Kauai
(808) 822-3791
5:30-10 Daily

Cow meat in what I, Snorkel Bob, am told is the highest quality on Kauai.

### NORBERTO'S EL CAFE—$
Hwy 56 in Kapaa, Kauai
(808) 822-3362

A-1, down home Mezicano, this 1, right here in Kapaa on Kuhio Highway. You can't miss it. Dinner 5:30-9.

### ZELO'S BEACH HOUSE—$
Princeville Market Place in Princeville, Kauai
(808) 826-9700
10-9:30 Daily

Zelo's is low cafe in the tropics with espresso and wines, beer and hardcore nutritional sandwiches. Nearly all the regulars talk sincerely about stuff like envisioning world peace, or envisioning happy whales, or envisioning concentric karmas, or envisioning aural afterbirth, or envisioning the perfect decade, which was the 60s, and all like that. I, Snorkel Bob, rate the cakes and sandwiches and salads here very good. The ambiance rating: light and airy. The wine selection: for emergency use only. The coffee menu: ☆☆☆☆ Excellanté; e.g., Napili Brew Espresso, and Mocha Frosted (see Coffee Places).

**CASA DI AMICI**—$$$ on up
Kilauea, Kauai
(808) 828-1555
11:30-2:30, 6-9 Daily

Damn decent northern Italian in a beauteous setting.

**CHARO'S**—$$$$
Haena
(808) 826-6422
11:30-5, Lunch only

Past Hanalei all the way to Haena on the ocean side. Or was, before Iniki.

Clean and well-lit, this place sits 20 yards from the ocean and serves from a predictable menu with Mexican, burgers, chicken, steak and a lobster tail investment lunch at $40. With luck, the return is quick and easy, the loss limited to the cash out. Big dessert tray too. WARNING on the drinkaroos—$4.50 (and up), a couple rounds and some bugs can set you a C-note for you and the squeeze, and that's before tip, tax, tags, dealer prep, destination charges, flooring, commissions, et al.

But even though you might get gouged on some over-promoted, heavily-packaged, dead-average groceries, don't forget the added value of this place: Charo. I, Snorkel Bob, get that hubba hubba feeling just looking at those puffy lips and all that lip gloss. Boy oh boy, what I, Snorkel Bob, could do with those from 8 to 10. I, Snorkel Bob, advise mouth breathing when snorkeling, but not in a camera pose, especially in a low slung tutu. But boy oh boy, my, Snorkel Bob's, hormones still stand up at attention for that kind of lift and spread. Gosh, she sure is some bombshell hunk o' little woman. Isn't she?

**BRICK OVEN PIZZA**—$$
Hwy 50 in Kalaheo, Kauai
(808) 332-8561
11 am-10 pm, Tu-Sun

Pizza, hospitality and complimentary pepperoncinis.

## POMODORO—$$$
Kalaheo, Kauai
(808) 332-5945

Up the steps of an aggressively forgettable office lowrise and across a nonskid floor awaits a quaint, fa fa interior so intimate you'll feel like whispering. This is the kind of place that makes me, Snorkel Bob, want to SCREAM BLOODY FREAKING MURDER!%%$$##??)(@! But the groceries are exceptionally well done.

## SINALOA TAQUERIA & MEXICAN RESTAURANT—$$
Hwy 50 in Hanapepe, Kauai
(808) 335-0006
11-4:30 Lunch, 4:30-9 Dinner, Daily

Good Mexican on the way to Waimea Canyon.

## KALAHEO COFFEE COMPANY & CAFE—$
Toward Hanapepe 10 minutes past Poipu in Kalaheo, Hawaii
(808) 332-5858
6 a.m.-4 p.m. Mon-Fri, 6:30-4 Sat, 7-2 Sun

"Quality Food Takes Awhile" means it's slow. You may call ahead for sandwiches to go, but then what's the rush?
The place is crowded but roomy; a nice space shaped with pleasing materials for a good vibration. The menu is excellent, and the tuna samich was possibly the best I, Snorkel Bob, have had since the 1 Snorkel Mom made. A ruddy fellow 1 table over ordered the Tavern Pig Samidge, and from what I, SB, could tell, he was gratified. This is a great restaurant in a 3rd world of wanna be's.

## KALAHEO STEAKHOUSE—$$
Hwy 50 in Kalaheo, Kauai
(808) 332-9780
6-10 Daily

A good local steakhouse open nightly 5:30-9:30 for dinner. No reservations needed; 1st-come.

## HANAPEPE CAFE & ESPRESSO BAR—$
3830 Hanapepe Rd. in Hanapepe, Kauai
(808) 335-5011

Breakfast 8-11, lunch 11-2 Tuesday-Saturday, and dinner 6-9 Thursday, Friday, and Saturday. Pricey coffee and pastries served to 3 in case you miss lunch. Hawaiian slack-key guitarist every night. All served in funky, local Hanapepe town.

# THE BIG ISLAND

## QUINN'S—$
75-5655 Apalani Rd. in Kailua, Hawaii
(808) 329-3822
11 a.m.-1 a.m.—to midnight Sun

Quinn's is best known for good cooking and honest count, especially on the Catch of the Day and prime rib. Tropical ambiance in the restaurant downshifts to semitough at the bar, where I, Snorkel Bob, dasn't order a foo-foo tourist drink with a little paper parasol, lest my badass buddies will think me, Snorkel Bob, some kind of sissy in need of a beating. No siree, it's just me, Snorkel Bob, football, puhehe and the boys at the bar. And don't forget the shrimp continental with sauteed vegetables or the pepper steak with special sauce. Like my friend, Deadbolt Pakalolo, said, "My that's good!" That Deadbolt—sometime he talk just like Fred Astaire. Across from the King Kam Hotel.

## SAM CHOY'S—$$$$
73-5576 Kauhola Bay 1 (New Industrial) in Kona, Hawaii
(808) 326-1545

Sam Choy is a big, fat chef who emotes warmth and friendliness with major PR. He seems sincere, but in Honolulu he's booked weeks in advance, because it's a place to be seen, disqualifying it from any guide dealing with reality. The Kona store, however, is easier access and used to be a warehouse, which accrues merit right off the bat. Density is a push here, counterbalancing with demerits, but more merits accrue with the simple fixed menu of 3 entrees and same sideflies. All was deeelicious with A-1 salads, breads, presentation and service. And with BYOB, you may also enjoy a reasonable buzz without the usual gouge. At $20-25 per, a fun 1, this.

## KONA RANCH HOUSE—$$
75-5653 Oioli St. in Kailua, Hawaii
(808) 329-7061
6:30-2, 4:30-9 Daily

The Ranch House is famous for it's complimentary, homemade, corn bread, served at breakfast and lunch while you're deciding what to order, or maybe after you've decided, or maybe after you ask for it. It's a feedbag here, 3 meals, with a big menu. It's hard to mess up eggs, and they didn't. Moreover, the fruit boat here is not an alternate-sexual-preference charter, but is sliced-up mango, papaya, kiwi and such in a carved pineapple.

Those of you who like to peu-peu it up, can eat in the area known as Fine Dining, with the peace of mind that comes from knowing that your eat mates called ahead for reservations and arrived, like you, in a shirt with a collar and long pants. (What, no shoes?) The more slovenly among you will be consigned to an area called Casual (not to be confused with Trough'n Brew), where you can drop in any old time wearing last week's shmata if you want. 2 weeks without bathing is also optional. And a handful of jellybeans from the hostess desk on your way out is pure gravy. But what I, Snorkel Bob, really like... Well, we better work up to that.

**HUGGO'S**—$$$ to $$$$
75-5828 Kahakai Rd. in Kailua, Hawaii
(808) 329-1493
11:30-2:30 Mon-Fri, 5:30-10 Daily

Huggo's is right by the Royal Kona Resort, only a step and a stumble from me, Snorkel Bob's!

The fresh fish here is good as you'll get anywhere, and the grill is right, with even coals and low heat in case you want chicken or cow instead. And you can match perfectly prepared lobster with big-time adventure, shucking the shells over the rail into shallow surf, where big, fat, Huggo's-fed eels come up, out of the water for some shell reaming. This is communion with Mama Ocean and the kind of action I, Snorkel Bob, can't go without. And oh, the lemon butter sauce and frigid beer!

**KONA MIXED PLATE**—$
Kopiko Plaza in Kailua, Hawaii
(808) 329-8104
10-8 Mon-Sat, closed Sun

This place is next to Domino's and is the cheapest acceptable place I, Snorkel Bob, have found for lunch or early dinner. It's mostly deep fried or fried Korean that will quell your hunger, especially the Chicken Katsu sandwich with fries or 2 scoop rice.

## BIANELLI'S PIZZA—$ to $$$
Pines Plaza at 75-240 Nani Kailua Dr. in Kailua, Hawaii
(808) 326-4800
11-10 Mon-Fri, 4-10 Sat & Sun

Above the hubbub in Pines Plaza. We deliver. I, Snorkel Bob, eat about as much pizza as I, SB, eat blowfish bouillabaisse, but field agents report this 1 worth trying for those who do. (What? Fried sauce? Yes.) 8 clams and up, anchovies optional, like the calzones and pasta miscellaneii.

## LA BOURGOGNE FRENCH RESTAURANT—$$$$
Kukini Hwy in Kailua, Hawaii
(808) 329-6711
6-10 Mon-Sat

La Bourgogne is fa fa de blah blah, avec un petite peu peu on the side. It's the kind of place where women read the left column and say oh boy, and their dates read the right column and say ho boy. That is, of course, unless the date happens to be rich, rich, rich, like me, Snorkel Bob, and can spread some gravy around—make that sauce. Hey, go ahead and relax with the moolah you already saved on $9 a week for Mask, Fins, Snorkel, Gear Bag, Snorkel Map 'n Tips, No Fog Goop, Fish I.D., And The Legend of Me!, Snorkel Bob. I mean Really.

But more to the point, these fancy French groceries for rich people are very good, but PLEASE FOREGO the saddle of laaaaamb and the Cute Little Baby Duck in orange-lemon sauce. (Oh, those frogs.) Only 8-10 tables here, so reservations are de rigeur. Last seating time changes depending on traffic.

## BUNS IN THE SUN—$
Lanihau Center in Kailua, Hawaii
(808) 326-2774
5 a.m.-4p.m. Mon-Sat, 5a.m.-3p.m. Sun

Buns is a friendly bakery with a breakfast special. Egg, ham 'n cheese on a kaiser roll for a couple scones, or you can go to a croissant for 20¢ more. What's more? Pancakes, French toast, biscuits and gravy and a Hawaiian-style breakfast. Boxed lunches available for snorkel go, if you phone ahead.

**KONA INN—$-$$$$**
Kona Inn Shopping Village at 75-5744 Alii Dr. in Kailua-Kona
(808) 329-4455
5:30-9:30 dinner, 11:30-midnight, grill

The Kona Inn is medium-old Hawaii with koa-wood trim and ceiling fans in the key of low. The unobtrusive lounge has a good pupu menu and the calamari is tender, and for a few clams more you get a decent clam chowder. (Clams? In the tropics?) The dining room serves sitdown groceries with fancy prep.

**MICHAELANGELO'S RESTAURANT—$$$$**
Waterfront Row (aka Clone 39, because it's a wannabe like the pier in S.F. of the same #)
75-5770 Alii Dr. in Kailua-Kona
(808) 329-4436

An amusing slice of old Pompei here that successfully transcends the revolting gingerbread atmosphere of Clone 39. Michaelangelo's sits on top with a great view and non-obtrusive interior reminiscent of old Italy, or at least reminiscent of an old Italian restaurant in Little Italy. Pasta & pizza are mainstays here with the usual chickens and fishes.

**SIBU CAFE—$$**
Banyan Court at 75-5695 Alii Dr. in Kailua, Hawaii
(808) 329-1112
11:30-3 Lunch, 5-9 Dinner

It's good Indonesian at Sibu at moderate prices. Chilled cucumber soup, curry dishes with mild, medium or nuke sauce, Balinese Chicken or Gado Gado Salad with peanut sauce. I, Snorkel Bob, once made a jellyfish sandwich with peanut sauce at home. It wasn't bad with curry, too, and cleared my ears better than a nose blow at 20'. Tucked behind the Banyan Court shops with a few outside tables. Cash only. No reservations.

**OCEAN VIEW INN—$ Lunch, $$ Dinner**
75-5683 Alii Dr. in Kailua, Hawaii
(808) 329-9998
6:30-2:45, 5:15-9 Tues-Sun

Cocktails from sunrise to slake the early thirst. The good things at Oceanview are a) an honest pour and b) good Oriental and Hawaiian fare in a diner format. The bad thing is the line, usually out the door and down the street. And cheap! I, Snorkel Bob, saw a Hawaiian family of 22 get out for $100. You'll find the menu teeming with Portagee sausage and eggs, fried opelu or meatloaf with a side of poi. Cash only.

**ROYAL JADE GARDEN— $ to $$$**
Lanihau Shopping Center in Kailua, Hawaii
(808) 326-7288
10:30-9:30 Sun-Thurs, 10:30-10 Fri & Sat

Royal Jade is standard Chinese, sitdown or take-out. The 3-choice plate could be sweet/sour pig, egg foo who, beef and broccoli, egg rolls, for example, over rice or noodles.

**THE CHART HOUSE—$$$ and up**
75-5770 Alii Dr. in Kailua, Hawaii
(808) 329-2451
5-9:30 Daily

Open for dinner only, the Chart House is on the water in the hubbub and is like Chart Houses everywhere, with good steak and seafood. This 1 has a memorable view from the bar upstairs. Reservations recommended.

**BANGKOK HOUSES THAI RESTAURANT—$ to $$**
King Kamehameha Square in Kailua, Hawaii
(808) 329-7764
11-3 Mon-Fri, Lunch; 5-9 Dinner, Daily

What a good Thai restaurant ought to be, plus some surprises, some finesse, in a little place with clean floors, good waithelp. I, Snorkel Bob, 1 hot, sweaty, mean-tempered evening, had the Rainbow Salad (minced chicken, shrimp, pepper, scallion, beanthread noodles, cooled not chilled) and iced tea, then exited calm, cool and happy...well, happier.

**ALOHA CAFE—$**
Hwy 11 in Kainaliu, Hawaii
(808) 322-3383
8-8 Mon-Sat, 9-2 Sun Brunch

The cafe is inside the old Aloha Theater. It's a Cape Cod chowder house with a long wooden porch overlooking the Kona Coast, the coffee groves and deep blue sea from 2,000'. The breakfast menu has pancakes, omlettes, homemade muffins and tofu scrambles. Brunch is 9-2 on Sunday. The lunch and dinner menu's soups and breads, sandwiches, pasta, fish, cow and tofu are at popular prices. I, Snorkel Bob, do not eat pig meat unless it's sliced paper-thin and served delicately on a kaiser roll with some purple onion and crisp lettuce, like they do at Aloha Cafe. The Aloha serves espresso drinks and Kona coffee with fresh-baked cakes, tortes, and pastries.

### KUAKINI TERRACE—$$$
Keahou Beach Hotel at 78-6740 Alii Dr. in Keahou, Hawaii
(808) 322-3441
11-4 Lunch, 5-9 Dinner

The Kuakini Terrace has a Pepto Bizzzzmal (all you can glub glubblap argh eat) Seafood Buffet on Friday, Saturday, and Sunday for $21.95—what the hey, let's call it 22 clams. The seafood is 1st rate, with Alaska snow crab legs, sushi, lobster, oysters, et al, so if you can avoid swinery at the fishery, it's a soulful repast. Reservations required for the buffet. Menu service too, for those who fear the frenzy.

### ROUSSEL'S—$$ to $$$$
Waikoloa Village in Waikoloa, Hawaii
(808) 883-9644
11-2:30 Lunch, Daily; 5-9:30 Dinner, Tues-Sat

French Creole Cuisine; that's New Orleans style but not Cajun. It's mostly seafood, light and airy with memorable gumbo and trout almondine.

### IMARI—$$$$
Hilton Waikoloa Village on the Kohala Coast, Hawaii
(808) 885-1234
6-9:30 p.m. Daily

The teppanyaki is good, and the chef scared everybody with flames to the ceiling. But isn't that what the teppanyaki boys do, i.e., scare the peas out of everyone? I, Snorkel Bob, once watched a teppanyaki chef slice a broiling onion in mid-air and then deftly flip 1/2 onto my plate and the other 1/2 into my (ex, as we speak) mother-in-law's hair. I, Snorkel Bob, was impressed, not to mention entertained. But then he switched his paring knife for a meat cleaver and I, Snorkel Bob, for 1, went ski daddle. But that was not at the Hilton, where they only make big fires and alas, where the pork butt tastes like sushi, or so I, Snorkel Bob, am told. A sushi bar and private tables are available for those who scorn teppanyaki.

## DONATONI'S—*$$$$*
Hilton Waikoloa Village on the Kohala Coast, Hawaii
(808) 885-1234
6-9:30 p.m. Daily

Also in the Hilton, in the ultra fa mode. I, Snorkel Bob, have a hard time with waiters in tuxedos and stiff necks, but I'm certain it's a personal problem for me, Snorkel Bob. The question persists, however: How would these guys do underwater?

But the service is impeccable, possibly flawless, potentially perfect. You may itch at Donatoni's, but you dasn't scratch, considering the implications, ramifications, hallucinations (can this be real?). I, Snorkel Bob, crave the Scampi Con Prezzemolo e Limone, especially the part in the doggy bag, eaten the next night during the late movie, on the floor with chopsticks. If not scampi, I like maybe 1 Gnocchi Al Tre Formaggi, which, in English, is potato dumplings in cream sauce with dried tomatoes and cheeses. That creamy stuff won't stop your heart if you go slow. I, Snorkel Bob, like mine with a few bratwursts and some whipped cream and a 3-egg omelette on the side. It's okay if you snorkel. Snorkeling fights cholesterol. Don't you know?

## KONA PROVISION COMPANY—*$$$$*
Hilton Waikoloa Village on the Kohala Coast, Hawaii
(808) 885-1234
11-2 Lunch, 5:30-10:30 Dinner

This place is also in the Hilton but cuts waaay back on the fa fa de blah blah, the peu peu pu deu. It's steak and seafood normal style, i.e., you got your tables, your chairs, your menus, your waitpersons in civilian clothing and flexible necks.

## CANOE HOUSE—*$$* to *$$$$*
Mauna Lani Resort on the Kohala Coast, Hawaii
(808) 885-6622
6-10 p.m. Daily

The Canoe House is so close to the beach you may need extra socks. The Stone Grill is a hot-brick, tableside cookery that they plop the chicken, cow, fish, shrimp and/or vegetables on and cook to taste. A good 1, this.

**EDELWEISS** -$ Lunch, $$$ Dinner
Hwy 19 in Kamuela, Hawaii
(808) 885-6800
11:30-1:30, 5-8:45 Daily

This is a popular German place (It nevah hoppent!) mit der wiener schnitzel unt der saurkraut unt der schpudsels mit der mayo uber allus. Warm, this place, especially when it's cold in the rest of Waimea. After 7 you MUST wait in line, 45 minutes maybe. No reservations. (Veh iss you paypahss?)

**MERRIMAN'S**—$$ to $$$$
Opelo Plaza in Kamuela, Hawaii
(808) 885-6822
11:30-1:30 (Mon-Fri only), 5:30-9 Daily

Steak and seafood in the L.A. suburban chic contextual mode. (I mean, this isn't about food! This is about taste interacting with decor!) That's white on white in white with no blush. Classical music and nouveau peu peu ambiance make this place aggressively inoffensive. I, Snorkel Bob, just luuuuv the continental steak and seafood prepared by "a nationally renowned chef." Whodaguy? Reservations required for dinner.

**NAALEHU FRUIT STAND**—$
Hwy 11 in Naalehu, Hawaii
(808) 929-9009
9-6:30 Mon-Thurs, 9-7 Fri & Sat, 9-5 Sun

Waaay down south on the Big Island, John and Dorene Santangelo run a combo health-food/grocery store with tables and chairs on the front porch. You can buy groceries or a pizza or a samidge with fresh-pressed pineapple juice, or a pineapple-coconut loaf homemade by Dorene. What a girl.

**VOLCANO HOUSE**—$$$
Hwy 11 in Volcano, Hawaii
(808) 967-7321
11-2, 5:30-9 Daily

It's cooold up here at 4,500', but not so bad with a fire in the hearth and a view for lunch or dinner of the Kilauea Caldera. The caldera is the foremost crater that 1st erupted at the beginning of time. Lunch is buffet and I, Snorkel Bob, come here when I want to know I'm out of the water. Reservations required for dinner.

### NAUNG MAI THAI KITCHEN—$

50-2955 Old Government Rd. in Pahoa, Hawaii
(808) 965-8186
4:30-8:30 Sun & Mon, 12:30-8:30 Tues-Fri, 5-8:30 Sat

They don't call it "kitchen" for nothing; you place order at counter with #1 daughter. Mamasan cookum up on kitchen stove, flip side. You choose from 4-5 tables and sit, watch action in kitchen or action outside. Bangkok, Phuket and Chiang Mai varieties of Thai cuisine, here, plus vegetarian versions on request. I, Snorkel Bob, had something calamari and hot peppers and something chicken and hot peppers. Indubitably good, this 1.

### HARRINGTON'S—$$$

135 Kalanianaole in Hilo, Hawaii
(808) 961-4966
5:30-9:30 Daily

Near the harbor, open, light and tropical. Steak and seafood and a fresh catch. Live music Friday and Saturday maybe slack-key guitar or a contemporary/Hawaiian mix. Reservations a plus.

### FIASCO'S—$ to $$$

200 Kanoelehua Ave. in Hilo, Hawaii
(808) 935-7666
11-10 Mon-Thurs, 11-11 Fri-Sun

This place looks like an Irish pub with wood and brass. Plenty sandwiches and pasta too. Thursday is Country night to midnight. Live music Friday and Saturday, open to 1, no cover.

### KEN'S HOUSE OF PANCAKES—$

1730 Kam Ave. in Hilo, Hawaii
(808) 935-8711
24 Hrs. Daily

Ken's gets 5 stars from me, Snorkel Bob, on the late-nite-snack rating—countum ☆☆☆☆☆. Open everyday like me, Snorkel Bob, and Ken goes a step farther—24 hours a day! What an unbelievable house of pancakes.

**MIYO'S—$**
400 Hualani in Hilo, Hawaii
(808) 935-2273

Asian style sashimi, tempura, sesame chicken and so on with sideflies in the $7-10 atmosphere. A fresh-water-lagoon overview makes this a slice of the old east.

# MAUI

Kihei is more limited than Lahaina, especially after dark. But Lahaina has a few kinks. In summertime it's hot, maybe hotter than you ever imagined, maybe hot enough to ask yourself where you went wrong, maybe hot enough to wonder why you exist at that unfortunate confluence of place and heat. It's crowded, with gridlock on the sidewalks, rubber-necking mobs looking for what they might be missing. A fine grit gets under your skin, and a voice calls out to you, yeah, you, come on over here, I want to show you something. Otherwise it's a gentle, lovely place.

And oh, those colorful street people.

**SUNRISE CAFE—$**
693A Front Street in Lahaina, Maui
(808) 661-8558
6 a.m.-10 p.m. Daily

Next to the library in Lahaina. (Walk from the Pioneer Inn across the lawn). Cheap groceries, cheap atmosphere, but not bad. They get the fancy fare from somewhere else and serve it up for less. This format was first revealed to me, Snorkel Bob, by a bag lady under the sprawling banyan tree, who offered a baked potato, still warm, still wrapped in foil for only 10¢. I, Snorkel Bob, declined, having already eaten. The Sunrise Cafe's slightly exposed fare shows far less mileage. For example I, Snorkel Bob, got a perfectly sanitary spinach quiche (research only) with fruit, and an iced tea for about $6. Lunch and dinner, sandwiches and espresso. 6 a.m.-10 p.m., catering to the boat-trip crowd.

**AVALON RESTAURANT**—$$ and up
844 Front St. in Lahaina, Maui
(808) 667-5559
11:30-10 Daily

Avalon is cuisine of the Pacific Rim (Mexico, Asia, Polynesia), below Moose McGillycuddy's on Front Street. This display of white on white in white with ferns and pricey entrees is still popular and still good. 2 favorites here are steamed clams in garlic black bean sauce and Chinese chicken salad. Avalon used to be better, but then so did I, Snorkel Bob. I mean, an open air café with original fare and a great wine list is different than a crowded scene to be seen in. Still, it's amusing, especially during the week in nonpeak hours. Reservations required for dinner.

**MAUI TACO**—$
Lahaina Sq.—and in Napili, Kihei and Kaahuumaanuu Ceenterr
(808) 661-8883

*Talk turned to killing flies, especially the juicy bombers buzzing the fish bucket. One man stretched a big rubber band for a trial shot on a quarter pounder. He let go—splat to the ditch—with a perfect hit. Talk turned to killing men. Voices thinned. One man said he could kill if he had to, no problem. Another said you never know. Fatty said it was easier than swatting a fly, and that surprised him, how easy a man goes dead. He remembered that man more than any fly he ever killed. He enjoyed it more—more than one of them fat, hairy sonsabitches bumping his head when he's trying to think. Much more; it felt good, like a two-tone tattoo once the sting and blood get done with. 'Course now the motherfucker had it coming. The oasis got quiet then with no questions.*

*Yours truly*
*—WHIRLAWAY*

Okay, the place made me, Snorkel Bob, feel like I haven't felt in years, not since drydock in the outback of Paradise. It's not as bad as that, but not by much. It's a small, crowded masonry cell with a Wolf Stove (for Tacos?) that promotes low prices but isn't cheap and won't take credit cards. The hats are $15, in case you have to have 1. This is a glaring example of the Executive Chef madness plaguing Hawaii these days. Gifted direction here is credited to the Exec. Chef from Avalon, though the brochure lists 2 Latino names. But you have to ask yourself if a taqueria needs an executive chef. The effort might be wasted, since the only iotum of old Mehico apparent to me, Snorkel Bob, was the flies.

Many flies. Many many. And a line. And more flies. And a so-so burrito & soda for $9. And flies. Then again, this was in Lahaina. I, SB'm told the others are nicer. The ingredients are said to be fresh.

### ARAKAWA—$
736 Front St. by Bad Ass Coffee
661-8811
11-2 & 5-7:30 Daily but closed every 1st, 10th & 20th

In the Kishi Building Mall, which is to malls what those coffins for the night in Tokyo are to real hotel rooms. It's a long, narrow, florescent hallway similar to a modern airline entry ramp. Arakawa is at the end. No speaka too gooda de English, but Japanese fast food is much more like how it used to be than what it is, and it's a fur piece from Bugs freaking Bunny scaring kids on the corner. Katsu don, katsu curry, potsticker, yakitori, teriyaki, hekka AND MACARONI SALAD. In and out for $6 (or maybe $7).

### GERARD'S—$ to $$$$
174 Lahainaluna Rd. in Lahaina, Maui
(808) 661-8939
6-8:30 p.m. (last seating) Daily

I, Snorkel Bob was depressed by the Confit of Duck and the Veal Normande, and tears flowed over the Baby Duck de Foie Gras, the Helpless Veal Medallions, Hatchling Quail under Glass, Veal Brains on Rye. Not really, but the menu here is troublesome reading for an animal rights radical like me, Snorkel Bob, what with the 2 ducks, 2 laaambs, 3 veals and some quail. Besides facing ultra-foo cuisine in rude disregard of critter consciousness, you will spend abusively too, with the tax, tip, appetizers and wine. It's big dough here in the soft-voice mode, i.e., this place makes me, Snorkel Bob, nervous, possibly claustrophobic and potentially, marginally skittish.

On the other hand, I, Snorkel Bob, got it from good sources that the Ragout of Slugs with Wild Mushrooms and Burgundy butter is an excellent repast for those who care to eat that sort of thing. Matt Roving, long time snorkel buddy and confidant to me, Snorkel Bob insists that this dish is actually called Ragout of Escargot, etc, et al. I Snorkel Bob, explained that slugs are escargot. Oh no, they're not, said Matt Roving. Slugs don't have shells, he said.

But you don't eat the shells, do you? said I, Snorkel Bob. It's not that I, Snorkel Bob, ain't game. I am. It's just that I, Snorkel Bob, always felt that a thing must look good and smell good, or else I, Snorkel Bob, won't want to eat it. Enough butter and garlic on anything can lure you right in, tongue 1st. But then you got the sound of it: Ragout of Slugs. Gee. That's tough. I, Snorkel Bob, don't hear much difference between that and, say Night Crawlers in Creme Sauce, or maybe Toady Frog Frappé. Hey, how about some Jellyfish Bouillabaisse (on a bed of pasta)? Or some Filet of Salamanders with Crushed Centipedes and Capers on Top, Under a White Wine and Smegma Sauce? Well? How does that sound? With a side demitasse of Gissome at room temperature? Well? Huh? What do you say now?

Please. Forgive me, Snorkel Bob, for my apparently uncontrollable approach/avoidance compulsion/revulsion, which has nothing, nada, rein, zip, zero, nary a spec to do with the groceries at Gerard's, which many people like. And, it's up the street from Snorkel Bob's.

## MAKAI BAR—$ and up
Marriot Hotel in Kaanapali, Maui
(808) 667-1200
4:30-midnight Sun-Thurs, until 12:30 a.m. Fri & Sat

The Makai is well-lit with an ocean view and a good layout. That is, the bar in the center separates 4 sections of the room, so you can frequent the place (within reason, of course) and maintain a fresh approach. Besides critical separation, the central bar also allows strategic open space for easier breathing, eye contact and traffic control. Best of all is the adjunct pupu bar, with sliced boeuf on petite rolls, sashimi, sushi, poke, nachos, shrimp and maybe a few other items for only a few bucks. For some reason that's hard to finger, I, Snorkel Bob, have always liked this place.

## SEA HOUSE RESTAURANT—$$ and up
Napili Kai Beach Club on Napili Bay, Maui
(808) 669-1500
8-11 Breakfast, 12-2 Lunch, 5:30-9 Dinner, Daily

The Napili Kai Beach Club hasn't changed in 400 years. Captain Cook lunched here with guests when he was in town. And the place does capture the old Aloha comfort. I, Snorkel Bob, gravitate to the fresh fish'n chips in overview of a most beauteous body of water, Napili Bay. It's on the beach, on the bay, in the shade with cold beverage.

**HONOLUA STORE—$**
502 Office Rd. in Kapalua, Maui
(808) 669-6128
6 a.m.-8 p.m. Daily

Follow the road sign from the Lower Road—you're on the Lower Road heading north if you turn left out of my, Snorkel Bob's, place in Napili. From the High Road, take the Pineapple Hill Exit (Office Road). Anyway, once inside you wade through all the tourist chachkas in front, back to the hot lunch buffet. The mahi mahi, lasagna, beef teriyaki, many chickens, spaghetti and on and on come with 2 scoop rice for $4.95. What? Yes! Kitchen closes at 3.

**JAMESON'S—$ to $$$$**
Kapalua Golf Course in Kapalua, Maui
(808) 669-5653
11-3, 5-10 Daily

Standard lunch fare with seared ahi and caesar salads, burgers, and sandwiches. For dinner–fresh catch of the day in one of the chef's special sauces. A great view from this 1.

**KIHEI PRIME RIB—$$$$**
2511 S. Kihei Rd. in Kihei, Maui
(808) 879-1954
5-10 Daily

This place is about as good as it gets in Kihei, which is far from, say, the best sewage treatment in Lodi. XLNT steak, seafood and salad bar here with a sneeze shield big enough to defend against Bronco Nigurski with a head cold. And oh, the sunset view. Kihei Prime Rib is good eats in decent atmosphere and a dark bar. A cheap Early Bird Special from 5-6 provides adequate yin to the outrageous yang of THE FIRST $40 ENTREE I, SNORKEL BOB, HAVE EVER SEEN, except for the 1 at Charo's on Kauai. It's Surf 'n Turf, for those whose taste is in their mouths. Reservations a plus.

**KIHEI CAFFE—$**
1945 S Kihei Rd. in Kihei, Maui
(808) 879-2230
5 a.m.-3 p.m. Mon-Sat, 6 a.m.-3 p.m. Sun

Great double cappucinos, big sandwiches and a few hot dishes too. Good cafe atmosphere with outside tables for the passing parade of rental cars. All breads and pastries are baked on the premises, with emphasis on imaginative ingredients, freshness, flavors. Good crew, good groceries, no gouge, and strong jo (see Coffee Places).

## THE GREEK BISTRO—$
2511 S. Kihei Rd. in Kihei, Maui
(808) 879-9330
5-9:30 Daily

This is Greek with moussaka, lamb casserole, spinach spanakopita, salads and more. Dinner later than most in the neighborhood is sitdown or take-out. Good gyros and baklava made on the premises and most notable of all, a non-honkytonk atmosphere. Eye contact optional.

## THE NEW YORK DELI—$
Dolphin Plaza at 2395 S. Kihei Rd. in Kihei, Maui
(808) 879-1115
7 a.m.-9 p.m. Daily

The deli is way back in Dolphin Plaza, that obscure strip center with high turnover and many vacancies and now a franchise pizza odor reminiscent of Saddam Hussein's mustard gas. Also on the gauntlet are 2 slumlike snorkel pretenders who would scratch their asses left-handed while picking their noses right, if only they would see me, Snorkel Bob, do it first. Junk is what they have, and junk is junk at any price. Oh yeah, Dolphin Plaza has bronze dolphins in front and a wall mural painted by the artistically challenged, for atmosphere. Penetrate the slum and it's an honest sandwiches at the deli, with a fridge case full of salads, olives, kosher dills, salamis, balonies, turkey, hams, cheeses and all like that, with carry-out cold soda and beer too. But just thinking of penetration that deep gives me, Snorkel Bob, the Kihei sleazy willies.

## RADIO CAIRO MAUI—$$ to $$$$
Rainbow Mall on South Kihei Road in Kihei, Maui     **CLOSED**
(808) 879-4404

Help! Mr. Wizard! I, Snorkel Bob, don't want to be a cynical sumbitch forever! But here we have a restaurant with A) an obscure, possibly stupid name with emphasis on the MAUI, as if that once-exotic address can fulfill a fantasy like, say, Cairo used to do, or something. And B) a menu revolving around a culinary oxymoron (African cuisine) with more obscure names for items that have nothing to do with Africa.

To whit: 2 orders of Kilimanjaro seemed appropriate for a couple noncarnivores just off the savanna out by the old Waikapu Dump. It's a mountain of mashed potatoes (Get it?) with molten cheddar flowing down the side to the meandering stream of congealed cornstarch and sugar gravy in the littorals. Oh, yeah, and don't forget the boiled vegetables strategically placed like boulders around the mountain. 28 clams for some iffy hash can be a disappointment.

It's enough to convince me, Snorkel Bob, that anyone who experiences great restaurants in America should be disqualified from sampling in Hawaii. Oh, you say, but Hawaii is America. I, SB, will not respond to that, other than to say a satellite colony offshore could be more imaginative. Meanwhile, this place is extremely popular, maybe because it has accoustics like the bus station and eye contact is mandatory. You will be checked out. On checking back, however, I, Snorkel Bob, found the king naked once again.

### THE FAIRWAY—$
100 Kaukahi in Wailea, Maui
(808) 879-4060
8:30-11 & 11-4 Mon-Sat, 7:30-12 & 12-4 Sun

A good breakfast in scenic overview of the never-ending repartee among people, about golf. Excellent place for sunsets, cocktails and recovery from endless fairways.

### SEAWATCH RESTAURANT—$$ to $$$$
Wailea Orange and Emerald Course in Wailea, Maui
(808) 875-8080

Excellent standard repast in regal overview of the biggest ocean in the world. The Baked Brie en Croute con Pineapple Salsa is a known stimulant. The wine list here is very good but just as overpriced. Entrees run the predictable gamut and the sugar orgy on the menu will make your incissors throb.

### UKULELE GRILL—$$
In the old Maui Lu at 575 S. Kihei Rd.
(808) 875-1188

A true sampler of the bon vivant will neither poo poo nor praise on the basis of mere appearance. Yet the Ukulele Grill, A.K.A. The Longhouse at the Maui Lu, was an arid dump at high noon, and now it's prettier'n a fo-dolla ho at night, trussed and atwinkle in those little white lghts. An estute raconteur knows as well that every menu has its highpoint. Here, the Pan Fried Oysters de Peu Peu are amusing with touristic Hawaiian music and a couple 3 brewskies.

Yet misfortune reared her unlovely head on the crab cakes–like canned tuna from the radar range, these are most unyum. With the tempered expectations most suitable to these balmy shores, however, I, SB, went ahead with din and found the grilled fish undamaged to a golden turn. Alas, the menu refouls with Braised Baby Duck and Roast Rack of Laaaamb. I, Snorkel Bob, could prolong these pros and cons, but in a nutshell: Yes, this can be good, if you order right.

### SUDA'S STORE—$
61 S. Kihei Rd. in Kihei, Maui
(808) 879-2668
6-12:30 Breakfast and Lunch Daily; 7:30-5 store hours

Way north on South Kihei Rd. with a gas pump, store and snack bar. The store started long ago for plantation workers. When Big Sugar left Kihei, Mrs. Suda got the store and got famous for her Chow Fun—noodles with scallion, pig and stuff. Also notable: Suda's Burger de Luxe, an honest burger with the works. About a buck and a half. Fries with mustardketchup go good with Burger de Luxe for another 75¢. But take my, Snorkel Bob's advice: Do not attempt Chow Fun, Burger de Luxe and Fries mustardketchup in 1 lunch. Ooh.

### AZEKA SNACK SHOP—$
Azeka Place Phase I in Kihei (Phase IX), Maui
(808) 879-0078

Phase I? What do they call the massive commercial tumor across the street, Phase II-IX? Don't get me, Snorkel Bob, started. The snack shop is how it used to be—outside, on the tarmac with greasy picnic tables. I, Snorkel Bob, am fond of the teriburger and the shave ice. The daily special is also tolerable, some days. Loco moco is the only breakfast choice at 7:30 a.m. 9:30-2 is lunch, but you can buy ribs until 5.

### CARELLI'S—$$$$
2980 S. Kihei Rd. in Kihei, Maui
(808) 875-0001
6-10 Daily

Good, this place, but who needs pasta shaped like a Neofundamentalist Self Portrait if it runs 90 clams? And black plates? Who died? I, Snorkel Bob, can tell you who—the soft-shelled crab at just the right moment with no apologies, fried shallow in olive grease with a hint of limón, a dash of sage, a wisp of saffron. Or was that alum and mint?

Anyway, it's a long time between soft-shell crabs this good, so once again it's a big-budget decor I, Snorkel Bob'm, all hot and cold over. The groceries are mainly good with high marks on espresso content and presentation. No reservations. 1st come. This is the kind of place typical now to Hawaii; you will be pissed off back home, remembering what you paid, but it's enjoyable at the time, because you're numb to price gouging.

**WAILEA CHART HOUSE—$$$$**
100 Wailea Iki Dr. in Wailea, Maui
(808) 879-2875
5:30-10 Daily

You'll know you're in Wailea when suddenly everything is perfect, clean and Republican. It's not very realistic, but then neither is a tropical reef, relative to the daily demands of life in America. The Chart House is a popular place here, across the main road from Wailea Shopping Village, in standard resort mode with very good entrees, including seafood. High comfort is available under the roof or outside with fountain and ocean views and a decent wine list. This place was Wailea Steak House before the fire. Chart House format changes little from 1 Chart House to the next, but I, Snorkel Bob, value the expected in a tourist zone where repeat business is not always a priority. It is here. Lahaina and Kahului also have Chart House restaurants.

**HARRY'S SUSHI BAR & LOBSTER COVE RESTAURANT—$$ to $$$$**
100 Wailea Iki Dr. in Wailea, Maui
(808) 879-7677

Across the courtyard from the Wailea Chart House, often good, fairly traditional, Japanese food. (See also sushi listings) 5:30-10 dinner with the sushi bar open 5:30-midnight.

**MAUI ONION—$ on up**
Renaissance Wailea at 3550 Wailea Alanui Dr. in Wailea, Maui
(808) 879-4900

The Onion is by the pool and is nice for lunch or a beer and (famous) onion rings. I, Snorkel Bob, grant a single but sincere rave to the Cobb salad here.

## THE FOUR SEASONS—$$$$

3900 Wailea Alanui Dr. in Wailea, Maui
(808) 874-8000

This place is very good for lunch. (See A Separate Reality)

## RAFFLES—$$$$

Renaissance Wailea at 3550 Wailea Alanui Dr. in Wailea, Maui
(808) 879-4900
6-9:30 Daily

Raffles at the Renwa is ultrafancy with the richest decor I, Snorkel Bob, have seen since scuba diving Cathedrals off Lanai (see Scuba Do). Raffles raves on groceries but skewers on price. The place was only fancy before the remodel, now it's perfect. They invited me, Snorkel Bob, to come see the new digs, maybe because they got so much business from my, Snorkel Bob's, 1st appearance. Who knows? I, Snorkel Bob, know they got off easy on the 1st go round, so a looksee was due.

Presentation here is emphasized if not stressed; I, Snorkel Bob, mean it's got to look good before you want to eat it, but this stuff inspires guilt. Eating it seems so primitive; matting and framing seems better. And I, Snorkel Bob, never had my silverware changed more often than my underwear—3 weeks' worth in hardly an hour and a 1/2!

The appetizers look like Miro paintings, with caviar spots, papaya strokes and a wildly dada flourish. The entrees are museum quality, with sideflies like Sesame Seed Spaetzle, Cilantro Pesto, Nasi Goreng Rice, Coconut Curry, Crab Rangoon, Fried Ogo and Grilled Shiitakes and Scallions, which always reads to me, Snorkel Bob, like Shitcakes and Scallions, but of course they're not, and most of the time I, Snorkel Bob'm, able to catch myself in time.

Bad news be brief, but DEMERITS be due: THE FOYER CORAL DISPLAY WAS TAKEN LIVE FROM DEEP WATER AND BLEACHED #!?!

And I, SB, hate to kick a horse, alive or dead, but: Hawaiian Estates Coffee @ $7 per 2-pack? How good can it be?

## PALM COURT—$$$$

Renaissance Wailea at 3550 Wailea Alanui Dr. in Wailea, Maui
(808) 879-4900
6-11 a.m. Breakfast, 6-10 p.m. Dinner, Daily

Open-air with dinner and breakfast buffets everyday, on any 1 of which you may see me, Snorkel Bob, after sunrise snorkel.

**PRINCE COURT—$$$$**
The Maui Prince Resort in Makena, Maui
(808) 874-1111 or (808) 875-5888
6-9:30 Daily

The dining is fine, the prices pricey, with linen, crystal and obsequious service. The chef's special is foo-foo at its best, with little Evian bottles for drinking water, so you know nobody's been snorkeling in it. ☆☆☆☆☆, this 1, if you really need a superiority fix.

**BUZZ'S WHARF—$$$ to $$$$**
Hwy 30 in Maalaea, Maui
(808) 244-5426
11-3 Lunch, 5-9 Dinner

At the base of Maalaea Bay. Coming from Kihei or Kahului, look for boat masts oceanside just south of the junction of Hwy 30 and North Kihei Road (Hwy 31). The harbor is good for a stroll after dinner. Buzz's has good seafood, good catch of the day, good ahi sashimi fish pupus. The steak pupu is most tender, and the pig meat ribs are tasty in the extreme, I, SB, am told. Also too good are Tahitian prawns, a house specialty at about $25.

**ARCHIES—$**
1440 Lower Main Street in Wailuku, Maui
(808) 244-9401
10:30-1:30 Lunch, 5-8 Dinner, Mon-Sat

Kau kau Japanese (udon, miso, teriyaki, tempura) with dinner under $10. Clean and well-lit, this 1.

**SIAM THAI—$ to $$$**
123 N. Market Street in Wailuku, Maui
(808) 244-3817
11-2:30, 5-9:30 Daily

Siam Thai is where my friends who love Thai cooking tell me is the best Thai cooking on all of Market Street, possibly in the whole wide world, except maybe for Saeng's place around the corner, but the votes are split on the issue. I, Snorkel Bob, run into personal divestiture problems with those hot runny sauces, but again you must discount my weakness. I, Snorkel Bob, humbly beg of you.

## SAENG'S THAI CUISINE—$$
2119 Vineyard Street in Wailuku, Maui
(808) 244-1567
11-3 Lunch, 5-9:30 Dinner, Daily

Saeng's is around the corner and up the street from Saim Thai. Why a 1-horse burg like Wailuku has 2 excellent Thai places in 2 blocks is a family story. Enough for now to say Saeng's place is big and open and every bit as good as you ever hoped Thai could be.

## FUJIYA—$$
133 Market Street in Wailuku, Maui
(808) 244-0206
11-1:30 Lunch, 5-9 Dinner, Mon-Fri; Dinner only Sat, closed Sun

This place is next to Siam Thai. They have good complete dinners with noodles, teriyaki, tempura, chicken, pig, cow. They have cold beer, neighborhood prices, hospitality and sometimes sushi when the sushi bar is open, which can frustrate a guy like me, Snorkel Bob, who deep down inside loves his little bitty fish buddies best of all in rice and nori, so I head down to Fujiya and what? No sushi? Why no Sushi? Oh. No sushi today. Maybe sushi no good today. I, Snorkel Bob, don't know, but when the sushi bar is open, the sushi is very good, especially with the new guy on the roll-ups who packs in magnum wasabi, so you can look him right in the eye as it melts down your brain stem but you don't blink, even with tears rolling, sweat beading, you snorting. And, gently, you assess: "Mmm...nice."

## TAKAMIYA MARKET—$
359 N. Market Street in Wailuku, Maui
(808) 244-3404
5:30 a.m.-6:30 p.m.  Mon-Sat, closed Sun

Takamiya is down the hill at the end of Market Street in Happy Valley. Takamiya's take-out lunch special could be why they call this topographical ebb Happy Valley. Contemplate chow fun (noodles), mahi mahi tempura, poke, poi, sashimi, kalua pig, lau laus. Chop sticks and shoyu to go, all at popular prices.

THE CHART HOUSE—*$$$* and up
500 N. Puunene Ave. in Kahului, Maui
(808) 877-2476
5:30-9:30 weekdays, open to 10 Fri & Sat

Like Chart Houses everywhere, this is a good 1 for relaxed atmosphere, good ventilation, consistent groceries, drinks, service and all. I, Snorkel Bob, like it.

KOHO GRILL & BAR—*$* to *$$$$*
Kaahumanu Shopping Center in Kahului, Maui
(808) 877-5588
7 a.m.-10 p.m. Mon-Thurs, to midnight Fri & Sat

A family place with okay prices, like entrees starting at $5. Also in Napili at 5095 Napilihau St. (669-5299).

MINUTE STOP CHICKEN—*¢¢¢*
They're Everywhere

MSC can stop your heart if you stop at the wrong minute. This greasefest can kill you any time if you eat too much of it too fast, especially if a man comes on the radio, tellin' me mo and mo, about some useless information, supposed to try my imagination—I cain't get no. Uh no no no... And you're chowing on the fly, shifting gears, signalling, keeping your beverage in the holder, trying to roll 1 without the hump in the center et al.

However, a busy Snorkel Executive like me, Snorkel Bob, knows the value of greasy chicken that makes no pretense. This is pretty good broasted (deep fried, then quasi-baked) chicken and potato wedges (same recipe); 3 pieces, chicken, spud wedges and roll for $3.65. This stuff can keep you on the go and then keep you on the go. More importantly and to the point is that after a few days of dropping $30-40 every meal because some clown calls himself a chef, or $60 if he's up there in the Executive Stratosphere, and it all tastes like the same low-voltage, high-margin crapola, well, then, Minute Stop Chicken attains ethereal meaning, most likely short of epiphany, but then in the 3rd world, you learn to appreciate proximities.

I, Snorkel Bob, like the Minute Stop on Dairy Road behind the 76 station. No reservations required.

## PAIA FISHMARKET—$
2A Baldwin Ave. in Paia, Maui
(808) 579-8030
11-4:30 Lunch, 4:30-9:30 Dinner, Daily

On the corner of Hana Highway and Baldwin Avenue, it's fresh, well-priced with marginal grunge yet homey, easy, non-fa, ultra-casual with above average wines by the glass and commendable beer choices. Do I, Snorkel Bob, like it? Yes.

## KIHATA RESTAURANT—$ to $$$$
115 Lower Paia in Paia, Maui
(808) 579-9035
11-1:30, 5-9 Tues-Sun, closed Mon

Kihata, across Hana Highway from the Fishmarket, is Post Modern Paia, fonky but neat and 1 of my, Snorkel Bob's, favorites, despite its high prices. The local-style chicken yakitori is impeccable, and the true bellweather of any Japanese restaurant is its ability to achieve the void through miso soup. Less is more, and Kihata miso leaves you with nothing but a warm, good feeling. Add 1 scoop rice and macaroni salad on the side. Lunch, dinner, take-out.

## FUKUSHIMA STORE
Haiku Rd. in Haiku, Maui
(808) 575-2762
6:30-8 Mon-Sat, 6:30-5 Sun

In downtown Haiku, Fukushima makes hotdogs like you never did. Steamum just right and serve with mustardketchup, pickle, onion for 85¢. Cold beverage and good wine and champagne selection here too.

## HAIKU MART
Haiku Rd.
(808) 575-2028
6:30 a.m.-9 p.m. Mon-Fri, open later sometimes Sat & Sun

Haiku Mart hamburgers are to hamburgers what Fukushima Store hotdogs are to hotdogs. Some towns got it wired. And Haiku Mart has an excellent wine and beer selection and deli buffet stocked daily with impressive stuffs prepared on the spot.

MAKAWAO STEAKHOUSE—$$$ to $$$$
3612 Baldwin Ave. in Makawao, Maui
(808) 572-8711
5-9 Mon-Thurs, 5-10 Fri, 5-9:30 Sat

The Makawao Steakhouse is upcountry with a 5-seat bar and an excellent seafood, beef and foul menu that I, Snorkel Bob, can recommend with conviction, without compunction or reservation. Furthermore, the place is comfortable with neither pretense nor foo-foo nor fa fa. I, Snorkel Bob, like it best after dinner when the crowd thins, the void eases in.

CASANOVA ITALIAN RESTAURANT & DELI—$ to $$$$
1188 Makawao Ave. in Makawao, Maui
(808) 572-0220
11:30-2, 5:30-9:30 Daily

Casanova Deli is adequate. The congealed pastas can be nuked back to presentable condition and are served with cold salads at room temperature. Casanova is also a good espresso place if you don't mind a noseful of B.O. and patchouli and all these white guys in knit do-caps. If you do mind you could go outside onto the deck, but then you get the noseful and the earful on art, life, meaning, and don't forget The Universe from people who kick that sort of thing around. Gobbledegook mostly, and often a rude scene, but always a scene.

Casanova Restaurant is a kick in the ass. I, Snorkel Bob, stepped inside and an extremely hip fellow at the door, who looked like he shopped exclusively on Melrose Avenue, said softly, "That's 4 dollars." What's 4 dollars? "Admission. It's 4 dollars to get in." Oh boy, I, Snorkel Bob, thought, a floor show. But rubbernecking inside 1 time showed up nothing but a handful of other hip shoppers rubbernecking me, Snorkel Bob, right back. I, Snorkel Bob, theorize that the females sized me up for you know what, and the males sized me up to see if I might be female. I, Snorkel Bob, mean that the place looks to be hetero, even though many of the fellows there wear radical-hip-waiter pigtails, shirts and pants that look like jammies and black leather shoes with paper thin soles. They didn't recognize me, Snorkel Bob, at night and out of water, no mask, no fins, no snorkel.

But anyway I, Snorkel Bob, asked the hip fellow at the door if it was 4 bucks just to drink a beer at the bar. "It's after 9," he said. Oh! Stupid me, Snorkel Bob. What the hey, 4 bucks is hardly enough money to hold up a story for. And the ultra-hip fellow at the door wasn't a bad fellow. As the dollars unfolded he told me confidential, "It's a happening here. We have waiting lines an hour long." I, Snorkel Bob, didn't press him for where exacalackaly is here; he looked so sincere.

But then at the bar another soft-spoken dude served a draft beer that looked fresh from a hot dryer (5 [five]–1, 2, 3, 4, 5 ounces.) He made excellent eye contact and nearly whispered, "That's 2.50." I looked 1 time to my left, then 1 time to my right, then straight ahead at the dude so he could go ahead and yell Surprise! and the party could start. But the dude done gone. 9 bucks for a beer was all I, Snorkel Bob, could think—that's $4 at the door and $2.50 each for 2 half-beers—with all these people glancing my way like they were trying to figure out what I, Snorkel Bob, was thinking, or something. Glub glub glub is what I, Snorkel Bob, wanted to tell them. That's what a full-time, hard-core, died-in-the-wool, bonafide, Olympic-class, ☆☆☆☆☆, waterlogged, fish-eyed, wrinkle-skinned, gill-breathing, slippery sucker like me thinks.

Oh hell; I, Snorkel Bob, went ahead on and blew the budget and ordered up the other half of my beer. But after spinning through the time warp turnstile at mach 9, Makawao to West Hollywood, I didn't have the stomach to check out the menu.

Back at the door inside 20 minutes, I, Snorkel Bob, asked the hip door fellow if It had happened yet, or was it still only after 9? By this time he was surrounded by another equally hip fellow, the bouncer. You can always tell the bouncer. He's the guy who looks like 1 of the floats in Macy's Parade, i.e. inflated, i.e. maybe overinflated with, for effect, the buttons on his shirt hanging on by the skin of their teeth. The 1st hip fellow turned quick to the 2nd hip fellow and they talked low, looking both ways, not like a surprise party was about to start but more like a deal was going down. The bouncer, to my amazement, inhaled. Then the 1st hip fellow peeled off 4 singles and gave them back to me, Snorkel Bob. "If you come back," he said. "You have to pay." Oh, I'll be back, I, Snorkel Bob, replied. But maybe not tonight. Or tomorrow.

But I, Snorkel Bob, went back, in the spirit of fair shakes. The same fellow worked the door, worn by time to quasi-hip; it's so tough to stay current in a stump-broke town like Makawao. At the door he went snake-eyed, stared off and spoke his revised mantra. "15 dollars. Different tonight. Must have a ticket. A show tonight." I, Snorkel Bob, said, "Wellll..." But he was somewhere else, long gone.

They call it Cashanova's in the neighborhood but I, Snorkel Bob, call it a shame shame shame.

### KITADA'S KAU KAU CORNER—$
Baldwin Ave. in Makawao, Maui
(808) 572-7241
6:30 a.m.-1:30 p.m. Daily

Kitada's has a local kitchen serving local-fare, plate-lunch style. THIS is kau kau.

## KOMODA'S BAKERY & STORE—$
3674 Baldwin Ave. in Makawao, Maui
(808) 572-7261
7-5 Mon-Fri, 7-2 Sat

Up the street from Kitada's and famous for malasadas (like donut holes, hot, greasy, dipped in sugar.) Tuesday is special malasada day, with other famous donuts available too.

## KULA LODGE—$ to $$$$
Haleakala Hwy in Kula, Maui
(808) 878-1535
6:30-11:15 a.m. Mon-Sat, 6:30 a.m.-3 p.m. Sun, 4:45-9 Daily

Up the mountain maybe 3500' and on the way to the summit of Haleakala. Mediocre fare with a high price and excellent view before dark. But even after dark the air is cool and crisp and an invigorating change from the heat, dust and tourism down in the flats, if you catch my, Snorkel Bob's, drift.

## HALIIMAILE GENERAL STORE—$$ to $$$$
900 Haliimaile Rd. in Haliimaile, Maui
(808) 572-2666
11-2:30 Mon-Fri, 5:30-9:30 Mon-Sun, Brunch 10-2:30 Sun

This place had a radio ad comparing it to Maxim's in Paris and Tavern On The Green in New York. But I, Snorkel Bob, been to New York, Paris and then some. You who been too, know you can walk those towns past nondescript places where, inside, some sax and bass are jamming casual and 20 people are relaxing over a cocktail. That's what I, Snorkel Bob, call happening. I, Snorkel Bob, got another call for a place with heavy media promo, bumper to bumper and shoulder to shoulder, see and be seen: crowded. In fact, I, Snorkel Bob, got a great idea for a bumper sticker: New York, Paris, Tokyo, London. Get it? It ain't Hailiimaile any more than it's Brownsville, Lodi, Bakersfield or Jessup.

But again keep in mind that every now and then I, Snorkel Bob, press my luck going from inside the reef to outside the reef—read the surge wrong and slide across on too little water, and all those scratches and gouges down my chest and belly, all those lumps and bumps cause a frame of mind I, Snorkel Bob, call Snorkel PMS. So I, SB, took my friend, Matt Roving, there. He said, "The beer is cold enough, but $6 apple pie is outrageous." That Matt Roving, always plowing up the hyperbole. I explained that it wasn't apple pie at all. It was Apple Tart. "That reminds me of when I had a job as a semiprestidigitator," he said. "I don't know. I

185

think that pie was worth $2.50, maybe $3. Maybe even $3.75 considering apples and all. But $6 is a reach, don't you think?"

"Hey!" I, Snorkel Bob, reminded him. "Don't forget the atmosphere!" Hailiimaile General Store would be considered stridently average in America, but you have to allow some credit for this kind of song and dance in Hailiimaile. Don't you?

# OAHU

RESTAURANT ROW occupies the 500 block of Ala Moana Boulevard between Punchbowl and South Street. Valet parking is $3, or $2 with shin guards. THIS is urban glitz in ultra-pop agglomeration with outdoor bars—The Cantina, Trattoria Manzo and The Row. NYN stands for Nothing You Need, a Sharper Image knock-off with little wooden jeeps for $35 with real suspension systems so when you run them through the sand you can feel the smooth ride in your hand.

NYN also has a faaabulous selection of potpourri jars and some little wooden airplanes just like the little wooden jeeps. They were 1 of the first with the print that's common as dog dukey now, the 1 showing the funky diner with neon over the window, and inside is Elvis as a soda jerk, and sitting at the bar is James Dean, Marilyn Monroe and The Hump. Forlorn down-and-outers, they shared the nitty gritty camaraderie of street-smart survivors. It was a scene from another, inverted universe, where these 4 were never famous but lived private lives just like the characters they portrayed. In the Restauran-Row universe it was only kitsch at the high end, $300. The price would have been right if I, Snorkel Bob, was airbrushed in there on a bar stool too. Then again, I, Snorkel Bob, lack the common requisite for that group portrait, i.e. rigor mortis, i.e. I, Snorkel Bob, still have a few more fins to kick, a few more bubbles to glug.

I, Snorkel Bob, did impulse on a bumpy little glass candle holder that fills with water and then all the dents and holes shimmer in candle light. It made me, Snorkel Bob, go all goose bumpy, aquiver and ashimmer myself. Alas and alack, my date was unimpressed. In fact, she broke a Superbowl record with 1) a headache, 2) the really heavy part of her period and 3) she just remembered she had to go home and wash her hair. Hey, it was only $17, not counting drinks and dinner.

KAPAHULU AVENUE, on the other hand, retains that lost, loving feeling of the old neighborhood before Honolulu got hyped, scammed, gouged. It's only a boulevard of cafes and shops off the end of Waikiki, into the neighborhoods near Diamondhead. Most cosmically karmically concentric to the Kapahulu realm is the existence in time and place of me, Snorkel Bob, at 700 Kapahulu Ave., at the corner of Date Street and nary a shuffle from:

## HELEN'S CHINESE FOOD—$
804 Kapahulu Ave. in Honolulu, Oahu
(808) 737-2055
9-9 Tues-Sun, closed Monday

Helen makes it happen here with 14 soups, 11 beefs, 10 chickens (you should know by now how I, Snorkel Bob, feel about eating ducks), 8 seafoods, 13 porks, 5 eggs, 4 chop sueys, 3 tofus and don't forget the fried noodles, look fun, wun ton, gau gee rice and, oh, the family lunch and dinner. Sitdown, family-style, old kind, nice, Helen's, homey setting, home-cooked Chinese.

## ONO HAWAIIAN FOODS—$
726 Kapahulu Ave. in Honolulu, Oahu
(808) 737-2275
11-7:30 Mon-Sat, closed Sun

Ono is only a 1/2 block up from me, Snorkel Bob, and boy oh boy oh boy. Mondo Combo for $5.75 gots laulau, kalua pig, pipi kaula, lomi salmon, haupia & rice or poi. But, large poi will run you 15¢ extra.

## RAMA THAI—$$ on up
802 Kapahulu Ave. in Honolulu, Oahu
(808) 735-2789
5-10 Daily

Nobody likes Rama Thai, they love it, especially the green papaya salad and chicken curry. Wednesday is buffet night for $13.95. Open for dinner only. Take-out too.

## KEO'S—$ to $$$
625 Kapahulu Ave. in Honolulu, Oahu
(808) 737-8240
5-10 Daily

Keo's also serves great Thai at popular prices. 1 other Keo's besides up the street from me, Snorkel Bob, is in Ward Center on Ala Moana (596-0020). Ward Keo's is open for lunch too.

## LA BAMBA—$$

847 Kapahulu Ave. in Honolulu, Oahu
(808) 737-1956
11-2, 5-9:30 Sun-Fri, closed Sat

Very good Mexican here, most casual, owner operated, and if you bring the sauce, the Triple Sec and the ice, La Bamba will lend you the blender and extension cord. Now this is my, Snorkel Bob's, kind of camping out.

Yet, however and although La Bamba got my, Snorkel Bob's, vote for very best Mexican in Oahu for years upon years, another truth suddenly surfaced, which was and is that Mexican and many if not most of all other restaurants in Paradise use **LARD** in everything. Can you imagine? There oughta be a law. Then again, with enforcement, who in Paradise could ever get anything done? Meanwhile, though La Bamba still tastes most excellent, the guilt-free and ever flavorful alternative resides only 1 block over and a few blocks closer to Waikiki and Diamond head from my, Snorkel Bob's, place. That alternative is:

## BUENO NALO—$ & ☆☆☆☆☆

3045 Monsarrat Ave. (which veers off Kalakaua just past the zoo. The cross street is Kanaina, at the base of Diamond Head.)
And also at 41-865A Kalanianaole Hwy. in Waimanalo
(808) 259-7186 and (808)735-8818

"We use no lard."—Lori & Andy Doka, owners.
Hey! The place is no big deal. No atmosphere, too much lighting and chrome and Formica overload would make it forgettable, if not for the honest fare that fills you up, keeps you going and doesn't feel like a truck parked on your chest when your done. EUREKA! For those of you too young or too modern to know what lard is, it's decocted pig fat. It comes in a #10 can and looks like opaque Vaseline. It will hurt you at the very least.

Bueno Nalo has served healthy for 20 years in Waimanalo in what used to be country between Makapuu and Kailua on the other side of Oahu. It still does near Makai Research Pier, Lani Kai and other good snorkel spots. Now you can enjoy a 7-Layer Vegetarian Wrap, Mahi Chimichanga Grandé, tacos, fajitas, pizza, tamales—the whole enchilada! In the old neighborhood!

I, SNORKEL BOB, AM GRATEFUL FOR BUENO NALO. Otherwise, it would be bitch bitch bitch. So in spite of the sterile setting and nonambience, BN gets this edition of Reality's **BEST OF SHOW AWARD YAHOO!** It made me, Snorkel Bob, feel good, and then you know what happened? I, SB, shuffled right next door (from the Diamond Head Bueno

Nalo) to discover that Lori Doka is not only wrapped way too tight (4 kids, 2 restaurants, competitive rough-water swimming to relax), but she also owns and operates:

**THE JUICE SPOT—$**
3045 Monsarrat Ave in Honolulu
(808) 739-7768

A good smoothie can keep you going and shouldn't be hard to find, but it is. The J Spot gives you 28 combos hovering under $4 that include 2 extra ingredients and for 50¢ each, you can add all the ingredients you want, including but not limited to:

> Bee pollen, brewer's yeast, calcium, egg protein, ginseng, lecithin, protein powder, rice bran, wheat bran or germ, oat bran, vitamin C, the power pack AND spirulina (not to be confused with pond scum or parrot squat but also not to be added lightly to an otherwise tasty smoothie).

I, SB, got the Tour de France with the Power Pack and knew exackalackaly how much poly, mono and saturated fat, calories, protein, carbs, dietary fiber, selenium, magnesium and vitamins A, B, C & X, Y, Z were flowing down my, SB's, gullet. 1 of these elixirs can fuel your love for the whole wide world all the way to happy hour, when things will get even better.

**OK CHO**
McCully Shopping Center (at Kapiolani & McCully)
1960 Kapiolani Blvd., 2nd floor, in Honolulu, Hawaii
(808) 947-2922

That's oak-choh, and it's dreamsicle pink vinyl with complimenting Formica splendiferous chrome trim and red and white checked vests on the waitpersons. And no, your lysergic acid diethylamide is not flashing back; the clocks are running in reverse. **THIS** is Korean. The yaki niku is superb, and the garnish is excellent and extravagant. Each table has a hole in the center, into which goes the hot coals, over which goes the grills, onto which go the squids, mushrooms, onions, shrimps, garlics, chickens, beefs and on and on.

It's a culinary adventure with exotic stops like Korean miso, which is like Japanese miso with some Belle Paise, fish sauce and jalapeños added. It's a good thing this place has neither A) smoke alarms or B) automatic fire sprinklers.

Once the grill heats up you go like hell or burn it all to a crisp. The denouement is at the end when you sit back sated and they take the coals away and it feels better than getting off an uptown bus. Ok Cho makes a trip to Honolulu worthwhile.

## MICHEL'S—$$$$ (+$)
The Colony Surf Hotel at 2895 Kalakaua Ave. in Honolulu, Oahu
(808) 923-6552
7-11, 6-9 Daily, Sun Brunch from 10-1

Also in the Colony Surf, in the finest fa fa de blah blah tradition. It used to be jackets and dresses only here, but what with steep growth curve on grunge, Michel's is down to jackets and dresses optional, or "dressy casual," as the man said. The top-drawer fellows at the door still set the tone with the softest how-do-you-do you ever heard. I, Snorkel Bob, must have appeared too casual, undressy, but it was okay. "Not to worry, Sir, if it's only a drink you want," said the silky host. I, Snorkel Bob, was led to a far corner not exactly behind the baby grand but close to it. Did I, Snorkel Bob, mind? Not on your patent leather, because the corner looked out on linen, crystal and perfect sunset to the horizon. Meanwhile, a whole gang of black-tie fellows seemed intent on my, Snorkel Bob's, every need, nay want in what can only be called le mode de plus parfait.

You will blow a wad o' dough here! But, it won't hurt, i.e. painless, if you arrive an hour before sundown and have an aperitif. Then have another. Then maybe 1 mo.

Then consider: steak tartare (30), sashimi (19), fresh Beluga caviar (86), fresh avo stuffed with crab (14). These are from the 1st section: Les Pupus. The ( ) is peu peu notation for $, because $ is such a gross, street-level symbol. (Get it?).

Then come the Salades, Potages, Garde-mangers, Legumes (avec Les Artichaui, Les Asperges, Epinard Frais, et Les Champignons, sauteed with shallots), Les Favoris, Viandes, Grillades, Rotis, Volaille, et Les Fruits de Mer, by which time the tails du Lobster don't look so steep at only (48).

I, Snorkel Bob, am here to say: This place is as ritz as it gets, anywhere, anytime. And oh! the salad bar! Only kidding. Dinner for 2 will run you 2 bills easy, 4 if you go slow and get careless on the wine list. Of course it's overpriced. For example, (12) for 1/2 dozen oysters is oysters at (2) per.

The waitgentleman is the nicest guy you ever met in your whole life and is happier to see you than your own mother would be. He is warm and caring and says Thank You at random intervals, which in time makes sense; he's grateful you're diving into the Cash Liability Hole! It gives him job security. With wine, your date can go to (1400) in a wink, (2,600) if you swing with 2 bottles. That's at (1200) the bottle for either the Chateau d'Yquem 1967 or the Chateau Margaux.

Plenty good grape juice in the pittance (30) to (35) range too, and I, Snorkel Bob, unequivocally, unabashedly, remorselessly and possibly urgently advise you, my friends, to let go. Let it fall away, in layers and all at once. Forget it. Leave it behind you, which is where it is. Face forward, with courage and happiness, and Dive Dive Dive!

Hey, you came this far. Moreover, the sashimi might be (19), but it is (dare I, SB, say it?) perfect. If the budget is too tight for a fling, that's okay—hang out happy hour with beer and oysters and get out easy for a (C), no sweat.

They have breakfast and lunch too, but I, Snorkel Bob, experienced fear at the prospect. Can you imagine a bill and a 1/2 for 2 over-easy like you never had before?

All in the Ward Warehouse, 1050 Ala Moana Blvd., between downtown and Waikiki, are:

**YUM YUM TREE—$ to $$**
(808) 592-3580
7 a.m.-11 p.m. Daily, to 1 a.m. Fri & Sat

Yum Yum has 4 other locations too: Kahala Mall, Westridge Center, Pali Palms Plaza and in Mililani Town Center. It's like Marie Callender's with a dangerous pie arsenal, and otherwise standard bill of fare.

**KINKAID'S—$ to $$$$**
(808) 591-2005
11:15-5 Lunch, 5-10 Dinner, Daily

This local favorite (formerly Horatio's) has a good steak and seafood grill, obliquely cut carrots and quasi-foo sideflies. I, Snorkel Bob, eat here with no hesitation. I do think twice, however, about the famous burnt creme. It's custard in a pewter dish with brown sugar, leading directly to bliss, then to guilt, toothache and fat. Only the name has changed.

**THE JUICE STOP—$**
(808) 597-8254
10-9 Mon-Sat, 10-4 Sun

For a mere pittance the guy slices apples and feeds them to his 4 megaton juicer for the freshest, cleanest pickmeup available in all of Ward Warehouse. Chowders and smoothies too make this place a rare and extreme ☆☆☆☆ stop. Not to be confused with The Juice Spot (above).

## QUINTERO'S—$ to $$
1102 Piikoi St. in Honolulu, Oahu
(808) 593-1561
11:30-3 Mon,Tues, Thurs, Fri; 4:30-10 everyday except Wed

Quintero's is among the best Mexican in town. The owners, cooks and groceries are all Mexican, with emphasis on freshness, presentation, taste sensation. Closed Wednesdays. (But do they use lard?)

## COLUMBIA INN—$
645 Kapiolani Blvd. in Honolulu, Oahu
(808) 596-0757
6 a.m.-11 p.m. Sun-Thurs, until midnight Fri & Sat
Breakfast, Lunch, and Dinner

Unchanged since '41, the diner and bar have been favorites for the duration. Complete dinner @ $6-8 is home-style, less for fries and a chocolate malt. Famous, this place, for shrimp tempura and local history, where innocence eavesdrops on corruption and vice versa. Right by the Honolulu Newspaper Agency, this place can be pivotal in the action, the info, the rendezvous, the chance meeting, the glance, the wink, the furrow, the knowing smile. Many international personalities hang immortal on the walls, including Frank Delima and Fasi.

## DOONG KONG LAU—$
100 N. Beretania St. in Honolulu, Oahu
(808) 531-8833
9:30-9 Daily

In the Chinatown Cultural Plaza with all your traditional Chinese favorites, mild or hot and spicy. Specialité de la maison is Hakka style. Extra very good, this 1.

## WON KEE—$$
100 N. Beretania St. in Honolulu, Oahu
(808) 524-6877
11:30-2:30 Lunch, 5-10 Dinner, Daily

Also in the Chinatown Cultural Plaza, Won Kee specializes in seafood. Also ☆☆☆☆☆ excellenté, this 1.

**MATTEO'S—$$$$**
364 Seaside Ave. in Honolulu, Oahu
(808) 922-5551
5:30-11 Dinner

In Waikiki advertising Classic Italian Cuisine in an intimate fine dining atmosphere, is better than advertising, say, All The Foo-Foo Your Plastic Can Stand.

It's good though, maybe even great, maybe even worth the price. Reservations required.

**JAMESON'S BY THE SEA—$$$ to $$$$**
62-540 Kam Hwy in Haleiwa, Oahu
(808) 637-4336
11-5 Lunch, 5-9 Dinner Mon-Fri; 9-12 & 5-9 Sat & Sun

Jameson's is kind of the best restaurant on the North Shore. I, Snorkel Bob, mean, how critical can you get that far out in the boonies? It's pricey, but what a view.

**THE CROUCHING LION—$$$ to $$$$**
51-666 Kam Hwy in Kaaawa, Oahu
(808) 237-8511
11-4 Lunch, 5-9 Dinner, Daily

The Lion is an old favorite but was better before the sheet-rock annex and parking lot jammed with tour buses. Still okay, this 1, especially if the tour buses are gone, and it's Winter, and they have a fire.

In Quick & Easy (look out for your life) am:

**ZIPPY'S–$**

They're everywhere and only qualify for my, Snorkel Bob's, Reality Guide to Hawaii because heavy proliferation generates temptation. Here are the pros and cons, high side 1st:
    1) Zippy's is cheap; $5 fills your tank.
    2) It's a rare chance to fully experience post-modern da kine;
        chili/rice, saimin, diet cola.
    3) Napoleon's Bakery alongside isn't bad.
    4) Open 24 hours, when most other places be shut.
    5) Breakfast good.

Liabilities are:
1) Sometimes wish tank still empty.
2) Sometimes da kine needs Pepto Biiizzzzmal back.

It ain't all bad, if you be careful with your menu impulse.

**FLAMINGO CHUCK WAGON—$ to $$**
1015 Kapiolani Blvd. in Honolulu, Oahu
(808) 596-0066
11-1:45, 5-9 Mon-Sat; 5-9 Sun

The Flamingo has a special called All You Can Eat that I, Snorkel Bob, hesitate profiling since any of you falling into that hole obviously need a lesson in a big way. It's stainless steel serving bins mostly, with a less durable server. They have a big steel bowl of fried chicken and a standing roast and 2 rows of vegetables from #10 cans.

# SUSHI PLACES

## KAUAI

### KIIBO
2991 Umi Street in Lihue, Kauai
(808) 245-2650
11-9 Mon-Sat, Lunch and Dinner; Dinner only Sun

Simplicity approaching complexity in the transcendent mode, like the Lotus/ when it falls in Autumn/ sends a ripple/ of gratitude. Not to mention fresh and clean.

### KINTARO JAPANESE RESTAURANT
4-370 Kuhio Hwy in Kapaa, Kauai
(808) 822-3341
5:30-9:30 Mon-Sat, closed Sun

Calmness emotes from the simple sitdown here; the scent, the glimmer, the hint, the pulse. Excellence in sushi in Kapaa.

### HANAMALU TEA HOUSE & ARA'S SUSHI BAR
Hwy 56 in Hanamaulu, Kauai
(808) 245-2511

Sushi is served at the Hanamaulu Restaurant Tea House and/or Ara's Sushi Bar, both inside the cafe, which is 1 mile north of Lihue.

# BIG ISLAND

### YU SUSHI
75-5770 Alii Dr. in Kailua, Hawaii
(808) 326-5653
5:30-9 Daily

Samurai sushi here, served with Perfection and Honor. Flying wedge sushi bar takes on 15 front line samurai at once! Victory arises from flawless cut, pickled ginger, wasabi smoldering with the heat of no heat. I, Snorkel Bob, seek calmness of mind, calmness of body as small beads rise on brow and roll in rivulets to the mighty stream...Nevermind! Let go. Eat, even in the heart of the hubbub (Clone 39).

### IMARI
Hilton Waikoloa Village on the Kohala Coast, Hawaii
(808) 885-1234
6-9:30 Daily

I, Snorkel Bob, enjoyed the atmosphere so much and had such a good time that I, SB, am willing to give Sushi Imari 1 mo chance. Stay tuned.

# MAUI

### HAKONE–$$ to $$$$
The Maui Prince Hotel in Makena, Maui
(808) 874-1111
6-9:30 Mon-Sat, closed Sun & Mon—Reservations required

Hakone is the best sushi place I, Snorkel Bob, ever visited—strong words from a frequent pissant like me, Snorkel Bob.

The Prince Hotel chain is worldwide and known for decor, comfort, landscaping and general beauty. The Maui Prince is reasonably (for a fah

fah de bla bla luxury hotel) priced at $250-$390 dollars a night for a partial view to oceanfront room. But the place has had a solitary feeling since it opened a few years ago. Maybe they don't advertise, or maybe the architecture casts the illusion. Fact is, it feels empty as a shallow reef in a falling barometer, so it attracts a guy like me, Snorkel Bob. And you may be hard pressed to find anything more ticklish to my, Snorkel Bob's, fancy, than my very own, private hotel, which is what The Maui Prince feels like.

What often makes a place memorable is a scene or a story, which is what I, Snorkel Bob, will tell:

Once upon a time there was a vast and epic hotel with a lobby of koa panels and woven Japanese rugs and art and flowers rounding a main courtyard with tropical landscaping. A delicate stream originated in the boulders there and flowed to a shallow pond 3' deep where many big koi lived. The pond spanned the courtyard in front of the boulders. Its embankments of pea gravel were raked like the bed of a Zen garden.

Above the pond on a gentle slope was a grassy knoll, where, evenings, a beautiful woman played piano most melodiously, evoking a perfect distant place. Beside her, a handsome man accompanied on the violin, candle-lit and with a spotlight too. A nautical legend visited once and got goose bumps.

Anyway, with a big old pond like that out in the country, the neighborhood frogs were very happy. In fact, they flat out got carried away with so much new habitat—and landscaping and classical music to boot. It came to a head when the damn frogs got thick as flies, so thick their wobbop, wobbop, wobbop drowned out the violin, threatened the piano.

So The Maui Prince got these 2 guys in hip waders—frog giggers is what they were, what they are—to wade out among the koi and perfect water lilies and gig. The giggers went when the frogs got sassy, just after dark, just after the gal on piano and her buddy on the gitfiddle got warmed up. In the end it was carnage: Dada da da da wobbop splat. Shoo be doo doo de wobbop splat.

Just thinking about it makes me, Snorkel Bob, hard pressed hungry for some sushi.

Which is what brought us here in the 1st place. The sushi chefs at Hakone are the best. Go in twice, even if it's 2 days in a row and they'll say, Hey, long time, no see, or some such charming American idiom. These guys come up with extra fancy sushis everyday, and even though the prices are maybe 15% higher, freshness, skill and atmosphere are higher than that. Can you tell? I, Snorkel Bob, like this place. Have an uni on me.

**SANSEI SUSHI**–$$$ on up
In The Shops at Kapalua
669-6286
Mon, Tues, Wed, Sat & Sun 5:30-11 with 25% off 5:30-6 & after 10. Thurs & Fri 5:30-2 (karaoke) with 50% off 5:30-6

Commonly regarded as the best sushi on the Westside. I, Snorkel Bob, shun such claims. But it is very good. Also very pricey without the discount.

**HARRY'S SUSHI BAR**—$$ to $$$$
100 Wailea Iki Pl. in Wailea, Maui
(808) 879-7677
5:30-midnight

Harry's is often very good.

**KOBE**
136 Dickenson St. in Lahaina, Maui
(808) 667-5555
5:30-10 for Dinner, sushi bar open until midnight

I, Snorkel Bob, had the Dynamite: scallops, vegetables and mystery mayo(!). It was very good. Also a sitdown Japanese restaurant, this place.

# OAHU

### YANAGI SUSHI
762 Kapiolani Blvd. in Honolulu, Oahu
(808) 597-1525
11-2 Lunch, 5:30-2 a.m. Dinner & Sushi bar, Daily; closed Sun

I, Snorkel Bob, consider this place close to Tokyo with its full Japanese menu. You may sit at the sushi bar or a table and be equally confused, but don't worry; alongside each item is a small picture so gaijin won't look too stupid. The exotics are here, but don't worry, it's not the hardcore disgusting stuff the Japanese love to stuff their gobs with, or maybe I, SB, just didn't know how to order nearly-hatched chickens. Arrrghh. It's very popular and a reservation won't hurt. Dining room and sushi bar.

## YOU MEKKA YOU OWN

The most common sashimi is ahi, which is blue fin or yellow fin tuna. You may have read awful stories about suburbanites getting nasty 20' worms stuck up their dukey chutes from eating sashimi. I, Snorkel Bob, don't doubt those stories, but what you should know is that those things come from A) exotic fish that are B) old or C) caught in polluted water. What is exotic? Isn't it obvious that speckled toad fish is farther out there than blue fin tuna? Not to say that any fish can be taken for granted. Fresh is the key.

If you eat fresh fish in Hawaii, especially ahi, you won't have a problem. I, Snorkel Bob, could visit Nebraska and have a ham sandwich from Kankakee that's 4 days old with plenty mayo in July and get sick like a dog. (But it looked so good!)

I, Snorkel Bob, have a friend in Ka Lae who is amazed that he can get pork steak for 1/2 off just because it's a few days old. He says he can put it on the counter and draw a circle around it and go away for an hour and it will walk out of the circle. Nevermind! he says. Cook it! Anyway, you get the picture. You eat good groceries, you feel good.

You can get good ahi at most local grocery stores throughout the islands. Safeway and Foodland can be good most of the time. Don't be afraid to ask, How old is that fish? I, Snorkel Bob, promise: It's not an indelicate question in the proper setting. I, SB, know of a supermarket chain here selling baaaad salmon, but that sort of thing is so easy to avoid, it looks so brown.

Freshness is just as easy to sense; if the slightest doubt rises, I, Snorkel Bob'll go ahead and smell that thang 1 mo time.

Ahi comes in steaks for cooking or blocks for sashimi. Get wasabi (green horseradish, powder or paste). If you get the powder, pour it on a plate and add water drops and mix it into a paste. Get cabbage, shoyu, chop sticks and a sharp knife. Slice everything thin, add shoyu and eat. And drink. Oh, get sake too. Or beer. You never had it like this in America.

A step beyond is aku. No sashimi this. Aku is for poke, diced in 1/2" cubes. I, Snorkel Bob, like aku for a change, but ahi poke shouldn't be sneezed at if no aku they got. A most joyous recipe is: Buy 1/2 pound of poke, ahi or aku—poke with onions, sesame poke, plain poke, shoyu poke. Put it in a bowl, then add a few shakes soy sauce, a few shakes cayenne pepper, a couple 3 tablespoon sesame oil, a smidgen or 2 sesame seeds. Stirumup. Eat. Not for everybody, only the lucky few.

Or, you can get fresh fish quick and easy at:

**SMP FISH MARKET**
45-1048 Kam Hwy in Kaneohe, Oahu
(808) 235-0048
9-9 Daily

SMP has aku poke and some stuff that looks like clam gizzards in seaweed and lizardfish eggs with unborn quail on top.

# KAUAI

**FISH EXPRESS**
Hwy 56 (3343 Kuhio Hwy) in Lihue, Kauai
(808) 245-9918
10-7 Daily

Ahi sushi can run $8 to $18 a pound, depending on weather, the catch and greed. It's higher in Winter.

**SAFEWAY**
Hwy 56 (4-831 Kuhio Hwy) in Kapaa, Kauai
(808) 822-2464

The ahi sashimi is usually good. Safeway's cone sushi 3-pack runs about $2.50, but I, Snorkel Bob, never tried it on account of the packaging had to run a 1/2 day, unless they did it local, and then it took a day and a 1/2. And who needs old rice and soggy nori? I, Snorkel Bob'm still waiting to try Safeway's 2nd selection, but I mention it here for the college educated who might think objectivity requires a taste: Spam Musubi Roll-Ups in a package (no kidding) for $1.39 in the deli department. Have at it.

# MAUI

**MAUI SEAFOODS**
800 Eha St. in Wailuku, Maui
(808) 242-6099
7-2 Mon-Fri, 7-12 Sat, closed Sun

In the Georgia Carpet Building, Wailuku Industrial Park. Best to call ahead for a prepared order, since hours sometimes vary.

**NAGASAKO FISH CO.**
1276 Lower Main St. in Wailuku, Maui
(808) 242-4073
6:15-11 a.m.

Call in advance.

# ESPRESSO & FRESH-ROASTED COFFEE PLACES

But first: A WORD ABOUT KONA COFFEE

It's good, if you can find the real McCoy. Mark Twain said:

"The ride through the district of Kona to Kealakekua Bay took us through the famous coffee section. I think Kona Coffee has a richer flavor than any other, be it grown where it may and call it by what name you please."—Letters From Hawaii, 1866

He found it. But that was before Hawaii was stricken by modern greed and was forced to pass a law requiring all coffee bearing the name KONA COFFEE to contain AT LEAST 10% Kona coffee beans. The remaining 90% can be Juan Valdez's floor sweepings and often is. Oh, honor, and its woeful absence.

That is, after paying $16 a pound for so-called Kona Coffee from any grocery store in Paradise, you will recognize on first brew that it tastes like crap. What do you expect at 10%? Some brands sell the real thing for just as much, but at least it's real. You must ask around, just as you did to find out who alone dispenses the highest quality snorkel gear in the world, and who blows smoke up your butt at TERRIFIC SAVINGS!

Rancor aside, let me, Snorkel Bob, say that coffee just caught on here. People who bought property at 1,000-1,800' elevation above Kona and a little farther south too, mostly had 1 of 2 ideas. The 1st idea has been a problem since the missionaries 1st landed, i.e.: "Boy oh boy, if I buy this apparently worthless tropical bush now for a song, I can sell it soon for a symphony, maybe with a chorus line and an overture and a few ovations if I'm really lucky."

The 2nd reason is equally taxing but less devious: "Boy oh boy, I think I'll live here." Anyway, they tried growing a few things and had luck with avocados, papayas, coffee, some lettuce and a few radishes. Then came the caffeine achievers with their bold dreams for a new tomorrow, beginning with a double espresso. Visitors here soon recognized a different character of Kona coffee compared to Brazilian, Columbian or Turkish.

The next unfortunate wave rolled over yodeling, "Hai! Domo arigato. Coffee please, to go with Mickey Mouse and baseball."

The Japanese market now wants about 250 pounds of Kona beans for every pound available annually. That's why it costs more than it's worth, I mean really.

Anyway, the big problem with coffee has been the harvesting, since each tree yields beans in all 3 phases of development concurrently, green, orange and red. Only red beans are ready for roasting. But if you machine harvest, you lose 2/3 of your crop. So you have no choice but to hand-pick, but then you're looking at workman's comp, pension plans and major medical, besides untold future generations of state bureaucrats.

So now they're working on a robot taller than the trees (10') with 8 arms like an octopus, with a photo optic sensor at the end of each arm. Its little silicon brain thinks, "Red, pick it; green or orange, leave it."

Anyway, they've been working on it for years now, and I, Snorkel Bob, suspect we'll see it sometime in the 00's.

Meanwhile, annual production here is 1.5 to 2.2 million pounds a year, which pales next to Brazil's 3.3 billion pounds a year. That's gross! And it's according to Nikki Ferrari, proprietor of Hawaii Mountain Gold Coffee Plantation in Holualoa.

Ms. Nikki says that if all the Kona coffee was brewed at once, all the coffee drinkers in the world could have just 1 cup, which I, Snorkel Bob, think is about the same size as an elephant. (See Whale Watch, Chapter 1, for other ratio realities).

F.Y.I., coffee beans and their phases are:

Cherry: Ripe bean with a red coat like a cherry, only with 2 little beans inside.

Parchment: Coffee beans soaked in water overnight and then dried either by sun or in mechanical dryers, cherry membrane still on but no longer ruddy red.

Green: Next step, parchment (dried skin) is hulled, leaving bean ready for roasting, grinding, brewing, drinking, sinking, thinking, wonderin' what I'll do when I'm through tonight; smokin', mopin', maybe just hopin', that some little girl will walk on by. Don't want to be alone but I love my girl at home, I remember what my little girl said. She said, my my my, don't tell lies. Keep fidelity in yo head. My my my, don't tell lies, when you done you should go to bed. Then I said "Hi" like a spider to a fly, jump right ahead in my web...bobobobom... She was common, flirty, she looked about 30. I would have run away but I was on my own. She told me later she's a machine operator. She said she liked the way I held the microphone. Something my my, something something like a spider to a fly, jump right ahead and something...*

Where was I?...Where am I, Snorkel Bob?...

Peaberry: A mutation caused by poor pollination. 1 bean in the cherry fails while the other goes round. This is da kine #1 and most expensive. Peaberry reminds me, Snorkel Bob, of me, Snorkel Bob, and my twin brother, What's-his-name, who went to college and got a j j j jj jjo jjjJJOBBB!

Now that you know about coffee, here is where you may recharge your primaries, back-ups and after-burners on 4 islands.

*cf. Mick Jagger, *The Spider and the Fly*

# KAUAI

### KALAHEO COFFEE COMPANY
In Kalaheo, Kauai
(808) 332-5858
6-4 Mon-Fri, 6:30-4 Sat, 7-2 Sun

This is the closest Latté to Poipu, good or otherwise, and this 1 is very good. (See Eateries)

### ZELO'S BEACH HOUSE
Princeville Market Place in Princeville, Kauai
(808) 826-9700
11 a.m.-9:30 p.m. Sun-Thurs, to 10 Fri & Sat

Cafe Zelo's has an excellent roaster, A-1 beans and a coffee menu that can pump your buzz with some taste sensations. I, Snorkel Bob, recommend it if you are in the neighborhood and up for an eye opener.

### VILLAGE SNACK AND BAKERY SHOP
Ching Young Village Shopping Center in Hanalei, Kauai
(808) 826-6841
6-3 Daily

In 1 of my, Snorkel Bob's, favorite stretches of mixed free enterprise on Planet E, Ching Young Village is unspectacular, unextraordinary, unhyped, unlit, unpackaged, unspoiled. It's old, natural, simple, low-key, top quality. Imagine that. Get good'n buzzed, then stroll up the street and absorb. Grill open to 2, sandwiches served to 3.

**LAPPERT'S**
1-3555 Kaumualii Hwy. In Lihue, Kauai
(808) 335-6121
6 a.m.-10 p.m.

May cause gagging with the sugar smell since sugar and butter by the ton is the main deal at Lappert's, in ice cream and teeth-throbbing cookies. But the jo is par excellenté and suitable for me, SB, and you, my friends, with no complaints (aside from those preventilated.) Stores in Waimea, Kapaa and Koloa too.

# BIG ISLAND

## MAUNA LOA ROYAL KONA COFFEE MILL AND MUSEUM
Mamalahoa Hwy. (Hwy 11) in Honaunau, Hawaii
(808) 328-2511
8-5 Daily

Tough to beat for buzz addicts who want more more more in color, history, displays and of course caffeine! Decaf is here too, but the hard core will ask: Why bother?

This is an old-style plantation (sugar) house with a tin roof. So if you go there like I, SB, did, in a driving rain, you'll please your auditory receptors with a bass line dirge moving directly to the bone marrow from the roof. You'll please your tasters too.

Mauna Loa, however, is the main marketeer of "Kona blend." This stuff has been stepped on 90% with unextraordinary beans. Smaller growers want the Kona name ONLY on the real McCoy. But money and influence blend to brew real power (Mauna Loa is Big and Old as the missionary family who started it) and you may be left holding the bag of mostly cheap beans behind a mostly false label announcing Kona Coffee. But isn't that how it goes when the Lord's work follows the wrong profit?

Anyway, the Mauna Loa showplace is commercial but not bad. The commercial line is mostly a full range of boring aloha clothing, but the place has a rustic feeling in a monsoon. (Who'll stop the rain?) I, Snorkel Bob, got a great book here on Pele, the volcano goddess, as painted by Herb Kane, and 1 of those eency teency potted plants that everybody says will die in 2 days, but it was only $3.40. And guess what it was, the little baby tree? What it is? What it will be? Kona coffee. I, Snorkel Bob, water it everyday and mist it too and then give it just enough direct sunlight. We talk of Kona at the 1800' level and of the not-too-distant future, when we will pick, parch, husk, roast, brew and then together savor the golden buzz, crafted by me, Snorkel Bob, and the little tree that could and of course You-Know-Who.

They have old photos at MLRKCM&M and some excellent displays of the process. The roaster is right there for scrutiny and maybe, if you're in the snorkel and caffeine groove, you will see it operate. I, Snorkel Bob, never got my timing right on seeing the roaster roasting, but I, SB, suspect it's heavier action than paint drying, grass growing or watching the parking meters in downtown Hilo run down and pop up: "Violation."

And they have a commercial percolator with fresh Kona coffee that will likely lead to a memorable javacation.

Go south from Kona on Highway 11 about 15 miles. Look for the big red barnish building on the ocean side. When you see the tree-house in the parking lot, you'll know you're at the right place. No admission charge here.

## HOLUALOA CAFE
76-5900 Mamalahoa Hwy (11) in Holualoa, Hawaii
(808) 322-2233
6:30-5 Mon-Sat, closed Sun

A cerebral crowd hangs here, pumps up on espresso, thinks way too hard and often expresses the process audibly before going home, some to think some more, some to fingerpaint, others to write down that special feeling of a thing right when they were really feeling it. Owner Meggi Worbach sustains an uncluttered atmosphere, and they seem to like it, the arteests. I, Snorkel Bob, do too.

## HAWAII MOUNTAIN GOLD COFFEE PLANTATION & MAC NUT CO.
Rte 180 in Holualoa, Hawaii
(808) 326-1111 for info. or to order coffee
10-5 Daily

Back north along Mamalohoa Highway, Nikki Ferrari's place is tucked into a cloud on a rainy day and feels like you'd imagine, tucking into a cloud with a cup of excellent jo.

On a clear day, you're sitting on top of the world, and with 2 cups of rare brew you will feel like the Queen, or King, even. The place overviews everything. Closer in, it assays 5 acres of coffee trees with a perimeter of the biggest Macadamia nut trees I, Snorkel Bob, ever saw.

100 years old, this place. And now the beautiful Ms. Nikki has all her family chachkas in the front room, in case you're interested. The parlor overlooks the greenery and sits adjacent to the coffee counter. I, Snorkel Bob, 1st gave Nikki demerits for serving powdered coffee whitener with

her coffee. On 2nd thought, I perceived another perfect touch. Only a Philistine would sip this stuff any other way than straight-up black. I, Snorkel Bob, mean rich, smooth and flavorful, what Mrs. Olson tried to fake with her lies, lies, lies.

## ALOHA CAFE
Hwy 11 in Kainaliu, Hawaii
(808) 322-3383
8-8 Mon-Sat, 9-2 Sun

In the Aloha Theater near the town of Captain Cook, the Aloha Cafe serves good coffee and espresso drinks. This is a great place that calls a spade a spade. Under cappucino on the chalk board is Killercino. Can you resist it? I, Snorkel Bob, hope the homefolks at the Aloha will soon chalk up some Owsley Light or some Orange Sunshine Dark or maybe even some Purple Microdot Latté.

## THE COFFEE SHACK
83-5799 Mamalahoa Hwy (11) in Captain Cook, Hawaii
(808) 328-9555
6-5 deli, 8-5 retail store, Daily

The Coffee Shack gets beans direct from Captain Cook Coffee Co., ie, with hardly time between the picking and the roasting and the brewing and pouring—8 different beans and espresso coffee. They pour Kona coffee free and have pastries and sandwiches for a few bucks to balance the acid in your stomach. But it's worth it, considering the taste and freshness, roasting and bagging on the spot.

This place is exackalackaly 4.8 miles from Captain Cook Coffee Co. in Holualoa town. Look for a sign painted on the front of the coffee mill to verify, or perhaps modify, my, Snorkel Bob's, logistical coordinates. Set your trip-o-meters on 0. Ready, go. The quaint setting under roof, no walls, overlooks a lush tropical valley and Kealakekua Bay, 1 of my, Snorkel Bob's all-time favorite snorkel spots, giving this place the proximity and vibe you're looking for.

## KONA KAI FARMS and KONA KAI COFFEE BAR
Hwy 11 and 81-6379 S. Kona Belt Rd. in Kealakekua, Hawaii
(808) 323-2911 main office and (808) 322-2115
7:30-5 Mon-Fri

2 more great stops for relaxing and rebuzzing on the best java for many miles around.

## WAIMEA COFFEE COMPANY
Hwy 19 in Kamuela, Hawaii
(808) 885-4472
7-5 Mon-Fri, 8-4 Sat, closed Sun

Quiche? In cattle country? Nevermind, this place serves cowboy espresso too. So it's marginal fa. What? Do you need rough and tumble all the time? Across the road from Edelweiss (see Eateries).

## CRUISIN' COFFEE
Kamehameha Sq. in Kona, Hawaii
(808) 329-0992

Great coffee with multitudinous myriadical variety AND good milkshakes. 24 hours.

# MAUI

## GRANDMA'S MAUI COFFEE
Upper Kula Rd. in Keokea, Maui
(808) 878-2140
7-5 Mon-Sat, 7-3 Sun

A country store on the way to Ulupalakua and Tedeschi Winery, Grandma's has sandwiches and fresh-roasted coffee. This place smells like it oughta and is the only place on Maui where you can get MAUI COFFEE. What? 35 clams a bag? It ought to be a controlled substance at that price. But I, Snorkel Bob, got a bag because good data is complete data, and a personal chat with Ms. Lily at Ono Farms rounded out the info. Ms. Lily holds that it ain't the coffee that churns your stomach. It's the chemicals. She says coffee is the most sprayed edible crop in the world, and unlike other produce you can rinse, coffee goes direct to the roaster, where the bug juice and assorted toxins and detrimentals get bonded to the beans and released when you least suspect it, early a.m., bleary-eyed, guard down.

Furthermore, she said, all this brouhaha about Kona coffee—why, they had to pass a state law requiring a minimum of 10 percent Kona beans in any coffee labeled Kona Coffee, because some packagers were mixing in 2-3 percent Kona beans with cheap junk beans. So now you get 10 percent for sure and that is maybe. Besides that, now they got a new regulation on all the cheapo beans coming in for the heavy mix and false label, that they get fumigated on arrival. We knew that, but isn't it nice to hear someone else rail for a change?

Which brings us back to MAUI ORGANIC COFFEE. You want silky smooth, easy lift, no thrusters nor boosters but rather a power coefficient equal to your most subtle delusions? This is it.

## MAUI COFFEE ROASTERS
444 Hana Hwy in Kahului, Maui
(808) 877-2877
7:30-6 Mon-Fri, 8-5 Sat, 9-3 Sun

The Roasters is now sitdown and is where most tourist places buy their coffee. So you get it 1 step unremoved at maybe a little better price. Beans are roasted on the spot. Deli lunch is optional til 4:30 on weekdays, 4 on Sat, and 3 on Sun. On the corner of Hana Highway and Dairy Road.

## THE COFFEE STORE
Kaahumanu Center  and Azeka Place in Kahului & Kihei
(808) 871-6860 and (808) 875-4244

In the middle of mall America, but it looks good, smells good, and makes excellent cappucino. Open 7 a.m. -9 p.m. Mon-Fri, 7:30-9 Sat, and 9-5 Sun.

## COCONUTS BAKERY & CAFE
Kukui Mall at 1819 S. Kihei Rd. in Kihei, Maui
(808) 879-0261
7 a.m. - 8 p.m. Sun-Thurs, 7 a.m.-9 p.m. Fri & Sat

Espresso et al with only Maui coffee and baked stuff as good as anywhere make this a must stop for my, Snorkel Bob's, sugar and caffeine needs. Passion orange muffins, cherry strudel, guava twists and Italian bread baked daily along with the old standards like Tiramisu, fruit tortes, cheesecakes and pies make the Gambardellas practically heroic in Kihei, considering the difficult leases, the traffic and sweltering heat.

## STANTON'S
Maui Mall in Kahului, Maui
(808) 877-3711

This mall pub (it's a reach, but tolerable) has parquet flooring and brass rails and specializes in cigars and humidors. Besides inexpensive breakfast and lunch, you may obtain great cappucinos.

## SIR WILFRED'S
Lahaina Cannery Centre in Lahaina, Maui
(808) 667-1941
9-9 Daily

Sir Wilfred's is surrounded by chaos, but it's a good coffee shop with take out and a lunch menu.

## KIHEI CAFFE
1945 S. Kihei Rd. in Kihei, Maui
(808) 879-2230
5-3 Mon-Sat, 6-3 Sun

In the old Island Fish House quonset hut, this place, and convenient to most of Kihei and Wailea. Breakfast served from 5 to 11 everyday but Sunday when you can get it til noon. An honest pour here, and just out the door and a step & stumble northward is my, Snorkel Bob's, place in Kihei.

# OAHU

## THE COFFEE LINE
1820 University Ave. in Honolulu, Oahu
(808) 947-1615
7:30-4  Mon-Fri

In the University YMCA, near the U of Hawaii, which accounts for the low pulse, the introspection, the wondering why? It's subdued with low-slung voices, no small talk and an air of marginal smarts. Mostly college students finding themselves here, but it's a good spot with good jo and decent entertainment in the Avant-Funk mode.

## JAVA JAVA
760 Kapahulu Ave. in Honolulu, Oahu
(808) 732-2670
10 a.m.-midnight Mon-Sat, 6 p.m.-midnight Sun

Just up from my, Snorkel Bob's, place in Honolulu, next to the funky antique shop. Live readings here, like when everyone knew what Maynard G. Krebs was, like, really all about. Also in Ala Moana Shopping Center at 941-2187.

# LUAU

Remember the luau on The Brady Bunch? Gosh it was swell, with the whole happy family sitting Indian-style in a half circle (to make room for the camera) around their very own pig with an apple in his mouth and all the beautiful plants and Hawaiians waiting on them hand and foot.

It ain't like that. It's more show biz here. In 1 sense it's more low-key than most people anticipate. For example, all the luau guests sit in chairs (usually the folding kind) at tables (also the folding kind), sometimes dining on table cloths (the paper kind) and sometimes not. That is, the mondo hunky Hawaiian guys you saw on The Brady Bunch, who carry the pig out in their inimitable, authentic, Hawaiian style have been replaced by a catering crew.

You should remember, though, they entertain up to 300 people an evening. For another example, you won't be served. All the luaus I, Snorkel Bob, know about are buffet. And the authentic Hawaiian style—the costumes, singing, dancing, stories and such are on a stage now, and the show starts when you're done with your luau repast.

Prelims begin with the removal of the pig from the Imu. The technique is exacting, since the meat can turn bitter if not properly handled. It's quickly pulled from the bones, diced and salted. The fat is usually mixed right in with tons of sea salt poured on for a ☆☆☆☆ heart attack pack. Hawaii has a longer average life span than any other state in America, but with higher incidence of heart disease and diabetes too.

Anyway, luau buffets range in quality and can be a culture shock for those from the suburbs. Besides Imu pig they have a white coconut pudding, which isn't bad once you get used to it. Lomi lomi salmon is cold with tomatoes, onions and salmon diced in. They all have sticky white rice and sometimes chicken long rice (rice noodles), or regular baked chicken. Salads, vegetables and sweets round it out, and it's usually good.

Most luaus I, Snorkel Bob, ever saw, were a combination of South Pacific cultures with heavy emphasis on Mai Tai* drinking. They're FREE, but hardly a bargain. I, Snorkel Bob, can get behind the boom ba ba boom and the coconut bras easy as the next guy and bellow "Yahoo!" for the dance review finale, because it's good. It just ain't a luau, not really.

Anyway, I, Snorkel Bob, won't list any luau not good. Some of these have 25 items on the buffet including tropical fruits and salads that should be fresh-cooked daily just like the Imu pig. The good luaus are outside on the water so you get sunset, twilight and starlight too. All require reservations. Here some luaus are:

## TAHITI NUI
Hanalei, Kauai
(808) 826-6277

In the middle of Hanalei with luaus Wednesday and Saturday nights—6:30 arrival for entertainment at 7:15. Dinner is chicken, kalua pig, lomi lomi salmon, homemade desserts. The show includes ancient and modern hula and Tahitian dancing too. Mr. Nui say seating only 150, but last night go 206, folks leaving town and all, maybe no more chance for see luau long time again. So? $40 adults, $17 kids 12 and under. You be luaued by 9:30, then go home. Full every show, so reserve early.

As seen on Good Morning America and CNN News. Not dressy but ultra casual, maybe come straight from beach in cover-up. Many people say Tahiti Nui is the best.

## LEMN'S LUAU
Anahola, Kauai
(808) 822-4854

This could be the twist you need for entertaining at least 100 of your closest friends. Private luau caterers, this 1. Mr. and Mrs. Lemn prepare everything, all you want, and bring it to you, 100 people minimum, starting at $12 per. Requires at least 2 weeks notice to order da pig. (Oink!)

## KAUAI COCONUT BEACH RESORT
Kapaa, Kauai
(808) 822-3455

Every night but Monday at $52 for adults, $30 for kids 6-17. Arrive at 6, done by 9 with a regular luau menu of kalua pig, teriyaki ribs, mahi mahi, chicken long rice, lomi lomi salmon, poi, fried rice and of course, much much more. 300 seats for a traditional Hawaiian show. For you total immersion buffs, da pig go in a hole 10:45 a.m. and come out 7 p.m., all different.

## NAMAHANA
Waimea, Kauai
(808) 338-1963

Namahana is another catering service mostly for south side fetes, but Princeville/Hanalei is a do, too, for a few dollars more. Namahana has no minimum, no maximum and preps the eats 1st, then brings them over. Smoked pork be Namahana claim to fame. So many people like it, maybe because smoking it lets more pig fat drip onto the coals instead of down the hatch, from whence it wends to arteries, giving rise to pop eyes, stolen breath and the unspoken yet understood announcement: I think it's the Big 1!

Nevermind. Most people like Namahana smoked pork better than any pig they ever ate. You can eat it here and take some home. Namahana will pack and refrigerate for you. You like sprouts and tofu in laulau? Okay, that. $9.25 per for a good party, kids 7-11 $7.50. 2 months advance reservation required.

# BIG ISLAND

### KONA VILLAGE LUAU
Kona Village Hotel in Kailua, Hawaii
(808) 325-5555

Friday only, this 1, 5-9. Adults/$66.50, kids 6-12/$32, kids 2-5/$24.50. Price includes house wine.

### ROYAL WAIKOLOAN LUAU
Royal Waikoloan Resort on the Kohala Coast, Hawaii
(808) 885-6789

Sunday and Wednesday, 6-8:45. Adults are $51.50. Children 6-11 are $22. 5 and under free. Seating begins at 5:30.

### MAUNA KEA LUAU
Mauna Kea Resort on the Kohala Coast, Hawaii
(808) 882-7222

Tuesdays only, 6:30-9. $60 for adults; $30 for kids 6-12; 5 and under free.

### KING KAMEHAMEHA LUAU
King Kamehameha Hotel in Kailua, Kona
(808) 329-2911

Tuesday, Wednesday, Thursday, Sunday, starting at 5:30. Adults are $52; kids 6-12 are $19.50; 5 and under free.

# MAUI

### OLD LAHAINA LUAU
505 Front St. in Lahaina, Maui
(808) 667-1998

The 1 luau maybe a little different is this. I, SB, by no means have seen all the luaus. Many hotels have them, and maybe convenience is a factor in choosing your luau.

Old Lahaina Luau makes more of an effort to replicate the old Hawaiian style. They put more uummph into research and presentation of Hawaiian custom and tradition. Michael at OLL says 25 items on the buffet include tropical fruits and salads fresh daily with kalua pig which is like Imu pig but they put the hot rocks inside the pig as well as outside to make it more roasted than stewed, I think. 7 days a week, adults are $57, kids 2-12 are $28.50. Includes a fresh-flower lei.

### ASTON WAILEA LUAU
Aston Wailea at 3700 Wailea Alanui Dr. in Wailea, Maui
(808) 879-1922

A Broadway production of a luau, with glitz, showmanship and good groceries. Tuesday, Thursday and Friday, 5 to 8:30. Adults pay $52, kids 6-12 cost $26. Under 6 is free.

### ROYAL LAHAINA LUAU
2780 Kekaa Dr. in Kaanapali, Maui
(808) 661-3611

This 1 goes 7 days a week, 5:30-8. Adults $62; kids 6-12, $28, under 5 free.

# OAHU

### THE ROYAL LUAU
Royal Hawaiian Hotel in Honolulu, Oahu
(808) 923-7311

A popular favorite on the beach with that old time feeling, sunset cocktails and Mai Tais.* On the greensward it's soft, pink and perfect so you can swill down 3 or 6 with hardly a hesitation. Then... It happens: The Royal Polynesian Extravaganza! Whoa, Dogies! Monday night only. 6-8:30. $78, unless you're 5-12, then it's $48.

### THE POLYNESIAN CULTURAL CENTER
Laie, Oahu
(808) 293-3333

The Poly Cult Center has a razzle-dazzle buffet and show with exotic groceries, like the napping piglet with the apple gob and citrus halo. And all the poi you can eat is better than all the mud and wallpaper paste you can eat. It's $59 adults, $39 kids 5-11, everyday except the Lord's day. Luau buffet starts at 5:30, ends at 7. The show goes 8-9:30. The price includes admission to the grounds and an Imax Theater ticket. The Poly Cult Center is in Laie, 38 miles around the other side from Waikiki.

### GERMAINE'S LUAU
Campbell Industrial Park, Oahu
(808) 941-3338

Germaine's is 45 minutes west of Waikiki, past Pearl Harbor at a private beach house in Campbell Industrial Park, which doesn't sound Polynesian, but these great big fat guys with itty bitty gitfiddles make up for that. Real pop and touristy, this 1, but an honest deal since all the poi you can stomach is included at $46 for bigs, $25 for smalls (6-12). 6 to 9:30 daily except Monday. Price includes 3 comp cocktails.

* Beware the dreaded Mai Tai. Even if you've experienced the I'll-never-do-that-again syndrome; you ain't seen nothing yet. It's not just the rum (distilled SUGAR cane), it's the pineapple juice (1 of the heaviest concentrations of SUGAR in all of nature) and, for that extra sweet taste you love, extra SUGAR is added. They go down like lemonade. The SUGAR rush is sweet (May I have another, please?), but the withdrawal and depression the next day (from the SUGAR) should be clearly anticipated and awaited in a room with a low ceiling, no rafters, no ropes.

**OKAY**, that's a bunch o' luaus and either you can pick 1 or keep shopping on your own because I, Snorkel Bob, can't take it anymore!

How much salty, soggy, greasy pig do you think I, Snorkel Bob, can look at? Oh sure, you want me to check them all for you, like the 1 where they got this fat chick in a grass skirt who looks like she eats with 4 hands and this guy dressed up in a papier maché costume who's supposed to be a local gremlin, but he looks more like a dwarf with elephantiasis and borderline psychosis. And all these big, sweaty, local boys are grinning at me, Snorkel Bob, with promises of thrusting back in time to the fire and fury and pulsating rhythm and seductive maidens and ferocious warriors exploding in a blaze of color! More Mai Tais* keep coming on with all you can eat and then eat some more! 2 Shows Nitely and much much more... HEEELLLPP!

# 5
# Places to Stay

# BED & BREAKFASTS

Most hotels in Hawaii are big with many rooms, many guests, tour directors and what often feels like a Camp Hawaii frame of mind. I.e., you feel compelled to do it all, keep the jam pumped, the cash flowing, the mind-set loud and physical. If you succumb to this error in judgment, the lost potential for serenity, reflection and growth may be profound.

In fact, removal from pre-packaged "activity" often varies directly with discovery, adventure, speed rush. Some grist for this mill may be:

BED & BREAKFASTS: I, Snorkel Bob, was for years sour on the cutesy concept, the House Beautiful atmosphere, the clutter and chachkas, the storybook atmosphere where tourists speak in whispers and observe the other guests as if this is the show and you're in it. I.e., I, Snorkel Bob, found it expensive, stifling, overcooked, confining and, above all, dull. On painful reassessment, however, I, SB, was made to realize that this deep resentment in my, SB's, subconscious mind, could be traced to a single weekend at a Bed & Breakfast in Northern California recommended by my, Snorkel Bob's, longtime snorkel buddy, Matt Roving. No further names need be mentioned, except the 1 this place should have been called: Sleepy Hollow Convalescent Center. Sheesh, I think Matt Roving must take drugs. But unlike the other guests at Sleepy Hollow, his are only recreational.

Anyway, when Bed & Breakfasts were suggested as a component of Reality in Hawaii, I, Snorkel Bob, with scorn and a snicker, said, "Pshaw!" But darn if the mermaid making the suggestion didn't turn my, Snorkel Bob's, head around. Oh, you think, she was only goldbricking for a ride with a megastar like me, Snorkel Bob. So? She had the skills to teach me, SB, just how much fun a B&B can be.

I, Snorkel Bob, now have a few favorites, like the Bamboo House in Pahoa, or Barbara Campbell's place in Kamuela, or Nathalia Richmond's place near Haleiwa. Yet another paradox arises: A listing here of what's good might render it not so; displaced in a heartbeat by the teeming refuse yearning to be free. Gone in a flash could be the country quiet and simple access to a clean place with a host who knows the neighborhood.

It would be better if you found your own guest cottage on a private estate or a house on the beach or a room with private bath for under $55. Because don't we value greatest what we earn? And who needs crowds?

The services listed here mostly book air, room and car packages. They use brochures, and I, Snorkel Bob, know that a brochure can tell a lie. But the B&B business depends on repeat business, so this should be a safe bet. Book far in advance with:

# BIG ISLAND

## HAWAII'S BEST BED & BREAKFASTS
P.O. Box 563
Kamuela, Hawaii 96743
(808) 885-0550 or (800) 262-9912—FAX: (808) 885-0559

Barbara Campbell lists places high on charm, location, landscaping, cleanliness and hospitality. Rooms, small inns and private cottages mostly range $95-250/night. Personal checks and Discover only, pre-payment required.

# MAUI

## HEAVENLY HANA INN
790 Hana Hwy in Hana, Maui
(808) 248-8442

Heavenly Hana Inn ranges $175-$235/night with continental breakfast. You must call between 9 a.m. and 5 p.m. HST.

## SILVER CLOUD GUEST RANCH
Thompson Rd. up past Grandma's in Ulapalakua on the way to Tedeschi Winery and Kenaio in Upcountry Maui.
(808) 878-6101

I, Snorkel Bob, had a particularly hard week with moneygrubbing sleezedogs trying to skim the cream with junk gear, plagiarism and assorted crimes and misdemeanors against the spirit of good service and a fair deal. You have no idea what a desperate, greedy level of competition has evolved here in Paradise. And then, as if blood and sweat weren't enough, I, Snorkel Bob, had to go all the way up to Ulapalakua to check out some obscure bungalow on a hillside.

Wowie zowie; inside 10 minutes and a cocktail or 2, things changed more dramatically than the before and after shots of an Imu pig. Nice nice nice this 1, with the misty greenery and postcard views untrammeled by the honkytonk and slick-to-make-you-sick bull fodder of the hubbub so far below: even it looked nice. Small rooms with kitchens and an old, lodge feeling and simple tables and chairs out on the deck line this silver cloud with decompression. Call ahead. I, Snorkel Bob, can't remember if it's $135 or $531. It didn't matter.

# OAHU

### ALL ISLAND BED & BREAKFAST
823 Kainui Dr. Kailua, Oahu 96734
(808) 263-2342 or (800) 542-0344

Tell Ann what you want & what you'll give. $55-$75 gets a room in a private home; $75-$85 earns a studio, and $85-$115 rents a cottage. Tell her your dreams and fantasies, in the limits of good taste, of course. She recommends. You reserve. The hostess mails you a brochure and welcome letter. 3-night minimum, 700 listings, all islands.

### HAWAIIAN ISLANDS VACATION RENTALS
### AND BED & BREAKFAST
1277 Mokulua Dr. in Kailua, Hawaii 96734
(808) 261-7895 or (800) 258-7895—FAX: (808) 262-2181

Rick Maxey has the history on his listings, e.g. the 1924 beach-house hideaway of John Walker, architect of the Bishop Museum and Honolulu City Hall. Apartments, studios, rooms with private entrance and bath or entire homes start around $55/night per person. Sometimes the houses are a better deal per head; e.g., John Walker House is $350/night and sleeps 6.

# CHEAP DIGS

If those exotic country hotels that look shabby but neat look like good hideaways, like refuge for you who've had it up to here with the spouse, the kids, the job, the bills, the station wagon, the ingratitude, the routine, nay the rut, the grind, the life...

They are, excellent hideaways that is. Why, a guy could move up here and never be seen or heard from again for probably 2 or 3 months. Oh, they'll get you in the end. But you always knew they would, so why not hole up with some cheap liquor and bug spray and see what might change?

# KAUAI

## THE TIPTOP MOTEL
Lihue, Kauai
(808) 245-2333

Right in the heart of downtown Lihue, the Tiptop has rooms for $44/night, down from $50 since '93, and still with a cafe and bakery. Plate lunch local style at popular prices from 6:30 to 2 everyday but Monday. A can of bug spray is provided for any guest in need. What more could you ask in a hostelry?

# BIG ISLAND

## THE KONA HOTEL
Rte. 180 in Holualoa, Hawaii
(808) 324-1155

The Kona Hotel makes escape fiscally plausible at $20 a night for a single. It looks funky, as in groovy, but soon a pervasive and moist subfunk will prevail, primarily in the musty, moldy, crawly mode. But what the hey at 20 clams a sundown you can afford payments on a dehumidifier and some bug spray.

It has several features that I, Snorkel Bob, find particularly refreshing. Namely, no swimming pool, no bellhops and no room service. And it's only a step and a stumble to a 6 pack and some couch wine from the room at the side downstairs. A double will run you $26. Community bath. They claim you need reservations, and hey, it's a cash deal.

## HOTEL MANAGO
Hwy 11 in Captain Cook, Hawaii
(808) 323-2642

$39 a night for a double with a private bath. It goes up from there: Add a couple bucks for the 2nd floor (consider the view), and if you want extra fancy or better odds on a last jump (3rd floor) you're looking at $44 a night. Reservations suggested here. It's a funky country hotel worth a night or 2 for fun in proximity to all the groovy stuff up on the high road—Highway 11.

# MAUI

### NAPILI VILLAGE HOTEL
5425 Lower Honoapiilani Rd. in Napili, Maui
(808) 669-6228

The NVH is the kind of place you often expect but have a hard time finding. It's clean, well-lit, 1/2 a stumble to the beach, no rats, clean sheets and all like that. $89-109/night with a kitchen, and Alissa and Rick have a car deal from $26/day based on a 7-day stay. The 400 sq. ft. rooms are neat with a king and foldout queen, so 4 friends can share in 2s if they're close. 4 newly remodeled de Luxe units now achieve the perfection honeymooners long for. Butler service is available too, if you bring your own butler. And hey, guess what? An **INTERNATIONAL SHRINE** is on the premises of NVH? Yes! It's me, Snorkel Bob, Himself.

# A SEPARATE REALITY

### HILTON AT WAIKOLOA —THE HOTEL

The Hilton at Waikoloa is the kind of place that puts a guy like me, Snorkel Bob, in a bind. I, Snorkel Bob, like to go directly inside, figuratively speaking, through the truth gap. I.e., you can look at the double truck centerfold in Mondo Travel Magazine at this scene, which is the Hilton at Waikoloa, and it's not just perfect, it's ultra-plus perfect in the radical extreme. The palms and ferns are perfect with perfect balance, distribution, leaf to stem ratio, ambient mist and moisture drippage, no white flies, mealy bugs, root rot, nematodes or plant scale and none of the slimy stuff that oozes out the base of the fronds and certainly no centipedes and extra especially no 9" centipedes that look like small dinosaurs and make you wish you were back in Nebraska. Like I, Snorkel Bob, said: Perfect.

It's the kind of photograph where they smear a little vaseline on the lens for dream haze, and the Beau and Young Princess on the steps gaze dreamily into each other's beautiful eyes knowing that the Hilton at Waikoloa is the only spot on Planet Earth perfectly matched to their kind of beauty.

Alas and alack, however. The double truck foldout is 2D. Like it's 3D antecedent, it's sighful, not to be confused with soulful. Perfection like this tends to leave me, SB, speechless.

Lucky for us, longtime pal and waaay back #1 snorkel buddy, Matt Roving, came along for the ambience report.

"It's a museum with a cash bar," he said, bellying up to our 1st stop on the river. I, Snorkel Bob, reminded him of the incredible logistics of building a perfect set with a river running through it in the middle of a barren lava flow. "Yeah," he said. "It's like Ben Hur at happy hour."

I, Snorkel Bob, often lose patience with Matt Roving. But sometimes he hits the nail on the head.

And there we sat, still life at The Landing, surrounded by perfect pillars wrapped in perfect coach whipping with 2-inch manila line; surrounded further by slatted tables and captain's chairs in koa. (Sheesh. $14 a foot this stuff.) The perfect cobalt crystal wine goblet was plastic, but that's life on board.

Matt Roving drummed his fingers on the perfect koa table top. "I don't know," he said. "I think maybe they ought to pipe some sludge through the river there and bring in some gondoliers and some winos with some squeeze boxes. And rats. Yeah, rats! And some big old alley cats to take care of the rat problem. Then they'd have some reality."

It was time to move on. We waited at the landing for the next boat. The little boats run on underwater cables, so the people in captain's outfits at the dummy wheel can't go off course. The little skippers do perform 3 real functions, however: 1) dock line 2) stop 3) go.

Or you can opt for the monorail running parallel to the river. Matt Roving said no matter how perfect it looked, it was still Bay Area Rapid Transit to him.

It was a slow night at the Hilton Waikoloa. Our captain told us it was $450 million to build all the digs there. Matt Roving allowed a moment of silence for that kind of overhead so a couple of backyard snorkelers like Matt Roving and me, Snorkel Bob, could ride a plastic boat down a cement-bed river with a union bellhop in a sailor suit at the wheel for a few cold beers and some bar snacks at the far end. But the Hilton doesn't eat it all that bad; it used to be the Hyatt, until the bailout and new ownership by the Hilton.

"You ever fall into the moat?" Matt Roving asked our captain. Our captain thought it over and shook his head.

At the end of the line we bellied up yet again at the Kona Provision Company, urban nouveau decor, also in the perfect mode. Initial reconnoiter of the hostess podium paused on a lovely girl, the hostess, just out of school and new on the job. Behind the podium is a plastic cast of a marlin. 1656 pounds, the plaque says. 90" girth. 16' 7" long.

She smiled sweetly and cooed, "It's real."

"It's plastic!" Matt Roving bellowed.

"Pulleeze," I, Snorkel Bob, appealed.

"It's plastic!" Matt Roving (another truth crusader, however indelicate) insisted. "You think that's real? They phone in some specs, usually on the big side, to some guy in South Florida, and his computer spits out orders to the fish mold! They knockum out with a chopper gun and an air brush! It's got 2 halves with a seam, just like your modular shower stall!"

She looked worried, then saddened, then crestfallen. Matt Roving eased up, strode forward and rapped it hard with his knuckles. It resounded, hollow, a big plastic can shaped like a fish. "Bubba'n paint! That's all it is! Look at this! The gill plates are Bondo!"

Her eyes turned down, tears forming in the corners. "Aw hell," Matt Roving said, easing an arm around her shoulders. "It works for the guy who caught the fish." She attempted a smile, in the spirit of customer service. "What's your name, honey?"

Reality came at last at the bar of the Provision Co. The steamed clams approached perfection. No parsley in the Land of Perfect; dill sprigs here, with a double reverse wedge on the lemon. 2 more brewskies got Matt Roving relaxed. And when the perfect young hostess said yes, she was at least 18 and yes, some private snorkel tutoring would be nice, if only she could afford it, he explained the meaning of easy terms. Come together is what it did, all of it, just as the tender, succulent, perfectly sauteed calamari arrived.

It was enough to make me, Snorkel Bob, feel at home in the center of a misty-eyed double truck. Arriving at figurative Reality required a bit of slogging through the arid fringe. But vacation, relaxation and growth usually take a toll. Don't they?

## THE GRAND WAILEA

Also a Hyatt used-to-be. At 1st blush a guy might think this place ought to be called The Grand Niagara, on account of the vast and dramatic water falls lining the approach. Or The Wailea White House, with the attendants, valets, lieutenants and fair maidens waiting to greet you as you gaze and think, Oh My God! But you will no sooner mumble than the thought will begin anew. It's an sensory avalanche, this Grandiose Wailea in Overdrive.

You got the Lobby Bar, marble of course and round like the sun and nearly as big, with the ballroom lily-pond surround, with dugout canoe centerpieces complimenting the granite sculptures and festooning flowers in the billions, like stars in The Universe.

I, Snorkel Bob, will not blow-by-blow this 1. It's simply way too much in perfect taste. Heard frequently on the coconut wireless: "It's just like Disneyland!" It ain't, and that comment may be unfair to Disneyland. Maybe what I, Snorkel Bob, missed was a dark alcove with a nondescript cafe, sawdust floor, tepid draft beer at 75¢ a glass, some barflies, a blue haze & a juke box with obscure 45s.

But I, SB, will not indict our unusual capitalist compatriots from Tokyo, the owners. No, because also on the wireless is the legend that 100% occupancy for 30 years (10,950 nights) will break the place even. And a stroll through the great halls is soothing, past the piazzas, gardens, alcoves, cupolas, kiosks, nooks and crannies, past the mosaics and murals, especially the 1 bigger than bigger than life, Prometheus Unbound in Hawaii (an industrial-romance-size rendition of Maui the demigod lassoing the sun in order to tow the rock up from the sea).

Nor will I, Snorkel Bob, critique in retentive detail the highs and lows of the extravaganza, like the Tsunami Discotheque's newspaper ads, "Of course you'll be there. The question is will we let you in?" Pulleeeze–hard to believe this is literal translation from the Japanese. Or the poolside chapel's (poolside chapel?) sensitive absence of denominational reference and missionary zeal, which absence comforts those of us of the Druid inclination. ("That's funny," said the elegant and tasteful hostess. "You don't look Druish.")

Or the Spa Grande and Terme Wailea (sounds terminal, no?) where you can get loofah-scrubbed stem to stern before the baths and cascading waterfalls from 7 a.m.-8 p.m. @ $59/guests or $100/nonguests, before or after the exercise room or the racquetball/squash court.

Or the water slide or swimming pool. Or, alas, the courtesy telephones everywhere so you can call anywhere, except long distance, which came as a shock to me, Snorkel Bob, they made me feel so pampered otherwise.

$380-495/night, depending on optionals, like regency breakfast, butler service, tea, cocktails, fa fa et al. I, Snorkel Bob, endorse a visit. This may be the last of the big-fin models.

## THE FOUR SEASONS

It's a tough verdict on this place too. Okay, it's nice, but Doric columns in Hawaii? It's like when John Madden says, "Okay, now that's a fullback. That's what a fullback is supposed to look like. You see that mud? Shirt's all torn up, blood all over the place, all the paint scuffed off his helmet—look at that! No teeth up front! That's a fullback! I like that! He just made the All-Madden team!"

But the 4 Seasons has no bamboo thicket, no dirt floor, no grass skirts. It has Doric columns, relentless Grandeur and fixtures big enough to dwarf a snorkel giant like me, Snorkel Bob. Who comes up with this stuff?

And why did they lay the place out like an airscoop on a blown hemi, which is what the tradewinds feel like jamming down the throat of the 4 Seasons like it was a 4-barrel Holly racing carb that could give you scratch in 4 Gears if only you could get this bucket moving.

Howsoever, just down the yellow brick steps is the Pacific Grill, a favorite place for me, Snorkel Bob, to luncheon, business of course. And just around the bend past the Health Club and Library is the Games Bar, a neighborhood favorite where homestyle recreation thrives in an atmosphere of uptown fa, with pool, shuffleboard and a bar if you're 21.

For your logowear needs, both expensive and very expensive, your stemwear, gems and trinkets, or maybe just some Pepto Bizzzzmol after dinner, you have the vast and elegant shops with names like Selections, Viewpoint, Don't You Wish (Not really. I, Snorkel Bob, made that last 1 up.)

And with the Recession of '95, '96 & '97 the 4 Seasons has a quaint, echoing charm, kind of like Xanadu without the crowds.

**ALI BABA & THE 40 THIEVES HOTEL**
or
**CASA BLANCA ARMS**
or
**THE ROAD TO MECCA**
or
**KEA LANI SUITES & HOTEL**

Kea Lani? With mosque domes? And parapets? And medieval troop turrets for defense of the fortress? The external ambience report reads in a word: Sheesh. I, Snorkel Bob, mean somebody is trying very hard at something. But who or what remains a mystery, a big 1.

Indoors is much better, similar to the opulence and grandeur and it's-never-enough mode of contemporary tropical overkill. But maybe not quite so overbearing is this 1, with fewer googahs, fewer multi-million dollar antiques strategically placed to compound your Oh-my-God experience. The retail shops fit the generic high-ticket hotel mode, but 2 iota make this place stand out: 1) the deli/coffee shop with its little bitty Colavita olive oils and eency teency balsamic vinegars to go with baguettes that taste amazingly French, which in this case is not rude. The cold deli is A-1 too, and the bevy of edible chachkas you didn't know you needed goes on and on. The coffee is most potent, most tasteful. And: 2) the Kea Lani restaurant, which I, Snorkel Bob, rate up to snuff but moreover excellent on those nights when the groceries are backed by the saxophone of John Zangrando. Soprano, alto, tenor and baritone, John Z knows how to apply a musical theory. I, Snorkel Bob, hesitate to recommend anything, but you could end up in the foolish zone if you don't check out these tunes. You must call and ask: Where Johnny Z be?

## THE SHERATON AT KAANAPALI

You may pause at the entrance and wonder: Where's the beef? Where in the world did they sink the $150 million in the recent renovation? Well, the place was getting old, so maybe the dough went toward noncosmetics. I, Snorkel Bob, will give the designers this: the Sheraton now feels like a high-ticket hotel in Hawaii instead of a fantabulous Disneyrama fantasy wet dream that closes in on you after a beer or 2. In fact, I, Snorkel Bob, love this place, in spite of its acres of meandering swimming pool, because:

YOU CAN PARK HERE TO SNORKEL BLACK ROCK AT THE SHERATON! And if that ain't love, then what?

# 6
# S.O.S.
# Snorkel Bob

# Vital Numbers

## KAUAI
EMERGENCY. . . . . . . . . . . . . . . . . . . . . . . . . . . . . .911

**Hospital:**
Emergency (24-hr). . . . . . . . . . . . . . . . . . . . .245-1010
Wilcox Memorial. . . . . . . . . . . . . . . . . . . . . .245-1100

**Doctors:**
Kauai Medical Group. . . . . . . . . . . . . . . . . . . . 245-1500
Kauai Pediatrics (Lihue). . . . . . . . . . . . . . . . . 245-8566

NOTE: Kauai Medical Group in Wilcox Hospital off Kuhio Highway and Kauai Pediatrics keep normal business hours. If you go crash boom after hours or on weekends, or anytime at all in Princeville or Hanalei–night or day–your nearest and onliest access on Kauai to the Miracles of the A.M.A is the Emergency Room at Wilcox Hospital in Lihue. OPEN 24 HOURS WITH A COMPLETE LINE OF CASTS, SPLINTS, INJECTIONS, X-RAYS, FORMS, DRUGS, STEEL RODS, STERILE GAUZE, DISINFECTANTS, RUBBER GLOVES, TONGUE DEPRESSORS, TWEEZERS, SCISSORS, SCALPELS, NEEDLES, SUTURES, CLAMPS, HOSES, PRESSURE GAUGES, MONITORS, O2 TENTS, DEFIBRILATORS, JUMP STARTERS AND SMALL CUPS.

**Airlines:**
Aloha . . . . . . . . . . . . . . . . . . . . . . . . . . . . . . . . 245-3691
Aloha Island Air (charters and scenic tours). . . . . . . . . . (800) 652-6541
Hawaiian . . . . . . . . . . . . . . . . . . . . . . . . . . . . . . .(800) 882-8811
American . . . . . . . . . . . . . . . . . . . . . . . . . . . . . . (800) 433-7300

**Airports:**
Lihue Airport . . . . . . . . . . . . . . . . . . . . . . . . . . . . 246-1440
Princeville Airport . . . . . . . . . . . . . . . . . . . . . . . . 826-3040
Federal Express . . . . . . . . . . . . . . . . . . . . . . . . . .(800) 238-5355

**Rent-a-Car:**
Thrifty . . . . . . . . . . . . . . . . . . . . . . . . . . . . . . . . 245-7388
Hertz . . . . . . . . . . . . . . . . . . . . . . . . . . . . . . . . . 245-3356
Budget . . . . . . . . . . . . . . . . . . . . . . . . . . . . . . . . 245-1901

Dollar . . . . . . . . . . . . . . . . . . . . . . 245-3651
Rent-a-Wreck . . . . . . . . . . . . . . . . . . . . . . 245-6411

**Taxi:**
Kauai Cab Service . . . . . . . . . . . . . . . . . . . 246-9554
Limo Limo (Limo service) . . . . . . . . . . . . . . . 822-0393

**Theatre & Music:**
Kilauea Theatre & Social Hall . . . . . . . . . . . . . . 828-1722
Consolidated Plantation Cinema . . . . . . . . . . . . . 822-9391
Kukui Grove Cinema (Lihue) . . . . . . . . . . . . . . 245-5055

**Museums:**
Kauai Museum (Lihue) . . . . . . . . . . . . . . . . . 245-6931
Kilohana Plantation . . . . . . . . . . . . . . . . . . . 245-5608
Kokee Natural History Museum (Waimea Canyon) . . . . 335-9975
Hawaiian Mythology . . . . . . . . . . . . . . . .246-4441, ext. 1300

**Baby Sitting Services:**
Liz Hey (Sitter Services). . . . . . . . . . . . . . . . . 822-1177
Namiko Hamada . . . . . . . . . . . . . . . . . . . . . 822-5387
Laurie Shiraki . . . . . . . . . . . . . . . . . . . . . . 822-3625

# BIG ISLAND

**EMERGENCY** . . . . . . . . . . . . . . . . . . . . . . . .911
Kona Police . . . . . . . . . . . . . . . . . . . . . . . 329-3311
Hilo Police . . . . . . . . . . . . . . . . . . . . . . . 935-3311
Ambulance/Fire . . . . . . . . . . . . . . . . . . . . 961-6022
Hospital:
    Kona (24 hr. emergency) . . . . . . . . . . . . . . 322-9311
    Hilo . . . . . . . . . . . . . . . . . . . . . . . . 969-4111
**Doctors:**
Kaiser Advice Line . . . . . . . . . . . . . . . . . . . 329-4211
Kona Clinic . . . . . . . . . . . . . . . . . . . . . . . 327-2900
Kona-Kohala Health Care (w/Pediatrics) . . . . . . . . . 329-1346
Hilo Medical Group (24 hr. w/Pediatrics) . . . . . . . . 961-6631
Straub . . . . . . . . . . . . . . . . . . . . . . . . . 329-9211

**Airlines:**
Aloha (Interisland) . . . . . . . . . . . . . . . . . . . . 935-5771
American . . . . . . . . . . . . . . . . . . . . . . (800) 433-7300

Big Island (Private Jet) . . . . . . . . . . . . . . . . . . . . . 329-4868
Continental . . . . . . . . . . . . . . . . . . . . . . . . . (800) 525-0280
Delta . . . . . . . . . . . . . . . . . . . . . . . . . . . . .(800) 221-1212
Hawaiian . . . . . . . . . . . . . . . . . . . . . . . . . . . . . 326-5615
TWA . . . . . . . . . . . . . . . . . . . . . . . . . . . . (800) 221-2000

**Airports:**
Keahole-Kona . . . . . . . . . . . . . . . . . . . . . . . . . . . 329-2484
Waimea . . . . . . . . . . . . . . . . . . . . . . . . . . . . . .885-4520
Hilo . . . . . . . . . . . . . . . . . . . . . . . . . . . . . . . 935-0809
Federal Express. . . . . . . . . . . . . . . . . . . . . . .(800) 238-5355

**Rent-a-Car:**
Budget at Keahole Airport . . . .935-7293(info);329-0971(reservs)
   Hyatt . . . . . . . . . . . . . . . . . . . . . . . . . . . . . .885-2881
   Hilo . . . . . . . . . . . . . . . . . . . . . . . . . . . . . . 935-6878
   Waikoloa . . . . . . . . . . . . . . . . . . . . 885-1234, ext.2881
Alamo in Kona . . . . . . . . . . . . . . . . . . . . . . . . . . .329-8896
   Keahole Airport . . . . . . . . . . . . . . . . . . . . . . . 329-2662
   Hilo . . . . . . . . . . . . . . . . . . . . . . . . . . . . . . 961-3343
Honolulu RAC in Kona (Cheap) . . . . . . . . . . . . . . . .329-7328

**Taxi:**
Paradise . . . . . . . . . . . . . . . . . . . . . . . . . . . . .329-1234
Marina . . . . . . . . . . . . . . . . . . . . . . . . . . . . . .329-2481
Limousine Service (Luana) . . . . . . . . . . . . . . . . . . 326-5466

**Theater & Music:**
Kona Community Players . . . . . . . . . . . . . . . . . . . . 322-9924
Hilo Community Players . . . . . . . . . . . . . . . . . . . . 935-9155
Kahilu Theaters . . . . . . . . . . . . . . . . . . . . . . . . . 885-6017

**Museums:**
Hawaii Tropical Botanical Garden . . . . . . . . . . . . . . . 964-5233
Kona Historical Society . . . . . . . . . . . . . . . . . . . . 323-3222
Kamuela (Waimea) Museum . . . . . . . . . . . . . . . . . . 885-4724
Lyman House . . . . . . . . . . . . . . . . . . . . . . . . . . . 935-5021
Parker Ranch . . . . . . . . . . . . . . . . . . . . . . . . . . . 885-7311

**Weather:**
Hilo . . . . . . . . . . . . . . . . . . . . . . . . . . . . . . . 935-8555
Island Wide . . . . . . . . . . . . . . . . . . . . . . . . . . . 961-5582
Human Voice . . . . . . . . . . . . . . . . . . . . . . . . . . . 935-5533

## Parks and Camping:

City of Refuge . . . . . . . . . . . . . . . . . . . . . . . . . . . . 328-2288
Volcanoes National Park . . . . . . . . . . . . . . . . . . . . . 967-7311
Eruption Message . . . . . . . . . . . . . . . . . . . . . . . . . . 967-7977
Hawaii State Parks (Cabins, Permits) . . . . . . . . . . . . 933-4200
Puukohola Heiau National Historical Site. . . . . . . . . 882-7218
County Parks (Permits, Pavillion Use) . . . . . . . . . . . 961-8311
Hapuna State Park . . . . . . . . . . . . . . . . . . . . . . . . . 882-7995

## Baby Sitting Services:

Barbara King . . . . . . . . . . . . . . . . . . . . . . . . . . . . . 326-1231

# MAUI

**EMERGENCY** . . . . . . . . . . . . . . . . . . . . . . . . . . . . . 911
Hospital . . . . . . . . . . . . . . . . . . . . . . . . . . . . . . . . 244-9056
**Doctors:**
Kihei Clinic (24 hours) . . . . . . . . . . . . . . . . . . . . . 879-1440
Pediatrician (Kihei) . . . . . . . . . . . . . . . . . . . . . . . . 879-5288
Doctors on Call (Hyatt Kaanapali) . . . . . . . . . . . . . 667-7676
West Maui Health Care Center . . . . . . . . . . . . . . . . 667-9721

## Airlines:

Aloha . . . . . . . . . . . . . . .877-5025 (info);244-9071 (reservs.)
American (Maui) . . . . . . . . . . . . . . . . . . . . . . . . . . 244-5522
American . . . . . . . . . . . . . . . . . . . . . . . . . (800) 433-7300
Delta (Maui baggage) . . . . . . . . . . . . . . . . . . . . . . 877-5025
Delta . . . . . . . . . . . . . . . . . . . . . . . . . . . . (800) 221-1212
Hawaiian Air . . . . . . . . . . . . .871-6132.or . . (800) 882-8811
Century Aviation (private jet service) . . . . . . . . . . . 877-7059
Airport Pager . . . . . . . . . . . . . . . . . . . . . . . . . . . . 877-6431
Federal Express . . . . . . . . . . . . . . . . . . . . . . (800) 238-5355

## Rent-a-Car:

Alamo . . . . . . . . . . . . . . . . . . . . . . . . . . . . . . . . . 871-6235
Budget . . . . . . . . . . . . . . . . . . . . . . . . . . . . . . . . . 871-8811
Dollar
    Kahului Airport . . . . . . . . . . . . . . . . . . . . . . 877-2731
    Kapalua Airport . . . . . . . . . . . . . . . . . . . . . . 667-2651
Kihei RAC (snorkel cruisers, cheap) . . . . . . . . . . . . 879-7257

**Taxi:**
Sunshine Cab Co./Rick ("Real Nice Cadillac cabs") . . 879-2220
Arthur's Limo (Kihei, Wailea, Kaanapali) . . . . . . . . 871-5555

**Theater & Music:**
Maui Philharmonic Society . . . . . . . . . . . . . . . . 244-3771
Maui Academy of Performing Arts . . . . . . . . . . . 244-8760
    Box Office . . . . . . . . . . . . . . . . . . . . . . . 244-8762
Baldwin Theatre Guild . . . . . . . . . . . . . . . . . . . 242-5821
Maui Community Theater . . . . . . . . . . . . . . . . . 242-6969

**Museums:**
Bailey House Museum . . . . . . . . . . . . . . . . . . . . 244-3326
Sugar Museum . . . . . . . . . . . . . . . . . . . . . . . . 871-8058
Baldwin House . . . . . . . . . . . . . . . . . . . . . . . . 661-3262
Weather:
Haleakala, Hana . . . . . . . . . . . . . . . . . . . . . . . 871-5054
General . . . . . . . . . . . . . . . . . . . . . . . . . . . . . 877-5111
Marine . . . . . . . . . . . . . . . . . . . . . . . . . . . . . 877-3477
Haleakala National Park:
Headquarters (Human Voice/7:30 a.m. to 4 p.m.) . . . .572-9306

**Baby Sitting Services:**
Kihei Keiki Sitters . . . . . . . . . 879-2522; Lahaina: 699-3812
Babysit Service of Maui . . . . . . . . . . . . . . . . . . 661-0558

# OAHU
**EMERGENCY**. . . . . . . . . . . . . . . . . . . . . . . . . . . .911
Hospital:
    Emergency (24 hr) . . . . . . . . . . . . . . . . . . . 547-4311
    Queen's Medical Center . . . . . . . . . . . . . . . . 538-9011
**Doctors:**
Doctors on Call . . . . . . . . . . . . . . . . . . . . . . . . 926-4777
Waikiki Health Center . . . . . . . . . . . . . . . . . . . 922-4787

**Airlines:**
Aloha . . . . . . . . . . . . . . . . . . . . . . . . . . . . . . 484-1111
Aloha Island Air (prop-jets) . . . . . . . . . . . . . . . .484-2222
Hawaiian . . . . . . . . . . . . . . . . . . . . . . . . . . . .537-5100
American . . . . . . . . . . . . . . . . . . . . . . . . . . . . 833-7600
Delta . . . . . . . . . . . . . . . . . . . . . . . . . . . (800) 221-1212

**Airports:**
Honolulu International Airport . . . . . . . . . . . . . . 836-6411
Federal Express . . . . . . . . . . . . . . . . . . . . . . 395-3339

**Rent-a-Car:**
Thrifty . . . . . . . . . . . . . . . . . . . . . . . . . . 836-2388
Hertz . . . . . . . . . . . . . . . . . . . . . . . . . . . .831-3500
Budget . . . . . . . . . . . . . . . . . . . . . . . . . . .537-3600
Dollar . . . . . . . . . . . . . . . . . . . . . . . . . . .831-2330
Alamo . . . . . . . . . . . . . . . . . . . . . . . . . . .833-4585

**Bus Service:**
THE BUS . . . . . . . . . . . . . . . . . . . . . . . . . . 848-5555

**Taxi:**
SIDA (over 500 cabs) . . . . . . . . . . . . . . . . . . . 836-0011
Limousine Service:
SIDA (and a few limos) . . . . . . . . . . . . . . . . . . 836-0011

**Theater & Music:**
Blaisdell Center . . . . . . . . . . . . . . . . . . . . . . 521-2911
Honolulu Symphony . . . . . . . . . . . . . . . . . . . . 537-6191
Honolulu Community Theatre . . . . . . . . . . . . . . . 734-0274
Honolulu Theatre for Youth . . . . . . . . . . . . . . . .839-9885
Manoa Valley Theatre . . . . . . . . . . . . . . . . . . . 988-6131

**Museums:**
Bishop Museum . . . . . . . . . . . . . . . . . . . . . . 847-3511
Contemporary Museum . . . . . . . . . . . . . . . . . . 526-1322
Hawaii Maritime Center . . . . . . . . . . . . . . . . . . 523-6151
Honolulu Academy of Arts . . . . . . . . . . . . . . . . 532-8701

**Weather:**
Oahu . . . . . . . . . . . . . . . . . . . . . . . . . . . . 836-0121
Honolulu . . . . . . . . . . . . . . . . . . . . . . . . . . 833-2849
Marine . . . . . . . . . . . . . . . . . . . . . . . . . . .836-3921
KPOI Surf Report . . . . . . . . . . . . . . . . . . . . . .521-7873
Time (What it is.) . . . . . . . . . . . . . . . . . . . . . .983-3211

**Baby Sitting Services:**
Aloha Babysitting Service . . . . . . . . . . . . . . . . . 732-2029
Sitters Unlimited of Honolulu . . . . . . . . . . . . . . .262-5728

VITAL NUMBERS are brought to you by Danway Tours, an affiliate of Luau On Wheels (location caterers for Snorkel Bob Movie Productions), and a subsidiary of Danway International, who brings you Speedrail (for all your guardrail/handrail needs), the Danway Party Pack (for the complete weekend) and the Danway DUI Kit (better safe than sorry).

Danway International now specializes in fancy-schmancy vacation rentals, usually on the beach. This, after significant divestiture as ruled by the Supreme Court of the United States of America (vis a vis John Doe v. Standard Oil of Indiana), bringing all Danway resources to focus on the most expensive & spectacular, fancy-pants fa fa digs in Hawaii. (808) 879-1895.

# HOW TO SPEAK PIDGIN

Most people define "tourists" as those other people in baggy shorts, dark sox and cornball aloha shirts with cameras slung round their necks. That's because most people are more soulful than tourists. That is, they can really feel the nuance and idiom of a place; they can blend in and are more world-wise than tourists.

So they feel compelled to adapt, to rise or fall to the local level, to speak the language. Be careful. Pidgin is not a legitimate dialect; it has no pattern, no standard syntax. It is just what it's called: pidgin—a loose and broken form. It is not a blend of 2 dialects but rather a basic exchange dependent on instinct and understood meaning, whether meaning is understood or not.

Those who speak it spot those who fake it in a New York minute, making you wonder how so much stink eye can come your way when you're cool enough to talk pidgin, after all. Like: "How's it, Brah. How's your da kine?"

You can't just butcher English and get pidgin. You must butcher it just right:

1. After nearly every phrase or sentence say "Yah?"
2. Substitute "da kine" for 98 percent of all nouns, both common and proper, 40 percent of all else.
3. Substitute "whodaguy" for 20 percent of all da kines.
4. Substitute "for" for "to."
5. Use "stay" for all location reference.
6. Say "um" or "im" for it or them.
7. Forget conjunctions.

For example: "Time for go getum da kine for Moko and Whodaguy, yah?" or "Da kine no moh stay, yah?" or "No no, Darryl and Wayne swimum deep for getum."

The Hawaiian language is not part of pidgin, although some Hawaiian words are commonly used by pidgin talkers and by English talkers too. Some common words and phrases are:

**Pau (pow):** Done, finished, fini, caput, all gone, no moh.
**Pau hana:** End of the day or end of the work time.
**Kapa Kai:** Turn over, capsize
**Shishi:** Urinate
**Maki:** Dead
**Puka:** Hole (remember puka shells?)
**Mauka:** Mountain or toward the mountain
**Makai:** Toward the sea.

**Ebba:** Beach

**Ono:** The best, also deep water game fish like Atlantic Wahoo.

**Kona:** South

**Imu:** Underground cooking method, an ancient and developed technique using rocks and dirt to form the oven and heat convection. Only certain rocks will not explode in the Imu. Pigs, turkeys and fish are commonly cooked in the Imu, usually wrapped securely in Ti leaves to keep the heat in and the fire out.

**Kiawe:** Big trees with gnarly thorns guaranteed to make you curse the missionaries if you step on 1. Local lore credits the missionaries for introducing kiawe for its thorns, so the natives would have to wear shoes, since barefoot was sinful. Kiawe displaced Koa, a rich grained hardwood famous for its beauty and now for its scarcity and high price.

**Lolo:** Crazy

**Paka:** Weed

**Pakalolo:** Used to be Hawaii's 2nd biggest industry. Now Hawaii's biggest with gross annual revenues of $10 billion, according to both U.S. Senators. Smokum Brah, Yah? Da kine lolo now come in many famous flavors: Maui Wowie, Kona Gold, Puna Butter, Kauai Electric, and it's famous for curing insomnia.

**Puhehe:** Da kine you-know-what.

**Luau:** Eatum 1 pig (See Luaus)

**Poke:** Raw ahi or aku diced in cubes and prepared with sesame seeds, soy sauce and/or other condiments.

**Tako:** Octopus.

**Saimin:** Like chicken soup but with long noodles and pigmeat. Eaten with chopsticks.

**Chow Fun:** Usually wide noodles with diced scallion and pigmeat, seasoned to taste with Tabasco or shoyu.

**You like beef?:** Do you want to fight?

**Bodda you?:** Simple question preceding Sunday punch.

**Lau Lau, Lomi Lomi Salmon, Chicken Long Rice, Burger de Luxe, Special Today:** Primary components of local cuisine, also known as Plate Lunch.

NOTE: Most proper nouns in Hawaiian describe a place in terms of its characteristics. For example, Maui's volcano is Haleakala, "Hale" meaning house, "akala" meaning sun, together meaning House of the Sun. Pukalani is "puka", meaning hole, and "lani", meaning heavens, adding up to Hole in the Heavens.

Anthropologists now theorize that many proper nouns endemic to modern American culture have evolved from this same system. Consider: Foodland, Burger King, Exxon.

# Maps of the Islands

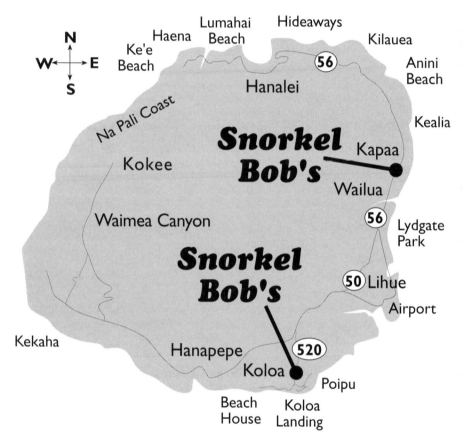

KAUAI

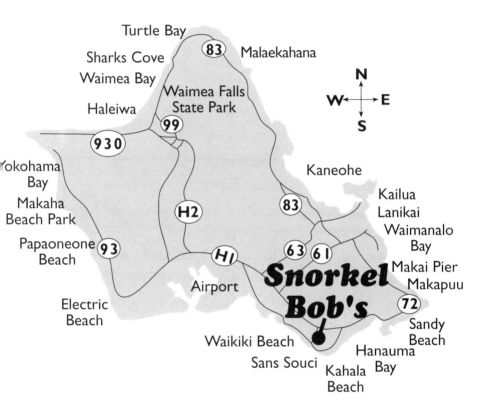

OAHU

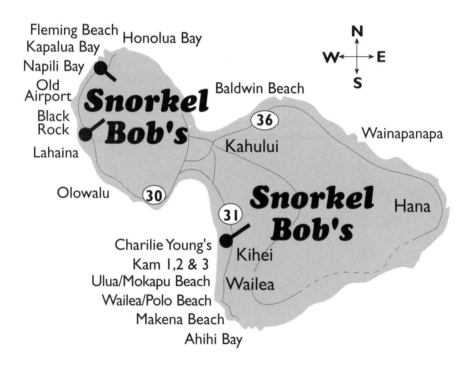

Fleming Beach Honolua Bay
Kapalua Bay
Napili Bay
Old
Airport
Black
Rock
Lahaina

**N**
**W** ← → **E**
**S**

Baldwin Beach

36

Wainapanapa

Kahului

**Snorkel Bob's**

Olowalu

30

31

**Snorkel Bob's**

Hana

Charilie Young's
Kam 1,2 & 3
Ulua/Mokapu Beach
Wailea/Polo Beach
Makena Beach
Ahihi Bay

Kihei

Wailea

# MAUI

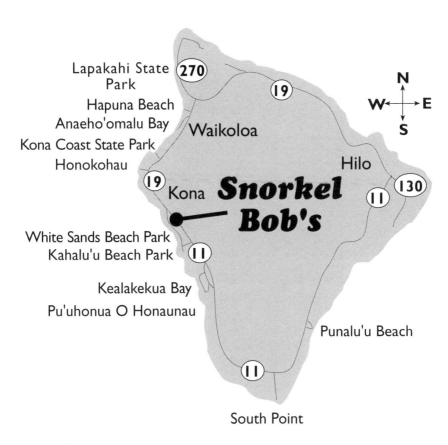

## BIG ISLAND

Photo by Anita

# ABOUT THE AUTHOR

From mid-Summer '48, to mid-Summer '62, Robert Wintner roamed the countryside of Southern Indiana stalking the giant crawdad, spotted salamander, baby catfish and other amphibians and reptiles. He was often accompanied by his dog, Tuffy, and on occasion by his duck, Quacky.

These formative years were highlighted by low-grade explosives, horse racing, diamond sales along the Ohio River, juvenile detention, camping with the girl scouts, stealing raw material for two entries in the All-American Soap Box Derby, and in '55, that ultimate communion, in which a boy first glimpsed the briny blue through an air space and a lens and said, "Oh, God. You can see everything."

The next eight years of formal education would have been avoided, if not for a more pressing avoidance at hand. Wintner endured the writing program at the U. of Mo. (known for its school of agriculture). His degree hangs today over his mother's TV. The next year brought lottery #198, three higher than the '71 quota for Vietnam.

Real life began on the Carolina coast, with boat work and shoreline self-sufficiency (fishing everyday). California came next; waning resources and shrinking potential led to desperate measures. Wintner sailed to Hawaii in '83 in pursuit of tropical fantasy. It didn't work. Finding himself all washed up and not even forty, he threw in the towel, deciding to forget fame and fortune in favor of a bag of groceries he could easily earn by dispensing snorkel equipment to tourists.

Robert Wintner has appeared on 60 radio shows, including three with Jan Coleman, WGN Chicago ("Robert Wintner is a born communicator.") and three with Roger Hedgecock, AM 1130 San Diego ("I always have time for Robert Wintner.").

Wintner has sailed two oceans, motorcycled two continents, experienced three realities, become legendary in Hawaii and on several occasions sat motionless for two hours. He is now on literary sabbatical on Puget Sound, where he snorkels in a wet suit and warms by the fire with Anita, Flojo, Dewey, Molly and Dino.

# Your Friend in the Tropics

## KAUAI:

**Snorkel Bob's Kapaa** ( just north of Coconut Marketplace)
4-734 Kuhio Hwy.
Kapaa, Hawaii 96746
808-823-9433

**Snorkel Bob's Koloa** (on Poipu Beach Rd, just past Old Koloa Town)
3236 Poipu Rd.
Koloa, Hawaii 96756
808-742-2206

## BIG ISLAND:

**Snorkel Bob's Kona** (by the Royal Kona Resort and Huggo's Restaurant)
75-5431 Kahakai St.
Kailua-Kona, Hawaii 96740
808-329-0770

## MAUI:

**Snorkel Bob's Kihei** (across from Kalama Park & the Big Whale on S. Kihei Rd)
34 Keala St.
Kihei, Hawaii 96753
808-879-7449

**Snorkel Bob's Lahaina** (just off Front Street)
161 Lahainaluna Road
Lahaina, Hawaii 96761
808-661-4421

**Snorkel Bob's Napili** (in the Napili Village Hotel just before Kapalua)
5425C Lower Honoapiilani Hwy.
Lahaina, Hawaii 96761
808-669-9603

## OAHU:

**Snorkel Bob's Kapahulu** (8 blocks from Waikiki)
700 Kapahulu Avenue
Honolulu, Hawaii 96816
808-735-7944

## ALL ISLANDS   8-5 Every Day
### http://snorkelbob.com

# Index

# And wait—there's still more!

**WHEN YOU** reserve your snorkel gear with me, Snorkel Bob, you ensure fulfillment of your tropical fantasy, or at least a best-effort approximation.

A visit to the Cybereef at

## http://snorkelbob.com

will give you more skinny, a dazzling retail display and a chance to safeguard you and yours against the ultimate tropical tragedy—no more snorkel gear. Ancient Hawaiian myth describes this condition as, *Da kine no mo stay*. Don't let it happen to you!

**WHEN YOU** take this step to ensure your family's fun, you will receive, **FREE IN THE ABSOLUTE, 1 Book 'n a Beach Chair.** The book shall be a tale of woe with a dash of adventure, a smattering of romance, a balance of frailty and heroics. Meaningless friction shall soil these pages. Smuts and gratuities shall flow like tears in Babylon, and in the end shall be: resolution. You may choose 1 book from the following page, and it shall be yours to keep forever. I, Snorkel Bob'm, here to tell you, this pulp goes great with the grease, the grit, the sweat, the flies, the azure blue and endless horizon. The chair shall be yours for a week.

Check it out.

You've come this far.

# More Books by Robert Wintner

You can order fiction by Robert Wintner, whose formative years cohere in THE ICE KING. The Bookwatch called this novel "a narrative voice at once powerful and lyrical, passionate and graceful."

The tales in HAGAN'S TRIAL AND OTHER STORIES were recommended by Publisher's Weekly: "Darkly comic, deeply ironic, these stories are a compelling chronicle. Wintner has a masterful touch, drawing his readers into each life with wit, irony and traditional story telling of the sort you'd hear rocking on an old front porch."

Exodus to Paradise and the yachting trials are recalled in the novel WHIRLAWAY. Two reviewers regretted the gratuitous sex and drugs, in spite of "vivid passages depicting harrowing open-sea crossings." Wintner also regrets the gratuities and hopes future passages are less harrowing if not less vivid. WHIRLAWAY follows two boomers from poverty downs, who think gainful employment is an oxymoron. They rob a bank the modern way and finace a sailing yacht. The future looks bright, with enough drugs to suspend the entire NFL, enough liquor to make sage brush soggy and women so loose they look boneless. The only thing missing is reality, but not for long. PG 23, in case you have any doubts here.

A third novel, HORNDOG BLUE, was favorably reviewed including a personal note from the ex-wife, who said, "I marveled at your literary ability. Did I already tell you this? I may have but have forgotten."

Robert Wintner does not have an MFA and has never attended a writers conference or lived in New York.

# ORDER FORM

| Qty | Title | Price | | Total |
|---|---|---|---|---|
| | **THE ICE KING** | **$12** | | |
| | **WHIRLAWAY** | **$20** | | |
| | **HAGAN'S TRIAL** | **$15** | | |
| | **HORNDOG BLUE** | **$12** | | |
| | **Order all 4 Books** ⬆ | **$25** | | |
| | **Snorkel Bob's Reality Guide to Hawaii** | **$15** | | |
| | Shipping & Handling ($3 for 1 book, $4 for 2, $1.50 each for 3 or more). | | | |

**Telephone Orders:**
Call (800) 262-7725
Have your VISA or
MasterCard ready.

**Fax Orders:**
(808) 735-3139
Fill out order
form and fax.

**Postal Orders:**
Coelacanth LLC
700 Kapahulu Ave.
Honolulu, HI 96816

**Payment: Please Check One**

☐ Check

☐ VISA

☐ MasterCard

**Expiration Date:**_____ /_____
**Card #:**_____
**Name on Card:**_____

Name _____
Address_____
City_____ State_____ Zip_____
Daytime Phone (     )_____

Quantity discounts are available.
For more information call (808) 737-2421